Advance Praise f

The Liza Minnelli Scra

"What good is sitting all alone in your room—except when you can have this book as a companion! It provides a wonderfully comprehensive tribute to a great performer and a beguiling personality."

—Michael York, star of *Cabaret, Murder on the Orient Express, Romeo and Juliet*, author of *Accidentally on Purpose* and co-author of *A Shakespearean Actor Prepares*

"Finally, the book that chronicles the scope of Liza's endless and boundless talent."

—Janet Leigh, star of *Psycho, Touch of Evil*, and author of *The Dream Factory*

"A very exciting way to tell the story of one of America's greatest stars. If you love Liza like I do, it is a must to have."

—Margaret Whiting, acclaimed singer ("It Might as Well Be Spring," "Moonlight in Vermont")

"Liza's life in the gossip columns and tabloids has tended to woefully and unfairly overshadow the Oscar, the Tony, the Emmy, and all the work she's done to earn such lofty accolades. She is, without question, one of the most electric performers of our time. In this superb and detailed scrapbook of the Minnelli career, Scott Schechter reemphasizes all those performances in loving detail. There are enough facts, tidbits, and surprises that even the most devoted fan of the indefatigable Liza will come away with an even deeper respect for the lady and the work she's done. When one is as talented as Liza, such an accolade seems not only justified but indispensable and long overdue. A star could not ask for a better tribute."

—Robert Osborne, columnist and critic for *The Hollywood Reporter*, and host of the Turner Classic Movies television network

The *Liza Minnelli* Scrapbook

The *Liza Minnelli* Scrapbook

SCOTT SCHECHTER

Foreword by Billy Stritch

CITADEL PRESS
Kensington Publishing Corp.
www.kensingtonbooks.com

CITADEL PRESS BOOKS are published by

Kensington Publishing Corp.
850 Third Avenue
New York, NY 10022

All Kensington titles, imprints, and distributed lines are available at special quantity discounts for bulk purchases for sales promotions, premiums, fund-raising, educational, or institutional use. Special book excerpts or customized printings can also be created to fit specific needs. For details, write or phone the office of the Kensington special sales manager: Kensington Publishing Corp., 850 Third Avenue, New York, NY 10022, attn: Special Sales Department; phone 1-800-221-2647.

NOTE: Every effort has been made to identify the copyright owners of the photos used in this publication. The author and the publisher apologize for any omissions and will make proper corrections in future editions.

First printing: November 2004

10 9 8 7 6 5 4 3 2 1

Printed in the United States of America

Library of Congress Control Number: 2004106177

ISBN 0-8065-2611-4

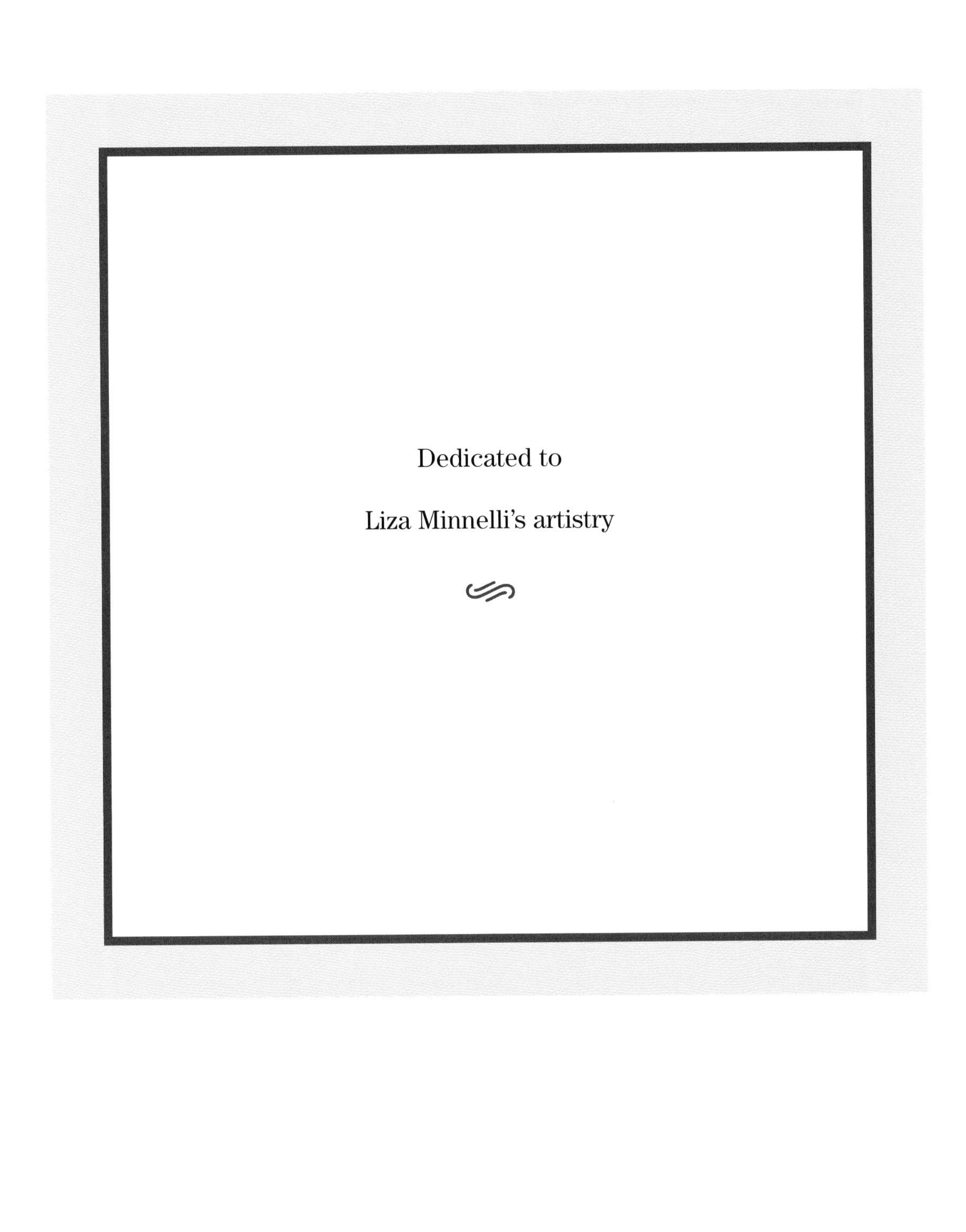

Dedicated to

Liza Minnelli's artistry

Contents

ACT TWO

EXIT MUSIC

Foreword

We all call ourselves *fans*, don't we? We're fans of movies, plays, television shows, books, sports teams—even our favorite foods. Perhaps the most intriguing form of fandom, however, is the admiration that develops for singular talents—individuals who, through extraordinary artistry, move us in such ways that our lives and perceptions are changed. It's not so much that a great actress, singer, or performer becomes the standard by which all others are judged; more accurately, it's that, for us, the artist stands alone, unique in every aspect, and no one else compares.

Come with me back in time to Sugarland, Texas, 1972. My passion for music was growing well beyond that of the average ten-year-old. I had discovered the great standards of Gershwin and Berlin, as well as classic movie musicals on TV. Then, suddenly, there she was: Liza Minnelli. An Oscar for her performance as Sally Bowles in *Cabaret* was followed by an Emmy for the television special *Liza with a "Z"*. Impressive? Yes. But there are no statues to celebrate what she had really achieved. Stepping out of the considerable shadows cast by her legendary parents, Judy Garland and Vincente Minnelli, proved that this was no ordinary twenty-six-year-old. She was "Liza"—she could command the attention of the world now, and her legion of fans was born.

Nearly twenty years later—March 7, 1991, to be exact—I was seated at the piano at Bobo's, a midtown Manhattan eatery, when she walked in the door. Naturally, I wanted to meet her, but I was also eager to make an impression. Taking a subtle approach, I began to play the theme from *The Bad and the Beautiful*. Suddenly, the famous figure that had transfixed me years ago was striding across the room . . . toward me. "Hi, I'm Liza," she said, as if we were both unaware of her superstar status. "How do you know that song?" I told her I had always loved it and that it was from one of my favorite movies. "One of my father's movies," she added, sounding as much like a fan as a daughter.

Our relationship began that night. While I am known today as her collaborator, accompanist, confidant, and any number of other things, I am most proud to call her my friend. And more than ever, I am still her fan.

Look elsewhere for the sensationalized drama of a life lived in the public eye. This long overdue tribute celebrates Liza's amazing career in loving detail, recording every step along the way. It's for the fans—the ones who know that Liza Minnelli's art is her life. And who know also that with every unforgettable performance, she gives the world her own love.

—Billy Stritch
New York, New York
May 2004

Opposite: Photos from the personal archives of Billy Stritch. Liza with some of her celebrity friends and associates, including: *(top, left to right)* Reba McEntire, in Nashville, early 1994; Steve Lawrence and Shirley MacLaine at the Desert Inn, Las Vegas, December 31, 1992; Sophia Loren, backstage at the Palais de Congrès, Paris, November 1991; *(middle, left to right)* Elton John at Lynn Wyatt's Birthday in the south of France, July 16, 1995; Billy Stritch, Academy Awards night, Los Angeles, 1992; Audrey Hepburn, UNICEF benefit, Miami Beach, summer 1992; *(bottom, left to right)* Bill LaVorgna, Liza's musical director, Houston, July 28, 1991; Charles Aznavour, 1993.

Overture

These photos show Liza rehearsing and performing in *The Diary of Anne Frank*. From Scarsdale High School Yearbook, 1961–1962.

Introduction

"I think the thing I like to do most in my life is to work, and to work hard." —Liza, 1978

Now in her fifth decade of performing, Liza Minnelli remains one of the world's most beloved entertainers. The star has been rewarded with every major accolade the industry offers—including the Oscar, Emmy, Grammy, and Tony Awards—among many other achievements. Miss Minnelli's greatest professional accomplishment, however, may actually be the multitude of devoted fans she has kept over the years.

This has happened despite the media's frequently focusing more on her personal life rather than her professional one. The attention is somewhat understandable: Liza May Minnelli was *born* famous, the daughter of the still beloved singing icon Judy Garland and the brilliant Academy Award–winning movie director Vincente Minnelli. Since then, the sometimes sensationalistic aspects of Liza's life (such as the health issues she has triumphed over) have continued to be publicized, putting the emphasis on the *wrong* side of the footlights.

This book seeks to rectify that scenario. *The Liza Minnelli Scrapbook* provides the solution by being the very first to concentrate on the artistic magic of Minnelli as a working star. The first half of the book (Act One) will present an overview of each decade of Liza's life, focusing on her career. The second half (Act Two) will be a more detailed look at her output in each media, from Broadway to films, TV, records, and the concert stage.

Minnelli's magic as a performer is one that has captivated this writer since 1975, when just a teen. The passion I felt for Liza's talent grew that year as I started seeing her appearances on various TV specials and series (including *The Mac Davis Special, Dinah!, The Tonight Show*); began buying her recent albums (*The Singer, Liza Live at the Winter Garden*); and going to movie theaters to catch her latest film, *Lucky Lady*. Yet the connection to her work was cemented the first time I saw her perform in person, on January 19, 1977, at the vast Latin Casino nightclub in Cherry Hill, New Jersey.

The clarity and power of seeing her live aside, what I walked away with most from the experience was a sense of someone who was in their element performing for the audience; how relaxed Liza was onstage; how much she talked with the crowd and responded to what they yelled out to her.

Turns out I was pretty observant for a fifteen year old: Liza Minnelli thrives on what flows back and forth between artist and audience. "This is the best game of tennis I know of," was how she succinctly put it, during one recent outburst of love in a packed concert hall. Yet even more than the power of her personality, the thing that makes Minnelli such a consummate performer is the fact that she *wants* to be entertaining her audience, to move them, to make them happy, or sad—to make them *feel*.

This desire to please extends to her offstage life. Being lucky enough to have spent some time with Miss Minnelli over the last twenty-plus years, I can see the truth in her reputation for being a kind, warm, and generous soul. Tales abound of her helping others and always making herself available for worthy causes over the years, including many AIDS charities and as a board member on the Institutes for the Achievement of Human Potential. Even people meeting Minnelli for the first time have benefited from her huge heart, as I observed backstage one night. I marveled at how perfectly

Liza attended to a young man's meltdown over his mother's recent passing, how she sat down and comforted him as he felt compelled to share his loss, how she took time away from the demands of her schedule to make certain another human being was all right. I don't mean to imply the woman is either a saint or perfect—she is a human being, after all, like all of us. Yet in an industry filled with horror stories about almost every star, Liza Minnelli seems universally known as someone enjoyable to work with, or to know, one without a "star" attitude. Liza's easy going and approachable demeanor offstage coincides with the personality she projects onstage.

Seeing Liza Minnelli in concert is akin to attending a love-fest, and it's not difficult to see why her fans are so devoted. How can you not respond to someone who loves you—and needs you—perhaps even more than you love and need them?

"I'm here for *you*. You're my life," Liza admitted to her audience during a concert in February 2003. It's easy to accept that statement as the utmost truth when looking at the vast body of work built by this icon; a career dating back to 1962, when sixteen-year-old Minnelli moved to Manhattan. It is hoped that *The Liza Minnelli Scrapbook* will prove that the driving force, and motivating factor in Liza's life has been, and remains, her calling: her work.

—Scott Schechter,
April 23, 2004

Act One

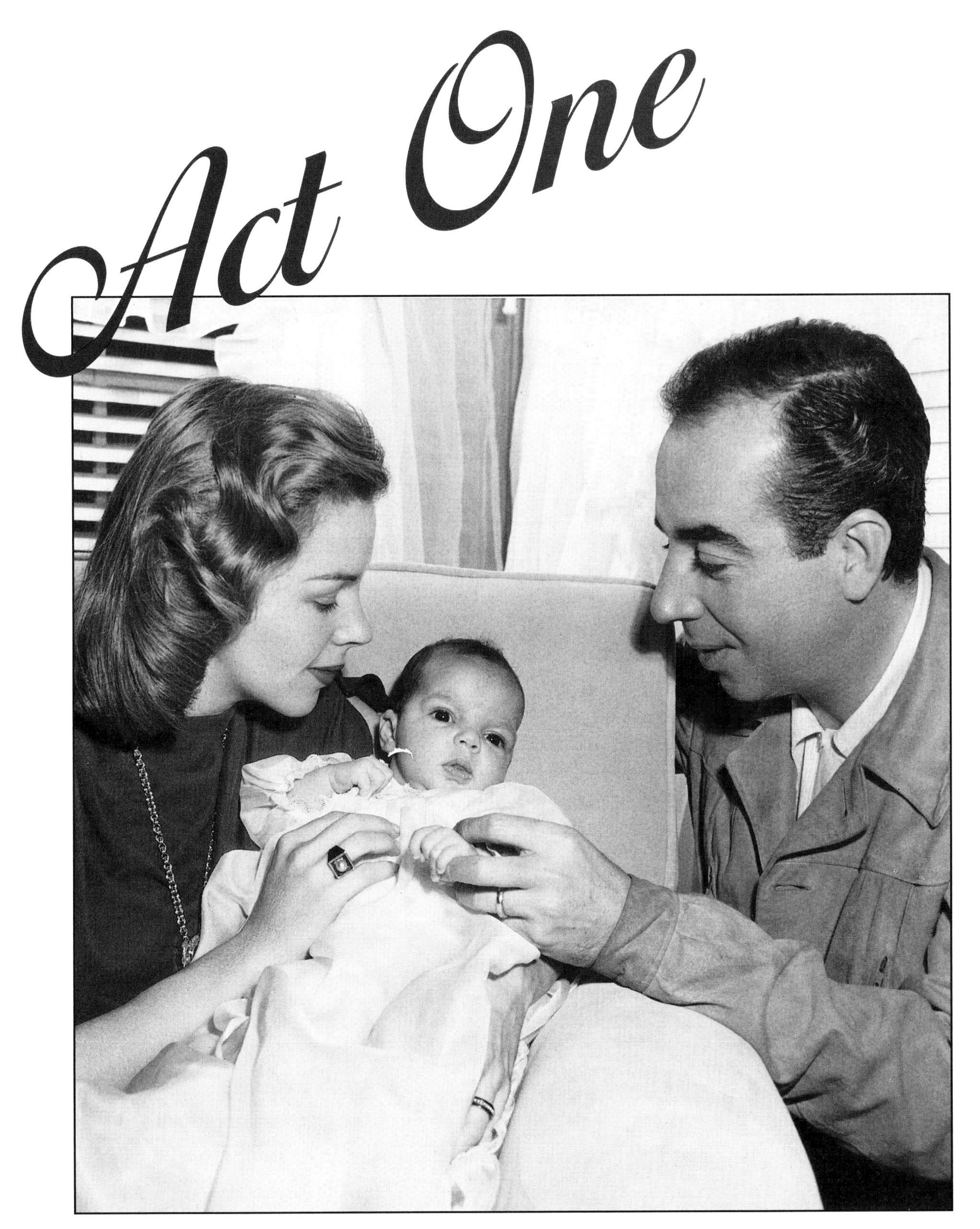

Proud parents with one-month-old Liza May Minnelli, during her first publicity portrait sitting in April 1946.

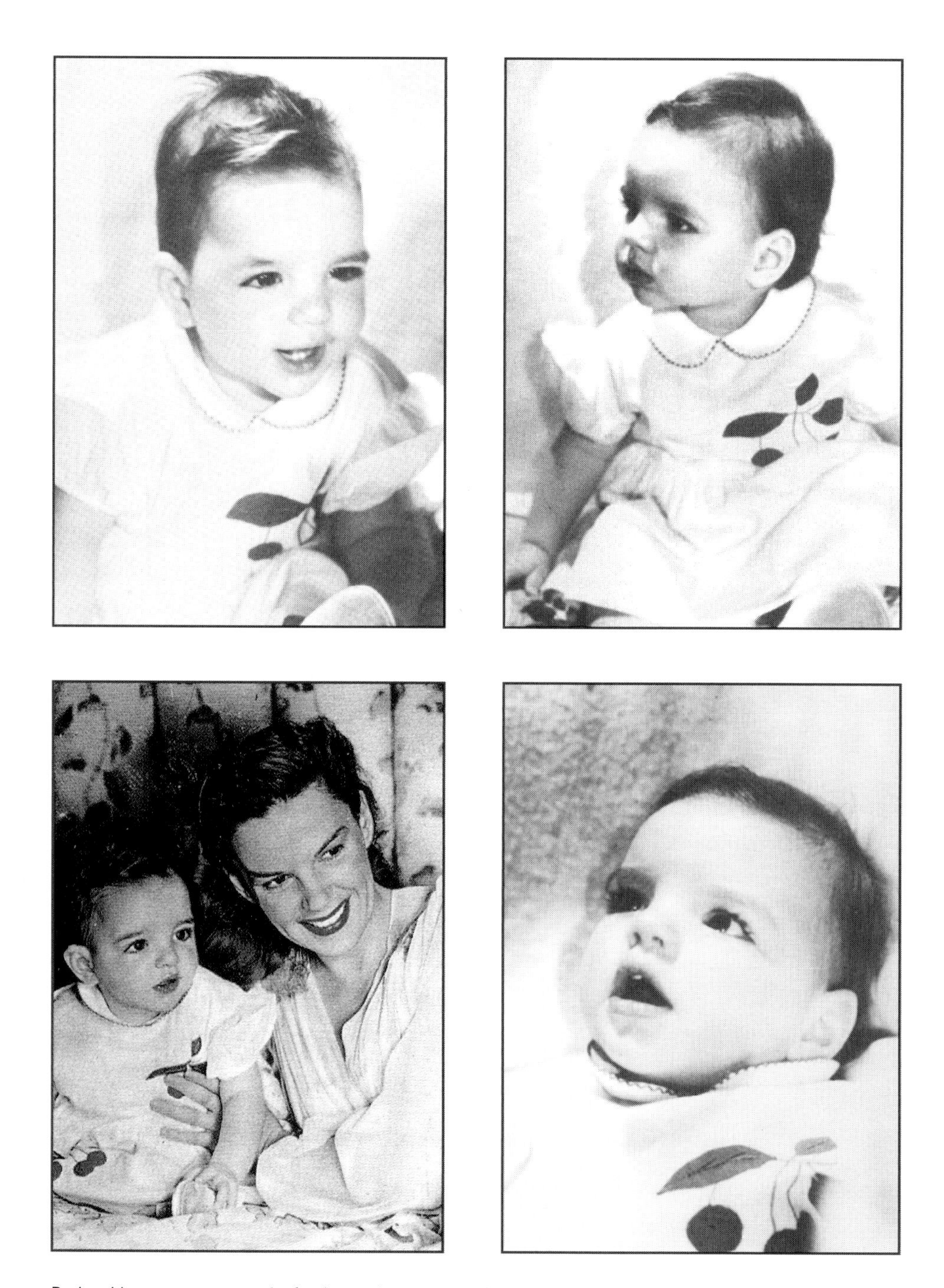

Baby Liza seems ready for her close-ups, alone, and in a two-shot with mama.

CHAPTER ONE

Liza's Life, 1946–1959 (An Overview)

Liza May Minnelli was born at 7:58 A.M. on March 12, 1946, at Cedars of Lebanon Hospital in Los Angeles, California, weighing 6 pounds, 10½ ounces.

As the offspring of Judy Garland, one of the most loved and talented entertainment icons of all time (forever known by nearly every human on the planet as at least "Dorothy" in *The Wizard of Oz*), and Vincente Minnelli, one of the greatest film directors of all time (*Gigi, An American in Paris,* etc.), Liza was ensured exposure from the beginning. Adding to this mix, her godmother was acclaimed singer-arranger Kay Thompson, who would later become the author of the famed *Eloise* children's books. It has been noted Minnelli served as the inspiration for the fictional youngster who ruled over the Plaza hotel in New York City.

As her parents were arguably the musical king and queen of MGM, little Liza was privileged to experience an industry environment that will perhaps never exist again: the studio system. A vast fantasy land—the business of creating illusions on film—was Liza's to explore, and it wasn't long before the young Miss Minnelli was herself part of "the factory's" celluloid magic.

In an unbilled appearance, Liza Minnelli's movie debut—at age two and a half—comes in the final scene of her mother's musical *In the Good Old Summertime* (1949). Liza doesn't appear very happy in costar Van Johnson's arms. It turns out the future film star realized on camera that she wasn't quite ready for her close-up. Minnelli later revealed she hadn't dressed fully; in the process of preparing for her first film, the child's panties were somehow forgotten, and so she wasn't completely comfortable during her brief time onscreen.

Even as a tot, Liza's joy and warmth were quite evident.

Liza's mother, Judy Garland, during perhaps her most breathtakingly beautiful period. Taken November 1942, a year before she began work on *Meet Me in St. Louis,* where she would fall in love with its director.

Liza's brilliant and beloved father, Vincente Minnelli, at perhaps his most handsome.

Twelve-year-old Liza with her dad, attending the premiere of Vincente's *Some Came Running* in 1958.

It would be many years before any further appearances by Liza were noted, aside from family performances inside the Minnelli household. Eventually Liza ventured out into the world to share her budding gifts. Putting on impromptu performances in the front yard, the child gave her all, hoping the people in cars zooming by would stop to applaud her singing and dancing. When one vehicle did finally slow down, the career of Liza Minnelli was nearly ended before it began: According to the star, the passenger of this car leaned her head out the window . . . and threw up. "My first review," Liza later joked.

Judy Garland's return to her vaudeville roots in 1951 gave Liza a chance to see the master at work—"lessons from the legend," as I call it. The child was thus able to experience life outside of Hollywood, one she would eventually favor—the life of a performer.

It was during Judy's second historic engagement at New York City's Palace Theater in 1956 that Liza May made her debut on stage, at age ten. While Mama belted "Swanee," Minnelli danced around Judy, a routine repeated often over the years. The child also made her official TV debut that fall, on November 3, 1956, when she co-hosted the first-ever telecast of her mother's movie *The Wizard of Oz*, along with the "Cowardly Lion," Bert Lahr. (Judy watched the live broadcast backstage while working at the Palace, with great pride and love for her daughter.)

Even though little Liza was getting tastes of various medias—film, stage, and now TV—following in either of her parents' footsteps was not something she spent much time dreaming about. This changed when the movies' greatest dancing director, Gene Kelly, performed impromptu with Liza at home. Kelly immediately stated his desire to hire Miss Minnelli to appear on his upcoming TV special. On April 24, 1959, the team of Kelly and Minnelli were seen singing and dancing on America's TV screens to "For Me and My Gal," the title song of Garland's movie with Kelly. This is the earliest known recording of Liza Minnelli singing, and the thirteen-year-old possessed a lovely, if slight voice. The surviving color videotape shows the trademark potent power was not yet evident, but that she did have a way with lyrics. She also moved with ease and seemed completely comfortable working on camera.

Gene Kelly rehearsing with Liza for her TV singing debut, April 1959.

What also seems evident is that *The Gene Kelly Show* confirmed the longing in Liza's heart to entertain, a longing first displayed for those people driving by her childhood home. The next decade would prove to the young lady that the family business is where she belonged. The 1960s would be the official start of Liza Minnelli's career.

CHAPTER TWO

Liza's Life: The 1960s (An Overview)

In 1960, fourteen-year-old Liza considered a career as a professional ice skater, but a Broadway show changed that. The conversion actually started a year earlier, when she was riveted by the legendary Ethel Merman the moment "the Merm" came storming down the aisle in the 1959 musical *Gypsy*. "Ethel, I'm with ya, honey," Minnelli later recalled her feelings at that moment. Still, it was seeing the 1960 production of *Bye, Bye, Birdie* that convinced Liza that she *had* to be on stage, singing and dancing. She'd never seen a large group of teenagers her age in a show before. It seemed as if the kids bouncing about up there were all part of one unit, one group that was having an incredible amount of fun. Having Hollywood parents made it clear to Liza that she wanted to be working in New York as opposed to Los Angeles: she'd found filmmaking tedious up to that point in her life. The young lady was also smart enough to desire work in a field that wasn't directly connected to her famous folks—the Broadway stage. Judy never acted in any book musicals or plays (a book musical is one that has a full story line, as opposed to a "revue" musical, which usually consists of musical numbers, tied together). Garland, however, did have great "live" solo successes at the Palace; Vincente had great success in New York theater and at Radio City Music Hall before his multiple movie hits, but they were as director-producer, not as a performer—and that had been back in the 1930s.

Rare color candid shot of Liza with her beloved mama, during Judy's legendary worldwide 1960–1961 concert tour.

Fifteen-year-old Liza apprenticed with the Cape Cod Melody Tent in the summer of 1961, following some months at the legendary High School of Performing Arts in Manhattan (where she developed a lifelong friendship and partnership with fellow student and future Oscar-winning composer Marvin Hamlisch. The school was later immortalized in the 1980 film *Fame*). This Cape Code stock company was based in Hyannis Port, Massachusetts, where Liza and her family were enjoying their summer vacation. Minnelli happily painted scenery and took bit parts in the choruses of such shows as *Wish You Were Here* and *Flower Drum Song*. Liza then graduated to an actual role in the company's last show of the season. Performing on August 23, 1961, in *Take Me Along*, as "Marie Macomber," she sang the number "I Would Die." The experience must have boosted her confidence—Minnelli signed with her first agent that summer (Stephanie "Stevie" Phillips). Then, while attending Scarsdale High School during the fall of 1961, Liza was cast in the lead role of the drama department's production of *The Diary of Anne Frank*.

The *Scarsdale Inquirer* called her portrayal "vibrant." An overseas tour for this cast of high school students was then personally financed by a local supporter of the arts (Mrs. Murray Silverstone, wife of 20th Century-Fox International's president). Liza Minnelli thus performed in Rome, Athens, and Amsterdam in the summer of 1962.

After securing her parents' permission, Minnelli moved to Manhattan late in 1962 at age 16½, living in a small apartment. She studied, including acting classes at a world-renowned actor's workshop, the Herbert Berghof Studio in Greenwich Village. She performed in a recital of Robert Frost's poetry on February 3, 1963. Not long before her seventeenth birthday (March 12, 1963), Liza was cast by director Danny Daniels and producer Arthur Whitelaw in her first New York production, the off-Broadway revival of the 1941 musical *Best Foot Forward*. (The original had introduced both June Allyson and Nancy Walker; Lucille Ball had starred in the 1943 film version.) Minnelli wowed *Forward*'s staff at her audition, singing "The Way You Look Tonight," and "They Can't Take That Away from Me." During rehearsals, the teenager was extensively interviewed, photographed, and pro-

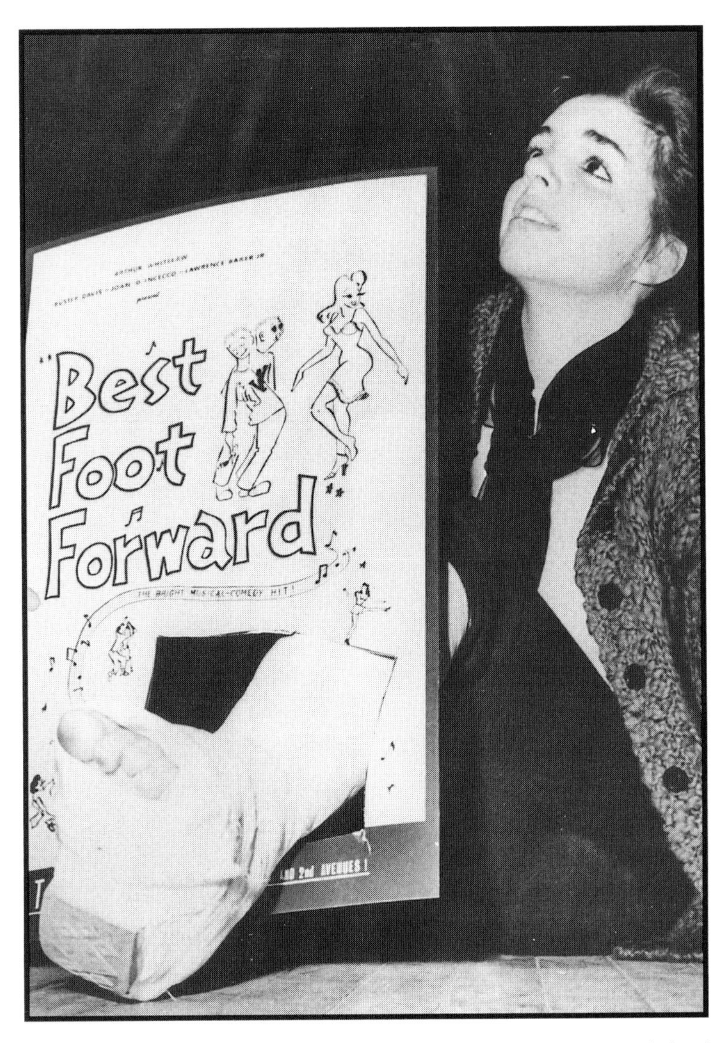

Minnelli's first monumental career moment. The original March 27 opening for *Best Foot Forward* was delayed nearly a week when Liza broke her foot while rehearsing. The show's savvy press staff—including friend and future media supporter Rex Reed—made certain to use the situation to their advantage.

filed, even if it was only because "Dorothy's daughter" was making her off-Broadway debut. Although she was the aspect of the musical being marketed to the public, the teenager was not the show's star. Liza was actually a supporting player, portraying "Ethel Hofflinger," a man-crazy young woman on a college campus—a part that showcased her verve with snappy one-liners, and gave her a couple of featured songs. One show-stopping ballad—"You Are for Loving"—was added for her as a solo near the end of the show. This was the only padding done to the part for Minnelli's benefit; the rest of the cast was also talented, and featured future film star Christopher Walken. During rehearsals, Liza indeed put her best foot forward . . . and broke it. The producers postponed the opening of the show for six days to accommodate her.

When *Best Foot Forward* opened on April 2, 1963, it can be honestly stated that a star was born, which was how the critics saw it. "She is easy and confident and accomplished and winning," wrote Walter Kerr for the *New York Herald-Tribune*. The rave reviews helped to offset the fact that Liza was only being paid the equity minimum of forty-five dollars a week for appearing in the show. The show also garnered Minnelli her first award: the Daniel Blum/Theatre World Award as one of the year's most promising young actresses.

On February 26, 1963, Liza officially began her recording career, cutting two songs from *Best Foot Forward* (she also later recorded the show's cast album). "You Are for Loving" actually became one of Liza Minnelli's biggest selling singles: over 500,000 copies, according to various newspaper reports. That success led to an offer to record for Capitol Records. On May 27, 1963, the teen began recording very "pop" oriented singles for Capitol, in New York. These initial tracks were fun, light tunes, obviously aimed at the youth market—songs such as "How Much Do I Love You?" "One Summer Love," "Day Dreaming," the wonderfully unusual "His Woman" with a samba beat, and several others. Offers to sing on TV came in (thanks to her off-Broadway smash and "You Are for Loving" disc), including *Ed Sullivan* and two guest shots on *The Judy Garland Show*.

Liza began planning other stage work, signing on for appearances in stock productions of *Carnival!*, the title role in *Time Out for Ginger*, and The *Fantasticks*, all in 1964. That was the also the year Capitol Records recorded and released Minnelli's first solo album, *Liza! Liza!* The disc was a superb mix of upbeat (and often offbeat) songs such as "I'm All I've Got" with beautiful ballads, including her first recording of "Maybe This Time," a song she'd later become identified with when it was added to the movie *Cabaret*. Like Barbra Streisand's early albums, the orchestrations were by the brilliant and acclaimed Peter Matz, who would also later craft the arrangements for Carol Burnett's variety hour, among many other credits. Matz's work seemed to prominently feature a very richly textured, brassy, Broadway sound that suited Liza's style perfectly. The album's June 25, 1964, recording of "Try to Remember" is an excellent example of the breathtakingly beautiful way in which the young performer combined a heartfelt, in-depth interpretation with a vocal musicality that is quite lovely and easy on the ear. To this day, the eighteen-year-old Minnelli's work astounds.

The teenager was soon recording a follow-up solo album in December 1964, having just completed her first concert engagement—one that would become legendary. After receiving an advance copy of *Liza! Liza!*, Judy Garland decided she wanted to share the stage with Minnelli at the London Palladium. The joint concert, set for November 8, 1964, sold out instantly, prompting the scheduling of a second performance a week later. The concerts were ultimately recorded by Capitol Records, and the second show was also videotaped for broadcast in England.

The cover of the program for the historic Judy-Liza concerts in London. Within months, Minnelli would be starring in her own Broadway musical, *Flora, the Red Menace*.

The resulting two-LP set of *Judy Garland and Liza Minnelli Live at the London Palladium*, released August 2, 1965, made mincemeat of the carefully constructed fifty-song concert, as did the fifty-five-minute TV version. Sadly, the poor quality transfer of the surviving footage (now available on DVD and VHS) exaggerates the slight dryness and roughness of Garland's vocal condition (by the film transfer not being at exactly the right speed, thus making movement just a tad slower and pitch a bit deeper than they really were). Worse still is the legend that continues to grow over how unsupportive Judy was of her dynamic daughter onstage. While Liza has admitted that each star realized that they were "dealing with a power out there," she also recalls "the enormous love" each felt for the other. A remastered two-CD set—presenting the entire two-hour-and-fifteen-minute concert for the first time ever—completed restoration in 2002, although it does not currently have a release date. It dispels the many myths that have grown over the years about these historic concerts, started by some journalists' off-target impressions of the shows. The Garland heard on the restored CD is in complete control of her talents, with her minor hoarseness gone by the second act. More important, the discs are splendid displays of the interactions between the artists and their audience, and between the two stars. The love these women felt for each other comes through, as does their humor—they are each other's best audience. The crowd is floored by what they experience, and the eighteen-year-old Minnelli clearly possessed the assets required to become a major star for a lifetime (if not as fully developed a performer as she would become over the years). These gifts included a powerful voice, great acting ability in her interpretations, and that certain unexplainable "something" that sets a star apart from a merely competent performer.

Returning to the U.S., Liza immediately began work on both her second solo album for Capitol, as well as auditions for a new Broadway musical, directed by George Abbott. Although other performers were sought as the leading lady (including

Liza Minnelli was becoming a star in the middle 1960s, with a record company, major agency representation, and a publicity firm behind her. This portrait was taken not long after she first cut her hair (1966) into what would soon become her trademark short shag.

popular recording artist Eydie Gormé), Minnelli had the show's songwriters on her side. Fred Ebb and John Kander would become one of Broadway's greatest and most successful songwriting teams ever. Equally important, they supplied Liza with her signature songs over the years, including "Cabaret" and "New York, New York." Minnelli made her Broadway debut as the title lead, and *Flora, the Red Menace* earned her rave reviews upon its May 11, 1965, opening. "Liza fulfills every expectation, singing and acting the role, winning bravos from the first-nighters," critic Judith Christ said on NBC-TV. The musical featured Liza's first Kander-Ebb hit, "A Quiet Thing," and Minnelli the *Menace* became the youngest winner of the coveted Tony Award for Best Actress in a musical, at age nineteen.

In September 1965, Liza Minnelli performed her first nightclub act. Live solo performances were a new Minnelli venture, and would become the main source of work for the rest of Liza's career. Despite all her successes with films, TV, and records, the star is perhaps best experienced and showcased in a live format. Her first nightclub engagement, at the Shoreham Hotel's Blue Room in Washington, D.C., was followed by her very first tour, which began that fall of 1965. Minnelli played all across the U.S., Canada, London, and Paris. Although not a concert format per se (which would usually consist of two acts and be performed in a theater or concert hall), this first tour of nightclubs gave Liza the chance to hone her skills as a live artist.

Liza with leading man Wendell Burton in her first starring movie role, as "Pookie," in *The Sterile Cuckoo* (filmed in the fall of 1968, and released in 1969).

Minnelli explored another new medium during the fall of 1966 when she began filming her first movie role, portraying the secretary to a famed writer in *Charlie Bubbles*. Albert Finney played the title role and also directed the film.

New records were also a way for Liza to increase her fan base. Her third and final solo album for Capitol Records—*There Is a Time*—was released in 1966, and was named Album of the Year by *Stereo Review* magazine. Musician Herb Alpert had formed his own label, A&M Records, and he signed the singer to a contract. *Liza Minnelli* was her first album for A&M, released in 1968. That was also the year she was cast in her first starring screen role.

Liza portrayed the title role in *The Sterile Cuckoo*, "Pookie Adams," a young girl going off to college and dealing with dysfunction and emotional problems stemming from a lonely, motherless upbringing. Minnelli won raves for her work—"a class by itself" stated the *Hollywood Reporter*—as well as an Academy Award nomination for Best Actress. *The Sterile Cuckoo* success was bittersweet, though, as Liza lost her mother in June 1969.

The 1960s ended with Minnelli appearing at the famed Olympia in Paris, performances that were filmed for television there and also recorded by Liza's label, A&M Records. Although only twenty-three when the decade ended, she had already achieved success in all media—movies, TV, records, Broadway, and live performances. Yet Liza's next decade would make the sixties seem like a dress rehearsal.

CHAPTER THREE

Liza's Life: The 1970s (An Overview)

The 1970s started off with an Academy Award nomination for Liza Minnelli's intensely dramatic and brilliant performance in 1969's *The Sterile Cuckoo.* Losing to Maggie Smith was a disappointment, but Liza already had completed another film at the time of the awards, the drama *Tell Me that You Love Me, Junie Moon.* The new decade also brought Minnelli her first U.S. TV special, simply called *Liza,* for NBC—for which she received her first and only *TV Guide* cover to date. The program aired on June 29, 1970, and is often forgotten, but her next special for the network would become one of the greatest successes in television history. Even more important, in early 1971, she finally began filming the role of a lifetime: the movie that would make Liza Minnelli an international superstar and media sensation.

Cabaret premiered on Broadway in 1966, and Liza had actually auditioned to play the leading role of "Sally Bowles" in that original production. Although not cast (the show's playwright and producer wanted a British actress), she immediately began singing the show's title song both on TV and in her act. The producers of the film version arranged to meet with Minnelli in December 1969, while she was performing at the Olympia Theatre in Paris. If Liza's musical arrangement and performance of "Cabaret" at that time weren't quite as compelling or complex as they would soon be, there was still enough there to convince the producers Minnelli *was* "Sally Bowles."

Publicity portrait for Liza's first U.S. TV special, *Liza,* 1970.

As the star of *Cabaret,* Liza received a vast amount of acclaim when the film opened in February 1972. Perhaps the official sign that Liza Minnelli was the biggest star in the world during this time came when she appeared on the covers of both *Time* and *Newsweek* magazines the same week. Not only was Minnelli the movies' newest sensation, but she was about to conquer all other media as well.

On May 31, 1972, Minnelli's second U.S. TV special was filmed before an audience in New York City. Entitled *Liza with a "Z,"* this "concert for television" was named for the song that Kander and Ebb had written for Minnelli's first act in 1965. That piece of special material attempted to correct the public's frequently calling her "Lisa," instead of Liza—with a Z. When the special aired September 10, 1972, on NBC (sponsored by Singer sewing machines), it was an immediate hit. Ratings were high, reviews were raves, and the soundtrack album released by Liza's new label, Columbia Records, would become Minnelli's second album to go gold following the soundtrack to *Cabaret.* (Gold records represent sales of between half a million and one million, which are thereafter awarded platinum records.)

Minnelli's movie star status was officially confirmed on March 27, 1973, when she won the Academy Award for Best Actress for her performance in *Cabaret.* The movie's other wins included Best Supporting Actor Joel Grey and Bob Fosse as Best Director. "Thank you for giving *me* this award. You've made *me* very happy," was Liza's way of making it clear that she felt she'd been given the award for her work, and not because

The Liza legend began with her Oscar-winning performance as "Sally Bowles," in the movie *Cabaret* (1972).

of sentiment over her mother's passing. If that were the case, Minnelli would have been given the award the first time she had been nominated back in 1970, mere months after Garland's passing.

Cabaret was a phenomenon, responsible for making Minnelli not only an Academy Award–winning actress and movie star, but also a multimedia sensation. Suddenly, everywhere she went, everything she did was written about, talked about, and overanalyzed. Every magazine wanted her; every TV show, film studio, and producer in Hollywood had to have her. Liza's brilliant acting performance made everyone think she was "Sally Bowles" off screen, when in truth, the star was much more focused on her career and less on being "divinely decadent" as "Sally" was. Liza's life was not about making sure that life was a cabaret, old chum, but about working for her audiences.

During Minnelli's film and TV ascent in the early 1970s, she frequently returned to the stage. In 1973, Liza played the London Palladium, and the following year performed her concert act at Broadway's Winter Garden Theater for three weeks. A special Tony Award for Best Personal Achievement was given to Liza for this record-breaking run (a huge $413,815 gross), and Minnelli took the show on tour in the summer of 1974. It was also being reported that banks would finance movies only if one of two "bankable" women starred in them: Barbra Streisand or Liza Minnelli.

Ready to concentrate on films full time (following a cameo in the movie *That's Entertainment!*), Liza flew to Mexico for the making of *Lucky Lady* in early 1975. The comedy co-starred Gene Hackman and Burt Reynolds, and the three played a trio of rumrunners seeking their fortune. Finally finished in the summer, Liza later admitted she "needed *something* after being on a *boat* for months" making *Lady*. Fulfillment came when she replaced an ailing Gwen Verdon in the Kander-Ebb-Fosse musical *Chicago*, during August and September 1975—with only a week's worth of rehearsal. Starring as "Roxie Hart," Minnelli wowed Broadway for five weeks by bringing her already legendary energy, style, and talent to the role. (Critics were requested to not review Liza in the show, since Minnelli didn't want to take any additional attention away from Gwen's pending return.) However, Liza's return to the big screen wasn't so lucky. *Lucky Lady* received mixed-to-poor reviews upon its release on Christmas Day 1975. The film's huge twelve-million-dollar final cost dictated it would not earn a profit despite packed theaters, thanks to the Minnelli-Hackman-Reynolds star power.

Liza did her best to promote *Lucky Lady* (including appearances on TV's *The Tonight Show* and *The Mac Davis Special*), flying back to the States from Italy, where she was making her next film, *A Matter of Time*. This new movie was a dream project: Liza was working with her favorite director—her father, Vincente Minnelli. It featured many of his trademark touches, lavish sets and spectacular costumes among them. Yet American International studios took post-production work

The follow-up film to *Cabaret—Lucky Lady* (1975)—was anything but lucky for lady Liza, although her reviews were raves.

A Matter of Time (1976) may have tanked at the box office, but it fulfilled a lifelong dream of Liza's to be directed by her father.

away from Vincente, forcing the Minnellis to disown the movie. The public followed suit: It was only *A Matter of Time* before the film was playing third-run theaters mere weeks after its October 1976 opening.

Liza was already completing the third of three movies she'd signed for as *A Matter of Time* was fading from screens: *New York, New York* had Minnelli playing a 1940s big-band singer who emerges as an early 1950s movie, recording, and concert star by the film's conclusion. *New York, New York* brought Liza full circle, since the movie was made (from March through December 1976) almost entirely on the MGM lot—the same studio she'd grown up at as a child. Word was that Minnelli, her costar Robert De Niro, and their director, Martin Scorsese, would all win Oscars for their work. This advance buzz was backed by nearly unanimous rave reviews—the *Philadelphia Daily News* called it "a towering achievement." However, though the marketing had audiences expecting a happy musical, they were instead treated to a dark one—despite its lavishness and brilliance in all technical aspects. (No expense had been spared in re-creating the 1940s, and the cinematography, scoring, and art direction were among the finest Hollywood had ever produced.) It was also felt the film was too long, at 155 minutes. Scorsese's original cut had been nearly four hours, due to the director's allowances for acting improvisation while filming. Negative aspects aside, Minnelli had what would become her second signature song—the title tune by Kander and Ebb—and another concert stable in their "But the World Goes Round" song. Still, the film's failure at the box office effectively stalled Liza's career as a top movie star.

Liza's one big movie musical made in Hollywood to date—*New York, New York* (1977)—featured her singing and dancing in the "Happy Endings" production number.

Returning to Broadway, and again playing a singer, Liza signed on for the stage musical *In Person*—which would be renamed *Shine It On* and then, finally, *The Act*. The show dealt with a former 1960s movie musical star making a comeback via her first nightclub act. There were controversial headlines during out-of-town tryouts over its director's inexperience with stage work, and the poor costume choices made for Liza. The show finally opened in Manhattan on October 29, 1977. The reviews praised Minnelli if not the show itself, calling it a concert and not a Broadway production. Box office business was brisk, however—people wanted to see Liza live, regardless of the vehicle. *The Act* was always sold out, even at a new high for Manhattan ticket prices: $25.00. The star won her third Tony Award for *The Act* in June 1978, a month before the show closed. Liza desired a new project, and thus refused to extend her year-long *Act* contract.

Liza crooning her Broadway hit "A Quiet Thing" to Kermit the Frog on TV's *The Muppet Show*, videotaped July 31, 1979.

Minnelli took to the road in September 1978, and rarely left it for the next twenty years. Live performing remained her favorite work, and it dominated her schedule. The 1978–1979 concert tour is considered by many to be a major Minnelli peak, both in terms of the two-act program of songs itself and the star being in superlative form and voice. In the summer of 1979, Liza also showcased her versatility by working with two vastly diverse entertainment entities—the Martha Graham Ballet Company, and the Muppets!

The fall of 1979 saw another milestone in Minnelli's career: She gave ten concerts at perhaps the most legendary hall in the world, Carnegie Hall. From September 4 through 15, 1979, Minnelli proved she had grown even more as singer and entertainer. *Variety* summed it up best by stating, "She arrives at what, in her mid-30s, must be a high spot in her career . . . She does most of the things one expects her to do, but she startles by doing them even better than can be recalled." In a venue so identified with Minnelli's mother—thanks to the everlasting monument that is the 1961 *Judy at Carnegie Hall* recording—Liza made her own mark on the historic hall. She also made her own recording of this event, even though it took two years to get the double-album *Liza Minnelli Live at Carnegie Hall* released, as Liza was not signed with a record company at the time. Immediately after the Carnegie run, Minnelli flew to California to videotape the second of three TV specials she'd star in for the 1979–80 TV season. *Goldie and Liza Together* teamed two old friends in an hour of song, dance, comedy, and even a dramatic scene. (Minnelli had befriended Goldie Hawn when she was a guest on Hawn's TV series, *Laugh-In*, eight years earlier.) Three days later, Liza was back on the road with her fifteen-month, forty-five-city concert tour, which concluded on November 25, 1979. That last night in New Orleans was filmed by ABC-TV for use in a *20/20* story on the star, and the night before, HBO had videotaped both of Liza's performances for one of the first episodes in their *Standing Room Only* concert series.

The entertainment industry is a crap shoot, full of dizzying heights and terrifying lows. Despite having a script that can read like an Oscar-winning film on paper, and all the greatest talents in Hollywood working both behind and in front of the camera, a movie may crash and burn at the box office. Liza faced that scenario during this decade, when her follow-up films to *Cabaret* failed to continue her career as a leading lady of the silver screen. Still, the 1970s marked the decade when Liza Minnelli became a household name and a true superstar, winning an Academy Award, an Emmy, and a second Tony Award.

The coming decade of the 1980s would prove to be challenging and life-altering.

CHAPTER FOUR

Liza's Life: The 1980s (An Overview)

The 1980s started with Liza beginning production in January 1980 on her third TV special for the 1979–1980 television season. *Baryshnikov on Broadway* paired her with the great dancer, Mikhail Baryshnikov.

After three years, Liza finally returned to the big screen in June 1980, when she began filming the comedy *Arthur* with Dudley Moore and John Gielgud, shot entirely in New York City. Minnelli played aspiring actress / working waitress "Linda Marolla," who captured the heart of multimillionaire "Arthur Bach," played by Moore. *Arthur* opened on July 17, 1981. The critics raved—"Miss Minnelli hasn't been seen to such good advantage on film since *Cabaret*," was how the *New York Times* put it—and most important, the movie grossed over 95 million dollars, making it among the biggest hits of the year. Liza was nominated for a Golden Globe Award, and was again profiled extensively in print and on TV. The media agreed that this was a great film "comeback." While not a cameo, her part was not the lead either. "I drift in and out of it," Liza admitted, "but I did it mainly to get to work with Dudley Moore and John Gielgud, who was a scream!"

There was another movie to promote at this time: an extended, restored version of *New York, New York* was reissued to theaters in the summer of 1981. "Now it makes sense," was how Liza herself summed up the three-hour-plus epic.

Concerts were where Liza's heart lay, and a 1981 tour schedule included another whirlwind of dates across the country and overseas, before her New Year's Eve concert in Las Vegas. One concert that was canceled, however, was a December 27, 1981,

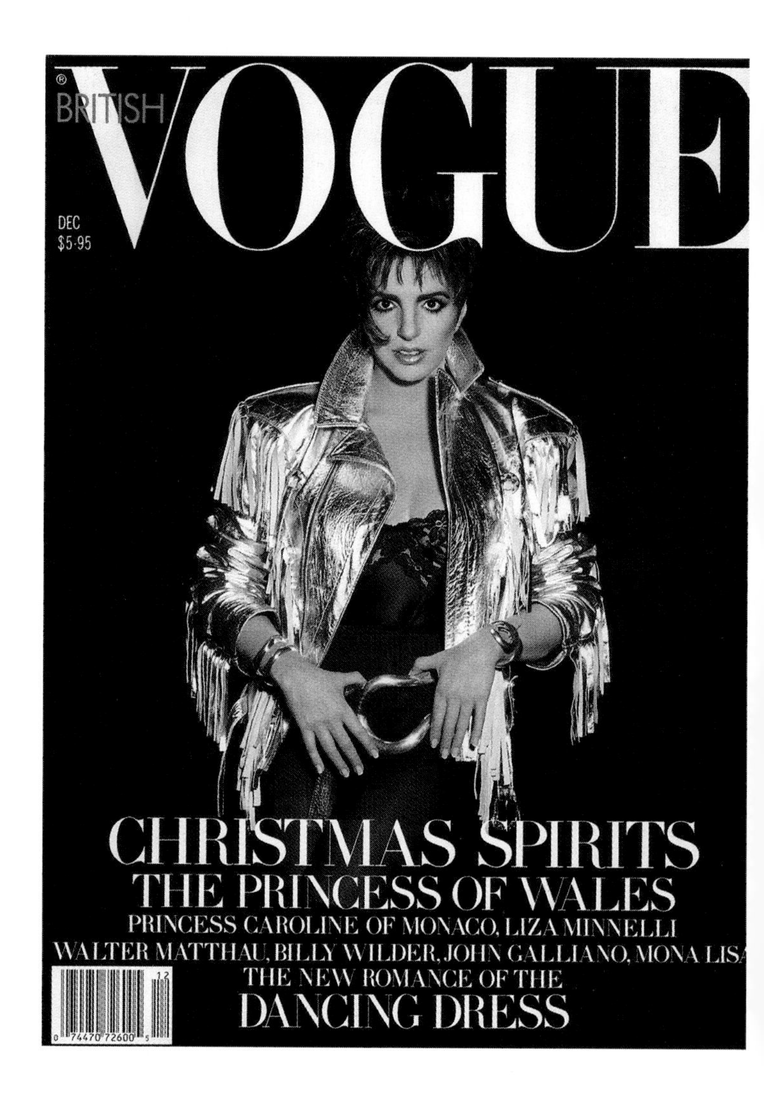

date at Carnegie Hall. It was to be a joint performance with singer-dancer-songwriter (and ex-husband) Peter Allen. The two would never share the stage in an official concert during the last decades of Allen's life (following joint appearances overseas in the mid to late 1960s).

Popcorn tasted good again in 1981: Liza returned to movies after a four-year absence in the hit comedy *Arthur,* starring Dudley Moore.

Given her hectic schedule in 1981, Liza admitted she was ready to take some time off for most of 1982. It was the first year she would do so since her career began nearly twenty years earlier. The following year, 1983, was also relatively quiet; the highlight was her co-hosting the Academy Awards that spring with Dudley Moore, Richard Pryor, and Walter Matthau.

Then, at the end of August 1983, it was announced that Liza had signed to star in a new Kander-Ebb Broadway musical, *The Rink.* Minnelli stated she was looking forward to playing a non-glamorous role, as "Angel," a rebellious ex-hippie who returned to her childhood, and to the volatile relationship with her mother, played by Chita Rivera.

The Rink opened on Broadway at the Martin Beck Theater on February 9, 1984. The show received mixed reviews—"All that talent, for what? A mishmash," was how the *New York Daily News* put it—but due to the public's desire to see Liza live, the show still did well at the box office. The strain of doing eight shows a week was making her tired, and Liza often slept until she had to leave for work. Then, on July 16, 1984, famed columnist Liz Smith—a constant Minnelli media supporter—announced that Liza had just entered the Betty Ford Clinic in Rancho Mirage, California, for help with an addiction to alcohol and prescribed medications. "I have a problem, and I'm going to deal with it," was her exclusive statement to Smith. Liza's sobriety has remained a top priority to this day, despite what you may have been led to believe. There would be relapses over the coming years, as there is no known cure for the disease of chemical dependency, but the star would continue to seek help for her illness, and would not shy away from the topic during interviews. With Liza gone from *The Rink,* the show closed, despite co-star Chita Rivera winning the Tony Award. Liza had been nominated in the same category.

The following year, 1985, was the start of Liza's first real comeback. In January, she agreed to return to doing concert tours, which kicked off on June 18, 1985, in Seattle. Minnelli spent a few weeks away from the concert stage in August and September of 1985, filming her very first movie for television. *A Time to Live* told the true story of Mary-Lou Weisman, the mother of a young boy who was dying from muscular dystrophy. The *New York Post* said it would be "impossible to imagine another actress" playing the part. Upon finishing the film on September 3, 1985—for which she would win a Golden Globe Award—she immediately went back on the road, to Wooster, Massachusetts, in concert with her newly reborn voice. Indeed, 1985 and 1986 marked one of the singer's best vocal periods ever. Minnelli's purity of tone equaled her powerful belt, producing a sound that was "pretty" to the ear, yet still emotionally devastating.

Minnelli marked a milestone on March 12, 1986, when she celebrated her fortieth birthday while performing in concert at the London Palladium. HBO again videotaped Liza's performance, and

quickly aired the concert *(Liza in London)* on their *Standing Room Only* series. Then on April 30, 1986, Liza shared the stage with Frank Sinatra for the first time, at the Golden Nugget casino in Atlantic City. After their own sets of solos, the duo closed the show with a mammoth medley of songs about New York: Yes, Liza duetted with her beloved "Uncle Frank" on the song "New York, New York." She also did additional solo concerts across the country throughout 1986, with her voice again in superb strength and form—she could do anything vocally, with a rich, musical clarity and power that was stunning to hear. Liza finished the year with two projects for the big and small screens. The first was the theatrical movie *Rent-a-Cop*, filmed in Rome during the fall of 1986. (The film flopped at the box office when released domestically in January 1988.) Then for PBS-TV, she videotaped a clip-filled tribute to her father's work that would air the following year, called *Minnelli on Minnelli*. (In 1999, she would star in a Broadway revue/tribute by the same name, to honor Vincente.)

In early 1987, Liza was back on the concert stage. One of the highlights of the year occurred between May 28 and June 18: *Three Weeks at Carnegie Hall* made Minnelli the very first—and only star to date—to ever sell out the legendary hall for fourteen consecutive concerts. Rave reviews were again the order of the day. "Her voice has never sounded stronger and surer," stated the *New York Times*. A two-CD set of all the songs (see Chapter Twelve, "For the Record," for a complete listing) were assembled for the Telarc label's *Liza Minnelli at Carnegie Hall* release. Along with taking the new Carnegie concert on the road, Minnelli made a movie in the fall of 1987. *Arthur 2: On the Rocks* was the sequel that reunited Liza with Dudley Moore as their beloved characters from the 1981 movie smash (the new film died at the box office in the summer of 1988). A successful first-ever venture by the star occurred in the fall of 1987, when Liza launched a fifteen-month-long stint as spokesperson for Estée Lauder's men's cologne Metropolis, complete with in-store appearances and a TV commercial. Minnelli was paid a noted $1 million for the spot, which was filmed at the following New York City locations: the Plaza Hotel, the Joyce Theatre, the Empire Diner, and the Fulton Ferry landing, where she was joined on screen by her then-husband, Mark Gero. Liza recorded a new version of the song "City Lights" from her Kander-Ebb musical *The Act* for the ad.

The fall of 1988 saw the start of a nearly two-year-long tour with lifelong family friends Frank Sinatra and Sammy Davis Jr. called *The Ultimate Event*. The concert had Sammy opening with his set of solos, followed by Liza's, then Sinatra's. Closing the show was a medley of songs performed by the trio, climaxing with "New York, New York." Their December 1988 stint in Detroit was videotaped as a Pay-per-View TV special,

(Opposite) Liza celebrated her fortieth birthday by performing a series of sold-out concerts at the London Palladium, later broadcast on HBO.

Liza with the Pet Shop Boys during the recording of her 1989 solo album *Results,* which remains one of her finest efforts.

airing on the Showtime cable network in February 1989. In England during Easter 1989, Minnelli moonlighted at midnight, running from London's Royal Albert Hall to a recording studio. She was making one of her most unusual, ambitious, and finest recordings to date: *Results*. The album was produced by the British pop trio the Pet Shop Boys; the style was very much a dance-club pop sound. It included the songs "Losing My Mind," "Rent," and "Love Pains." The album was certainly nothing one would associate with Liza Minnelli, but the singer was in flawless voice, lovely and melodic. Her unique storytelling style of singing was still completely apparent; she didn't change her way of singing to suit this different genre of music. *Event* costars Sinatra and Sammy approved of the album, with Davis proclaiming it "the hippest record around." Liza immediately began promoting her first (non-cast) studio album in twelve years. *Results* actually got them, especially in England, where the disc's first single, the Stephen Sondheim Broadway hit "Losing My Mind" from *Follies*, went to number one in the summer of 1989. *Results* reached Number 128 on the *Billboard* charts in the States, and Minnelli ended 1989 by receiving an honory "Living Legend" Grammy (this was a lifetime achievement award, for an entire body of work).

The 1980s had begun with an onslaught of TV appearances, and ended as such, with a valid attempt at stretching the public's view of what Liza Minnelli could do. In the coming decade, Liza would continue with more traditional ways of expressing her art, while battling life-altering health issues.

CHAPTER FIVE

Liza's Life: The 1990s (An Overview)

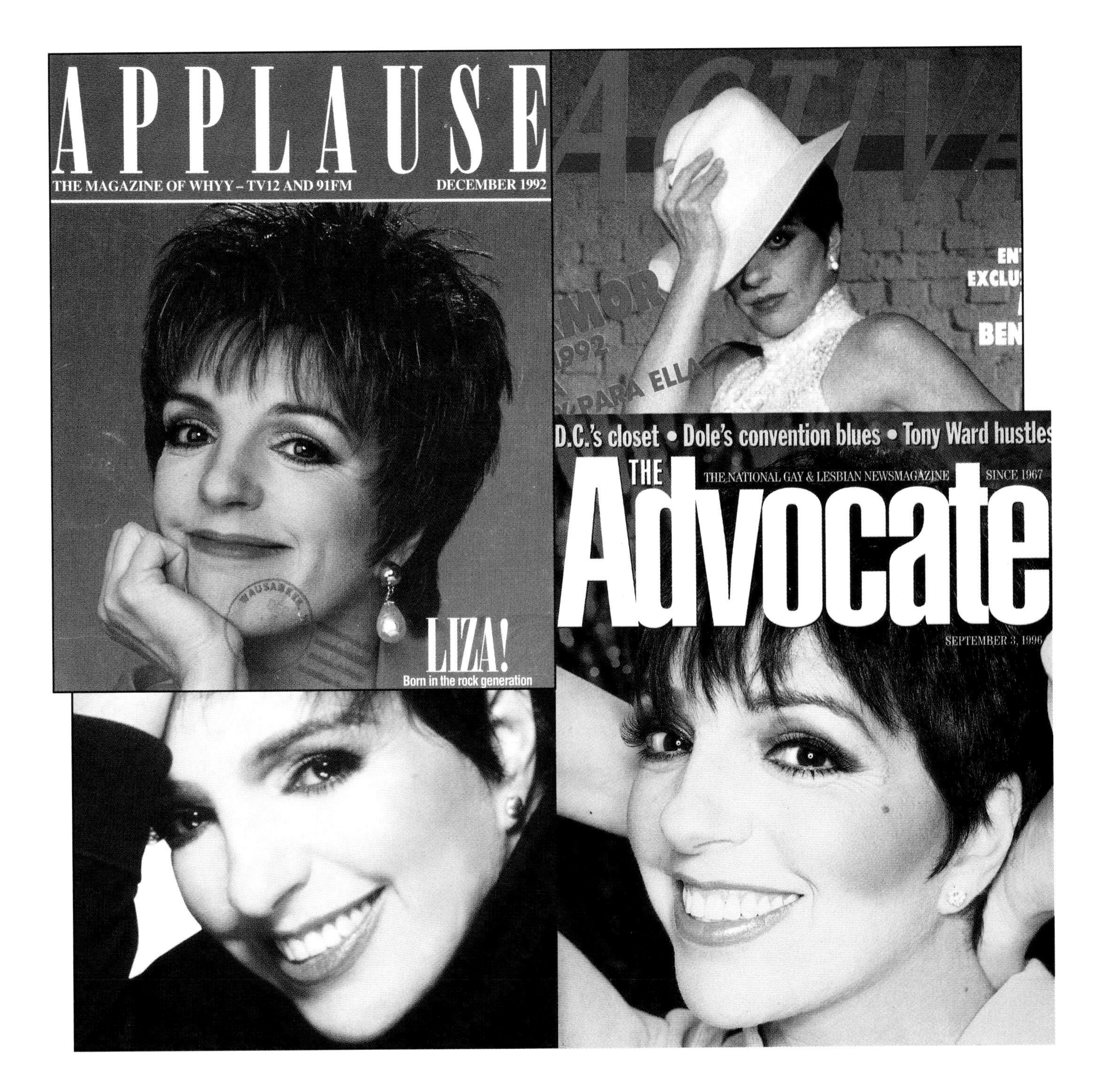

April 26, 1999
In Theater
GUEST EDITOR
Liza
HER PERSONAL SCRAPBOOK
HER CABARET FAVES
MEMORIES OF KAY THOMPSON
TELEKNACK
WEEK VAN 25 APRIL TOT 1 MEI 1997
Ze is de dochter van actrice Judy Garland en musicalregisseur Vincente Minnelli. Als driejarige dreumes maakte Liza Minnelli haar filmdebuut. En na een korte carrière als danseres en zangeres in nachtclubs, brak Minnelli echt door met de film Charlie Bubbles (1968). Haar acteertalent werd bekroond met een Oscar voor haar rol van Sally Bowles in de musical Cabaret.
Vrijdag laat ook Dudley Moore zich, in de komedie Arthur, door haar charmeren. Te bekijken op TV1 om 21u10.
Liza voor het altaar
JANUARY 13, 1997
NEW YORK
SHOWGIRL
The comedy and tragedy and strange

The first year of the new decade was spent fulfilling concert dates, and filming *Stepping Out*, a comedy-drama in which Liza played "Mavis Travis," a one-time Broadway performer teaching tap dancing to a lovable group of misfits. ("*Rocky* meets *A Chorus Line*" was how the the film was described.) The title tune, "Stepping Out," another Kander-Ebb effort, remains one of their best.

Minnelli then began 1991 by undertaking perhaps her most lavish stage project to date: *Liza Stepping Out at Radio City Music Hall.* Opening on April 23, the production featured a solo concert in the first half, and a dozen "demon divas" who joined Liza in the second act. Planted throughout the audience, the ladies—of all ages and races—joined Minnelli in singing and dancing on the Music Hall stage. Breaking every box office record in Radio City's history, the show brought in $3.8 million, making Minnelli the largest-grossing live act of 1991, beating even rockers such as the Rolling Stones.

Minnelli took the Radio City act out on tour, and also promoted her movie *Stepping Out*, which opened in October 1991. Paramount had lost faith in the film, deciding to hold it from spring to fall, and only made eight prints. It could thus only be shown in a few select cities.

At the time of the movie's Los Angeles premiere, Minnelli was given a star on the Hollywood Walk of Fame, arranged by her fan club, Limelight on Liza. Nancy Barr-Brandon started the club back in December 1964, then it was run from 1976 to early 1997 by Susan Meyer. (Soon the Internet became the best source for up-to-date Liza information, via websites and e-mail groups. See this book's Appendix for more.)

In 1992, Liza continued to tour the world with concert work, while promoting a new CD and home video/laser disc. She had personally supervised editing of *Liza Live at Radio City Music Hall*, culled from high-definition videotapes of her Radio City show shot earlier in the year. Both the video and the compact disc were successes. The VHS made the top of *Billboard*'s video charts, and the CD remains Liza's biggest selling solo album to date, according to SoundScan reports (which began tracking record sales in 1991).

A haunting publicity portrait, made during the filming of Liza's movie *Stepping Out*.

1993 continued Liza's concert career around the country. She also hosted the annual Tony Awards telecast on CBS. During this same period she performed a series of concerts at Carnegie Hall with French singing sensation and frequent musical partner Charles Aznavour. Minnelli was also part of an ensemble cast acting in a comedy-drama for the Showtime cable TV network, called *Parallel Lives*, in which she played a woman in charge of a college reunion.

On December 1, 1993, Liza was the main media presence for the first ever World AIDS Day, an effort to raise awareness and help for those afflicted with the disease. At the United Nations, she sang an anthem for the cause, "The Day After That," from the Kander-Ebb musical *Kiss of the Spider Woman.* Columbia Records released a single of Minnelli singing the song, as well as a VHS and laser disc of the music video. Liza made her directorial debut with this video. A substantial

Liza in a scene from the second of her three TV movies to date: *Parallel Lives* (1994), filmed in 1993.

portion of net profits from the release was donated to a key AIDS charity, AmFAR.

Most of 1994 was again spent touring. To commemorate the twenty-fifth anniversary of her mother's passing in June of that year, Liza appeared at the Stonewall 25 gay pride event in Central Park. Along with singing "The Day After That," she spoke beautifully about her beloved mama to the million people packed in the park. Those gathered greeted Minnelli's entrance with chants of "Ju-dy, Ju-dy, Ju-dy, Ju-dy . . . !" (This was in honor of their icon, who has been cited as a main reason behind the start of gay liberation—the Stonewall riots occurred as the drag queens were returning from Judy's funeral.) As Minnelli left the stage, the masses were cheering "Li-za, Li-za, Li-za, Li-za . . . !"

On December 17, 1994, the star had the first of three surgeries she would face over the years for replacement of her hips. There would also later be procedures to repair damage to her knee and back. These were all prices paid for the stresses caused by the thirty-plus years of dancing.

By 1995–1996, Liza's professional activities had become a welcomed and expected routine, with concerts still the backbone of her multimillion-dollar company, LM Concerts. Along with her appearances in theaters and concert halls, Minnelli had contracts with casinos in Las Vegas, Connecticut, and Atlantic City, which all called for her to perform a certain number of weeks each year. "A.C. is homier than Las Vegas. I love the sea, the beach, the boardwalk. I do a lot of work down there," Minnelli said in a print interview. In the spring of 1995, Liza filmed a TV movie for CBS, *The West Side Waltz*, based on the Broadway play about a group of misfits who find inner strength together. Co-starring were Shirley MacLaine, Jennifer Grey, and Kathy Bates (whom Liza had worked with in *Arthur 2: On the Rocks*).

Also in 1995, Liza signed a new recording deal with Angel Records, and began taping a CD of what she called "make-out songs." *Gently* features beautiful ballads and standards, the types of numbers she would sing at parties or at home with her friends, such as "It Had to Be You," "You Stepped out of a Dream," and "Chances Are." On March 12, 1996, Liza celebrated her fiftieth birthday in Paris, and began promoting the release of *Gently*, her first studio album in nearly seven years. Sales were fairly brisk (making the Billboard charts), even if the lady's voice was not as strong as it would soon be again. By summer of 1996, Minnelli's voice had regained its full power, as she embarked on a concert tour with her *Arthur* costar Dudley Moore, duetting on the theme from the movie. Solo concerts in the fall continued to reveal Liza at one of her peak periods vocally and physically.

Taking over Julie Andrews's role in the Broadway musical *Victor/Victoria* in January 1997, Liza began having vocal problems during the second week of the run. During her fourth and final week in the show, doctors demanded that she stop performing for fear of risking permanent damage to her vocal cords. Liza would still go on stage before the start of the show to talk with the audience and apologize for not being able to perform. Ultimately, because of her vocal condition, she wound up not performing her last few scheduled shows. What never seems to be mentioned in connection with *Victor/Victoria* is the fact that Liza Minnelli brought in nearly three million dollars to the box office, making the musical a sellout.

The only bright spot during this period was a 1997 Grammy Award nomination for Liza's *Gently* album. (Natalie Cole, Bernadette Peters, Rosemary Clooney, and Tony Bennett were her competitors; Tony won the Grammy.) Shortly after this, just as Liza was turning fifty-one, she faced difficult surgery: polyps had to be removed from her vocal cords. Tragically, the procedure was not successful, and Liza spent the next two years, 1997 and 1998, slowly rebuilding her voice, through work with vocal coaches and doctors. Astonishingly, the surgeon who operated on Liza's vocal cords was the same doctor who worked on Julie Andrews; Julie's fate would be worse, as she has yet to sing again.

Liza returned to concerts, performing in Atlantic City on May 16–18, 1997. While touring for a full year, she sought the help of a vocal coach to continue strengthening her voice. Following May 1998 engagements in Atlantic City and Las Vegas—and after some 1997 and 1998 concert dates had been cancelled—Liza finally allowed herself official time off, to heal her vocal cords.

A heaven-sent birthday gift reportedly appeared on March 12, 1999, when Minnelli miraculously sang on her fifty-third birthday. The richness and power missing from her voice for the last two years were back. She agreed to test the waters publicly by singing "Stormy Weather" at the annual Mac Awards in New York City on April 5, 1999. The resulting ovation over Minnelli's reborn chops could be heard down to Battery Park.

At an October 20, 1999, Manhattan press conference, Liza announced that she would be performing a Broadway tribute to the music from her father's films (including "Gigi" and "An American in Paris"). *Minnelli on Minnelli* would be remarkable for another reason: This tribute to her dad would be playing the Palace Theater, a venue closely identified with Judy Garland. If this weren't enough to signal that the show was a family affair, the show's initials even spelled *MOM*. One of the revue's many highlights included a duet between Liza and Judy on "The Trolley Song" from *Meet Me in St. Louis*. Liza sang along with Garland's voice from the soundtrack, while the film clip played. The first day of ticket sales broke the Palace box office record again, bringing in nearly half a million dollars. Minnelli was profiled extensively in print and on TV, including ABC's *20/20* where she told reporter Cynthia McFadden that this was indeed a "come*back*, a crawling, climbing *back*!" Following a week of previews, *Minnelli on Minnelli* opened on December 8, 1999, to multiple standing ovations from a star-studded crowd (including Gregory Peck, Rosie O'Donnell, Nathan Lane, and Mary Tyler Moore). The local reviews were surprisingly lukewarm, but the nationals noticed a fresher Minnelli. *USA Today*'s headline joyfully shouted the news: "Liza's Voice Is Reborn."

Liza's *MOM* tribute to Dad was given extensive media coverage during its December 1999 run on Broadway. Here Liza is shown singing two months earlier, at Radio City Music Hall's Grand Gala Reopening, October 4, 1999.

CHAPTER SIX

Liza's Life: Minnelli's Millennium, 2000–2004 (An Overview)

Minnelli's new millennium began with the star concluding the final week of *Minnelli on Minnelli* performances at the Palace Theater on Broadway. Wanting to share the show she was so proud of, Liza opened the road version of *MOM* with a four-night engagement in San Francisco. On her fifty-fourth birthday, the mayor of San Francisco declared March 12, 2000, "Liza Minnelli Day," as the star closed her engagement in strong vocal form and style. Liza then flew back to New York to continue promoting the *Minnelli on Minnelli: Live at the Palace* album that Angel Records released on February 29 (it had been taped the last week of her Palace run). A QVC TV appearance selling the CD was followed by an in-store signing at the Lincoln Center Tower Records, where the line of fans wrapped around the block (there had also been an in-store signing while Liza was in San Francisco). Looking lovely, Liza stayed many hours past her scheduled time, till she had met all the fans. Washington D.C.'s Kennedy Center was the next stop for the *MOM* tour, where CBS-TV videotaped her for a *CBS This Morning* segment. It soon became clear Liza wasn't actually as healthy as she was trying to be. Just after Easter 2000, Minnelli announced she was canceling the remainder of the *MOM* tour, due to physical pain preventing her "from doing the show my fans want to see and what I love doing for them so much." Taking the first official open-ended vacation she'd had in over fifteen years, Liza retreated to Florida, where she attended local ball games, and was a frequent visitor to area restaurants and theaters. This seemingly tranquil

time of Liza's life soon ended. On October 8, 2000, she collapsed while singing at home, and was rushed to the hospital. It was feared she'd suffered a stroke, but it was announced that Liza had actually contracted viral encephalitis, a serious and sometimes deadly inflammation of the brain. Minnelli's always amazing strength was perhaps tested as never before. Doctors reportedly told the star she was lucky to be alive—but added she might never talk and walk again, let alone sing and dance. Remaining in Florida for treatment, Liza was very low on the industry radar, as she was rarely written about during this time. Back surgery in March 2001 brought her home to New York full-time, after which she stated she was finally pain-free and ready to work. Making headlines, she sang "Maybe This Time" at an AIDS charity event, the first time she'd sung professionally in a year. Liza's longtime friend Michael Jackson then insisted that she be a part of his *30th Anniversary Celebration* CBS-TV special, being videotaped at New York City's Madison Square Garden in September 2001. Liza sang "You Are Not Alone" and a medley of "Never, Never Land/Over the Rainbow" (the first time in forty years that she'd sung "Rainbow") at the two Jackson shows on September 7 and 10, 2001. The next morning—9/11—the world changed, and Liza immediately did whatever she could to help heal the country. Singing "New York, New York" at Shea Stadium, Liza garnered cheers heard all over town. Minnelli also performed *her* song on *Rosie O'Donnell*, appeared on *Larry King Live*, and at Madison Square Garden.

Flying to London in January 2002, Minnelli's comeback concert was announced: *Liza's Back!* A tour was being planned, with London's Royal Albert Hall set as the first stop, in April. That spring, Liza Minnelli was the most talked and written about celebrity in the world. Audiences and critics went wild over the revitalized Minnelli: Her voice sounded vastly improved over even her finest 1999–2000 work. Liza was indeed "back," and booked into Manhattan's Beacon Theater for a week of concerts, May 31 through June 8, 2002. Clive Davis had her last two nights at the Beacon recorded for a fall CD release. While many other projects were being considered, one was announced on July 25, 2002, at L.A.'s House of Blues. The star had signed a million-dollar deal with Viacom's VH-1 cable network for a weekly hour-long musical-reality series—Liza Minnelli's first TV series. The deal called for ten episodes, with options for a total of forty shows in all (or four cycles of ten shows each) at $125,000 per episode, plus expenses such as wardrobe fees and other perks. VH-1 began filming various daily activities: rehearsals, shopping, attending social events, etc.

The *Liza's Back!* CD was released October 29, 2002, capturing all the excitement of Liza live, and the love between the artist and her audience. This love affair was again evident at Tower Records in Manhattan the day the disc was issued, when Minnelli signed copies for fans who again lined up for blocks to meet their idol. The next day it was announced that VH-1 was not continuing production of the *Liza and David* TV series (set to feature Minnelli with her then-husband, producer David Gest), before even a single episode was aired. Allegations flew across the media, as did multimillion-dollar lawsuits, which would ultimately be dropped by both sides in September 2003. All the facts have yet to surface, except that over sixty hours of footage had been shot, including the first of the scheduled weekly dinner parties at the star's Manhattan penthouse, on October 21, 2002. Liza admitted she was disappointed about not being able to perhaps have an impact on people across the country on a weekly basis. VH-1 also expressed regret that the public wouldn't be seeing the woman they had greatly enjoyed working with. Yet Liza actually returned to VH-1 in November 2003 as the first presenter on the network's award show *Best of '03*—proving that in the entertainment industry, anything is possible.

That sums up the latest on Liza, and on her life and career in general. Minnelli performed a December 2002 *Liza's Christmas Spectacular* at New York City's Town Hall, in superb form and voice—even better than she had been on Broadway in her *Liza's Back!* concert the preceeding spring. A twelve-show concert tour took place in various U.S. cities in February 2003, again revealing the star to be in superlative shape vocally. Many Minnelli projects were mentioned as being in the works, including movie projects. These included one by the makers of the hit *Four Weddings and a Funeral*, and a promise by Andrew

Lloyd Webber that Liza will play the lead in the film version of his *Sunset Boulevard* Broadway musical.

As of this writing, the latest projects in Liza's life are exciting ones: Minnelli has become MAC Cosmetics' new spokesperson. The company launched their biggest marketing campaign to date, via a fall 2003 launch of products with the star's name—and input—attached. Liza Lashes and the entire Liza line are now being sold across the country, as this living legend faces the world as a dynamic individual, with room for even greater growth. The icon is currently entering another new area by making her sitcom and TV series debut via guest appearances on the new Fox 2003–2004 series *Arrested Development*. Her comedic timing was praised by television critics and audiences, and rumors were rampant about two new albums, a summer 2004 concert tour, and confirmed offers for two TV series and a feature film.

Life just might turn out to be a cabaret for Liza May after all.

Publicity portrait used for the *Liza's Back!* tour and CD, taken summer 2002, revealed the lady looking as lovely as ever.

Intermission

The Many Faces Of...

THE LIZA MINNELLI LOOK

Liza Minnelli, singer, actress and daughter of Judy Garland, is a girl who likes clothes that have all the dash and flair of today—this minute —1965. That means fashions that are young, colorful, kicky; fashions that are designed with simple, clean lines and lots of style. Here's Liza to show you just such a look from Junior Sophisticates' summer collection.

Continued

Above: A white piqué coat-dress with a wide, notched collar, easy skirt, and belt that ties loosely over the hips. With it, Liza wears a white straw sailor hat, pale lemon leather shoes with a grosgrain silk tie. Dress, about $65. Right: Chrome-yellow three-piece outfit consists of a pleated walking skirt, a sleeveless, zippered overblouse, a long loose jacket. Try an enameled flower on the lapel. The outfit is about $90.

24

Liza often worked as a fashion model, appearing in magazines early in her career, including this spread in the May 29, 1965, issue of *TV Guide*.

CHAPTER SEVEN

The Liza Look

Only a handful of celebrities are lucky enough to have a signature style. Liza Minnelli excels in this area, for she has more or less kept the Liza Look for over thirty years. Since 1972—when the film *Cabaret* made her an international superstar—Minnelli has been instantly recognized for her dark hair and her equally dark, huge eyes, with those special Liza lashes. Two people were instrumental in helping the star develop her "Sally Bowles" look: veteran Broadway performer Gwen Verdon, wife of *Cabaret* director Bob Fosse, and Vincent Minnelli. Liza's dad poured over books and magazines from the 1920s and 30s, settling on a style inspired by film star Louise Brooks. This look has stayed with Liza, while evolving, as you'll see here.

The lashes themselves are such a part of her signature look that the MAC cosmetic company signed the legendary Liza to market Liza Lashes as part of her own line with the company, in the fall of 2003.

Minnelli's glamourous image is also due to the genius of the world's greatest fashion designers, especially two who have designed for her throughout her career. Halston first became known as the man who made Jacqueline Kennedy's famous "pill box" hats before taking the 1970s fashion world by storm via his fashion styles for the rich and famous. (Liza recently mentioned a contribution she herself made to the 1970s fashion world: the "invention" of hot pants!) The man who has handled most of Minnelli's current professional needs, Bob Mackie, became best known for his outrageous and sometimes comical designs for Cher. Both acclaimed designers kept Liza in sequins. Halston started the practice because he felt the beads worked well at hiding perspiration on a performer who sweats a lot on stage while belting out songs to the balcony.

Liza wasn't always a symbol of show-biz razzle-dazzle. In terms of her "packaging," she appeared very much as other teenagers did when she began being profiled and publicized in 1963 at age seventeen—favoring casual clothes such as jeans or slacks. Nor did Minnelli sport her signature short bob. As you see here, her hair was actually quite long throughout 1963 and into the following year.

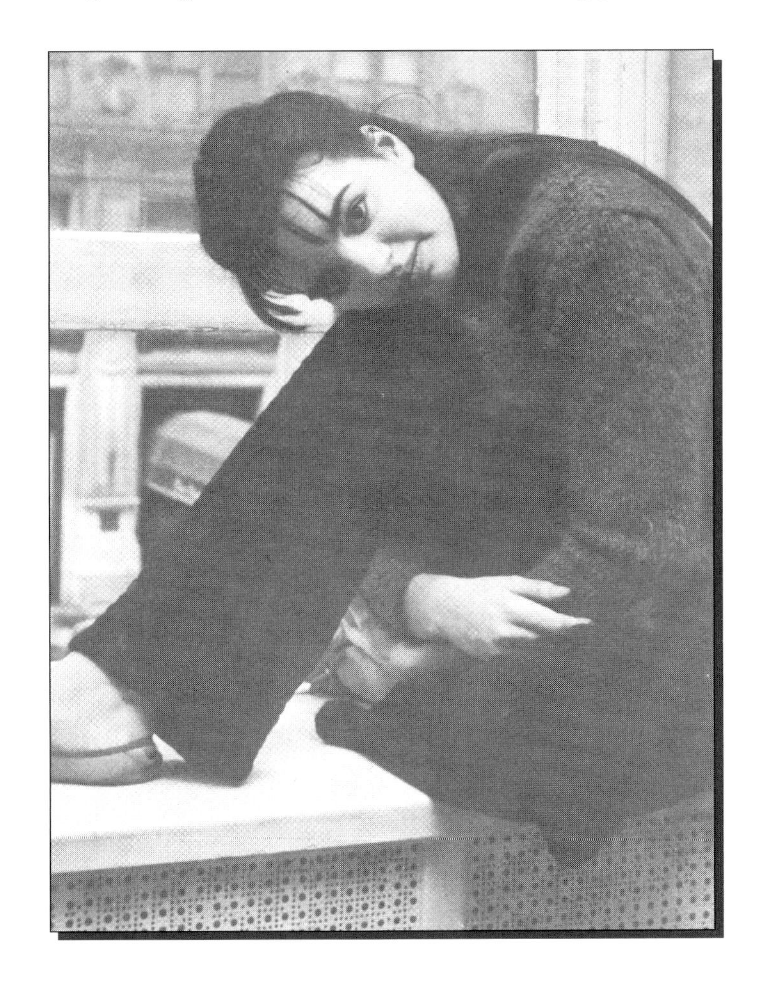

It wasn't until later in 1964 that the young lady reportedly got so fed up with her long locks that she cut her hair herself—requiring hours with a professional stylist to undo the damage she'd done. A shoulder-length look was kept for 1964 and 1965, before another change was made: a more important one.

Liza signing autographs in New York City, June 1965, during the time of her Broadway debut in *Flora*.

On March 19, 1966, a week after her twentieth birthday, Liza Minnelli first adopted the close-cropped "do" that she would become known for, even if the style hadn't quite evolved as it would by the early seventies.

Liza sporting her new hair do around the pool, while performing at the Sahara in Las Vegas, September 1966.

Liza continued trying new styles as late as 1970 and 1971, even adopting a longer, permed look as seen here.

Liza in January 1971.

By 1972, the Liza Look seemed locked in place, and has pretty much remained that way to date.

The hair alone wasn't the only unique aspect of her image. The huge false eyelashes became an equally important part of what people today expect Liza Minnelli to look like. "They're made out of some kind of thin wire," the star explained on stage in 1977. "The minute they get wet, they go right into your eyes. I'm all for glamour, but blindness? Skip it!" Minnelli said as she removed them from her sweat-soaked face. Makeup artist Christina Smith designed the lashes and the Liza

Look. (Smith wasn't a household name, but stars in Beverly Hills—such as Cher, Ann-Margret, and others—relished her skills at making them look their best.)

The lashes' lengths would vary from large to impossibly huge, as you can see from the photos here.

One interesting Liza hair period was 1977–1979, when Minnelli kept experimenting. Just before doing *The Act*, she had a longer, shoulder-length hair style that was very becoming. The star then changed to an equally fetching combed-to-the-side short look, with no bangs. Her 1979 "concert hairstyle" was also mesmerizing—the completely smooth-lined, solid "cap" of hair kept bouncing right back into place as she moved.

In 1979 and 1980, Minnelli briefly sported a new pulled-back, upswept hairstyle for appearances with the Martha Graham company, and also for the 1980 Oscars. (See the ad below, also.)

Liza Minnelli says that the things she remembers most about her childhood are "travel and my Capezio shoes." Here she is at age five in those favorite Capezio ballet slippers. And today, the legendary Liza wears Capezio hand-made-to-order satin Character shoes.

Soon to be seen in the movie, "Arthur," Liza with a Z is Zomething else!

For our newest Catalogue, send $2 (includes postage and handling) to: Capezio Ballet Makers, Dept. AD12, 1860 Broadway, New York, N.Y. 10023

Jack Mitchell

YOU'RE A STAR IN CAPEZIO®

Capezio's been dancing

In the early 1980s (and occasionally afterward), Liza's hairstyle favored "spit curls"—sort of "bangs" that came out onto the sides of her face. Sometimes there were two of them, and sometimes three, as you can see here.

Liza's "spit curls" made a dramatic—and cinematic—return in the movie *Rent-a-Cop* (1987), in which she starred with Burt Reynolds.

In 1982, Minnelli made headlines for getting a perm, and she became Liza with a Curl. In the summer of 1985, Liza's hair was dyed blond for a TV movie, *A Time to Live*, and she kept the look into 1986.

Liza adopted one of her most unusual—and effective—looks during the time she was promoting her *Results* album in 1989 and 1990. This look—with a long extension piece hanging down near the front of her face—was quite appealing in its effort to perhaps attract a younger demographic.

From 1990 to 2001, Liza usually sported the classic Liza Look. (Pixie hair cut, sometimes spiked, sometimes with spit curls, along with the

Publicity photo for *A Time to Live* (1985).

long lashes and the sequins.) In the summer of 2001, her hair was longer and had a flip to it, which she enjoyed showing off. For her September 2001 appearances for the Michael Jackson special, she wore a hairstyle fashioned after the "Aces High" number in the *New York, New York* movie.

Liza at Spec's in Cocoanut Grove, Florida, February 27, 1993, for a signing of her *Radio City* CD.

Lately Liza has been favoring the 1987 "Carnegie Hall" hairstyle (very spiky), but no matter what style her locks are, Minnelli proves her packaging can be compelling. All one needs to say is, "the Liza Look," and an image enters your mind of a pixie haircut, lush lashes, and an ensemble dripping with sequins.

CD signing for the *Liza's Back!* disc, October 29, 2002, at Tower Records in New York City.

The man who designed Liza's trademark sequined look, the great Halston, here with Liza in 1981.

Night and day—The latest Liza Look is her classic. Liza as the star of MAC Cosmetics' new fall 2003 campaign, Liza's own cosmetics line.

CHAPTER EIGHT

"Everybody Loves a Winner" — Liza's Major Awards

Liza with two of the most important men in her life, Oscar and Dad, the night she won for her performance in *Cabaret*.

Academy Award ("Oscar") for Best Actress, for her starring role in the 1972 movie *Cabaret*. Nomination for Best Actress for the 1969 release *The Sterile Cuckoo*.

Best Album of the Year was awarded Liza's 1966 album *There Is a Time*, by *Hi-Fi/Stereo Review* magazine.

Box Office Magazine's Top Box Office Draw of 1975.

David di Donatello Awards: Best Foreign Actress for *Cabaret*, and for *The Sterile Cuckoo*. Liza won a Special David award in 2002 for her body of work.

Emmy Award: Given to Liza for her 1972 TV special *Liza with a Z*. Liza was Emmy-nominated for her performance in the January 3, 1973, ABC special *A Royal Gala Variety Performance in the Presence of Her Majesty the Queen*, in the category of Outstanding Supporting Performer on a Music or Variety Program. She lost to Tim Conway of *The Carol Burnett Show*, but this was the same year/TV season she shared in the victory of *Liza with a "Z"* as Outstanding Variety/Music Program—she was given a statuette by the TV academy for being the show's star. Five other TV series or specials starring or featuring Liza received numerous Emmy Award nominations, including the 1979 episode of *The Muppet Show* she guested on; the 1980 specials *Goldie and Liza Together* and *Baryshnikov on Broadway* were both nominated for Outstanding Variety or Musical Program; and *Liza Stepping Out at Radio City Music Hall*, broadcast on PBS in 1992, brought Liza a nomination for Outstanding Individual Performance in a Variety or Music Program. The title song for the June 1999 CBS-TV special *AFI: 100 Years, 100 Stars—"Without You,"* by Marvin Hamlisch—was sung by Liza, and nominated for Best Original Song.

Golden Globe Awards: Best Motion Picture Actress, Musical/Comedy, in 1973, for her performance in *Cabaret*, and Best Performance by an Actress in a Mini-Series or Motion Picture Made for TV, 1986, for her performance in the TV movie *A Time to Live*. She also received four additional Nominations: Best Motion Picture Actress, Drama, in 1970, for her performance in *The Sterile Cuckoo* (1969); Best Motion Picture Actress, Musical/Comedy, in 1976, for her performance in *Lucky Lady*, (1975); Best Motion Picture Actress, Musical/Comedy, in 1978, for her performance in *New York, New York* (1977); Best Motion Picture Actress, Musical/Comedy, in 1982, for *Arthur* (1981).

Liza was presented the Liberace Legend Award in Las Vegas (by Siegfried and Roy), May 22, 1996.

Gold records—the *Cabaret* movie soundtrack and her *Liza with a "Z"* album.

Grammy Award—Liza received the Living Legend Grammy Award in November 1989 for her body of work in the music industry. There was also a nomination for Best Traditional Pop Vocal, 1997, for her album *Gently*.

Woman of the Year, 1973, Harvard's Hasting Pudding Theatricals, USA.

Highest Grossing Live Act/Engagement, of 1991: *Billboard* ranked Liza the highest-grossing act of 1991. Her engagement at Radio City Music Hall in April of 1991 grossed more than any appearances that year by any other performer anywhere in the United States, including such popular rock acts as the Rolling Stones.

Number One Single—Liza had a number one single on the dance charts in England in 1989, "Losing My Mind" (from her album *Results*).

Playboy Music Poll, Favorite Female Vocalist, 1976: Liza placed fifth in the 1976 *Playboy* Music Poll for Favorite Female Vocalist: 1) Phoebe Snow; 2) Roberta Flack; 3) Barbra Streisand; 4) Ella Fitzgerald; 5) Liza; 6) Flora Purim; 7) Shirley Bassey; 8) Cleo Laine; 9) Nancy Wilson; 10) Peggy Lee.

Theater Hall of Fame—Liza was inducted into the Theater Hall of Fame on January 29, 2001

Tony Award (Antoinette Perry Award): Liza has received three to date: Best Actress in a Musical, for her starring role in the 1965 Broadway show *Flora, The Red Menace*, her Broadway debut, at age nineteen. She remains the youngest recipient of that award, to date; Best Personal Achievement, for her January 1974 solo show at the Winter Garden; Best Actress in a Musical for her starring role in the 1977–78 Broadway show *The Act*. Liza also received a Tony Award nomination for Best Leading Actress in a Musical for the 1984 Broadway show *The Rink*.

Publicity portrait for Liza's hosting of the 1993 Tony Awards. Minnelli has three of the awards herself.

Act Two

PLAYBILL

MAJESTIC THEATRE

BEST FOOT FORWARD—STAGE 73

Cover page of the program for Liza's first off-Broadway show. Liza is one of the girls in the center, eighth from the right.

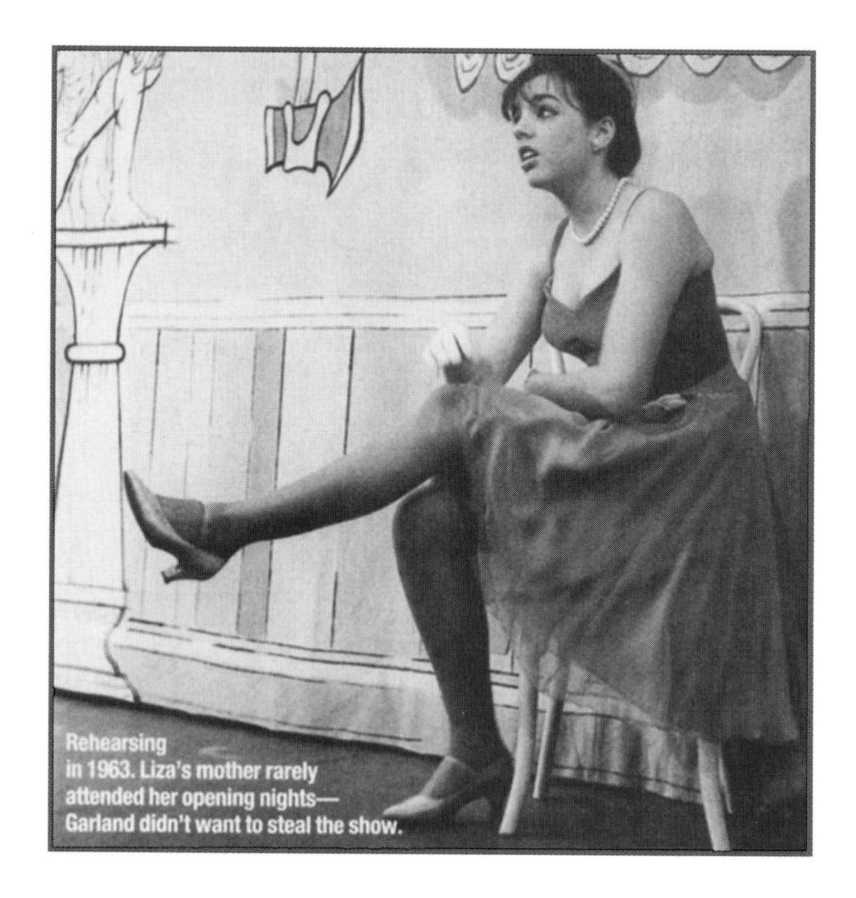

Rehearsing in 1963. Liza's mother rarely attended her opening nights—Garland didn't want to steal the show.

CHAPTER NINE

Broadway Baby: Liza's Stage and Theater "Book" Shows

Minnelli's heart may actually belong to Broadway. It was the art form that first captured her soul—despite growing up in Hollywood—and convinced her to pursue a show business career. She has portrayed about a dozen memorable characters on stage, in "book"—non-concert shows—most of them on Broadway. From 1963 through 1997, we'll look at the stage roles on which she has left the Minnelli mark.

As previously noted, before officially starting her career, Liza appeared in three summer stock shows in Hyannis Port, Massachusetts, in the summer of 1961: *Wish You Were Here*, *Flower Drum Song*, and *Take Me Along*. As a result of this stock work, Liza actually signed with her first agent, Stephanie "Stevie" Phillips, who would remain with Minnelli for many years. Also, following seven weeks of rehearsal after school, Liza debuted as Anne Frank on December 8 and 9, 1961, in the Scarsdale High School production of *The Diary of Anne Frank*. Thanks to a local sponsor, Liza and company then toured with the show in Israel, Greece, Rome, Jerusalem, and Amsterdam during July and August of 1962.

Best Foot Forward (1963)

Mere months after arriving in New York City to work in her chosen field, Liza Minnelli made her off-Broadway debut in a 1963 revival of the 1941 Broadway hit *Best Foot Forward*. Sixteen-year-old Liza was cast in the supporting role of man-hungry "Ethel Hofflinger" (a part that allowed her to showcase her singing, dancing, and acting talents) early in 1963, for which she was paid $45.00 a week—the equity minimum. The show opened on April 2, 1963, just after her seventeenth birthday on March 12. It played at the Stage 73 Theater at 321 East 73rd Street in Manhattan. Minnelli's reviews were rapturous:

"You want to get up on the stage, take her in your arms and tell her how good she is."
—George Oppenheimer, *Newsday*

"Liza Minnelli is certainly appealing. . . . She is easy and confident and accomplished and winning and also, I would think, a person."
—Walter Kerr, *New York Herald-Tribune*

"Liza is great! Liza sparkles!" **—Robert Coleman, *New York Mirror***

"About five minutes before the final curtain, Liza Minnelli stands alone on the stage singing a new song called 'You Are for Loving.' . . . Nothing else in the show can match those few minutes for sheer intensity of talent." **—Martin Gottfried, *Women's Wear Daily***

"We dig a rising star, Liza Minnelli . . . worth seeing, if only to remember back some day to having witnessed a Broadway star in her professional debut, in an eight-row theater, capacity 172, on the Upper East Side, back in '63." **—James Davis, *New York Daily News***

Liza received her very first award for her work in *Best Foot Forward.* She was one of twelve rising performers to receive the Promising Personality Award given by Daniel Blum's *Theatre World.* (Other recipients that year included Dorothy Loudon, later known as the evil "Miss Hanigan" in Broadway's smash musical *Annie,* and Stuart Damon, later known as Prince Charming in the 1965 *Cinderella* TV musical, and for his work on the ABC-TV soap *General Hospital.*) Minnelli began taking leaves of absence from the show in June 1963 to pursue other projects, such as videotaping appearances on her mother's TV series in Hollywood. In September 1963, she left the cast of *Best Foot Forward,* as offers for TV shows and records came to the new young star. There were even rumors of movie offers, but Liza decided to stick with the stage and the small screen for the time being. (Marcia Levant—daughter of Judy's MGM contemporary Oscar Levant—replaced Liza in *Forward,* and '40s film siren Veronica Lake became the new lead. The show still closed on October 13, barely six weeks after Minnelli left for good; clearly she was the real draw at the box office.)

Some of Minnelli's work in *Best Foot Forward* can actually be seen today. The teenager appeared on *The Ed Sullivan Show* in 1963 to promote the show, singing "Just a Little Joint with a Juke Box." It's miraculous to watch the surviving black-and-white videotape and marvel at Liza doing the actual number as she did it every night, and with the same dancers. While hardly the polished performer she'd become, the videotape makes it clear that the young lady has "it." Liza also recorded the cast album, preceeded by a session to make a single of her main solo "You are for Loving." (For the B side she sang the show's "What Do You Think I Am?") These two tracks are included on the most recent CD edition of the cast album (from Varese Sarabande Records). Minnelli's melodic vocal work is a thrill to hear, and this CD is a must-have for any Liza fan or fan of musical theater.

Carnival!
(1964)

Liza began touring in her first professional stock work from January 28 to March 22, 1964. It was the musical *Carnival!*, and she played the leading role of "Lili," originated on the New York stage by Anna Maria Alberghetti. The show concerned a naive young girl who joins a circus, and featured the standard "Love Makes the World Go Round". The road production played three theaters on the winter stock circuit in New York and New Jersey, including Long Island, New York, (mostly at the Mineola Playhouse). Another venue was the Paper Mill Playhouse, a 1,200-seat theater in Millburn, New Jersey. The notices were quite positive, including this one.

"By the time Liza sings her second number, 'Yes, My Heart,' the applause belongs to her alone." **—Mike McKay, *Newsday***

It was while at the Mineola Playhouse that Liza first met songwriters Fred Ebb and John Kander, later known for the scores of *Cabaret*; *Chicago*; *New York, New York*; and other Broadway and Hollywood hits. At this point they were mainly known for the song "My Coloring Book." Fellow cast member Marge Cameron (who later changed her name to Carmen Zapata) insisted the songwriters meet Minnelli. During a May 1964 interview with the press upon her arrival in Australia for concerts, Judy Garland mentioned Liza would be understudying Barbra Streisand in the just-opened Broadway musical *Funny Girl,* and that a show was being written especially for Minnelli. Both projects must have only been in the talking stages, as neither came to fruition.

Time Out for Ginger
(1964)

Not much information is known about this show, except that it was a comedy, with Liza playing the title role opposite Chester Morris. It played the Bucks County Playhouse in New Hope, Pennsylvania, where it opened on June 1, 1964.

The Fantasticks
(1964)

During this time, Minnelli also starred in a stock production of *The Fantasticks*, which toured four U.S. states and Canada for ten weeks. This mystical musical about young lovers was the longest running show in off-Broadway history. Liza's production began with two weeks of rehearsals at the Sullivan Street Theater in New York City. The tour's first stop was the Westport Country Playhouse in Connecticut on July 6, 1964. It was followed by a stand at the Tappan Zee Playhouse in Nyack, New York, where it played on July 10 and 13, 1964. There was a September engagement at the Coconut Grove Playhouse in Miami, Florida; a run in Ontario, Canada; and a final engagement in Mineola, Long Island, where it played during September and October. Liza's leading man was Elliot Gould (playing "The Boy" opposite Liza's "The Girl" role). Gould had recently starred in the 1962 Broadway musical *I Can Get It for You Wholesale*, and was married to another performer from that show, Barbra Streisand.

Liza and co-star Elliot Gould, both on and off-stage during an engagement of *The Fantasticks*, at the Tappan Zee Playhouse, July 13, 1964.

Flora, the Red Menace (1965)

Liza Minnelli made her Broadway debut in this musical, playing the title role of "Flora Meszaros," a young fashion illustrator in love with a man who was a Communist (played by Bob Dishy), set against the backdrop of the Great Depression. The show's legendary director, George Abbott, had

reportedly been considering Eydie Gorme for the role, and Liza seemed set to do the Broadway musical version of *Roman Holiday*, a remake of the 1950s Audrey Hepburn movie. As Minnelli told her fan club in 1965, "They wanted me [for *Roman Holiday*], but they postponed it, so I went back and auditioned for *Flora* again." Along with being Minnelli's first show on Broadway, *Flora* was also the first Broadway musical by the new songwriting team of Kander and Ebb. Starting out-of-town tryouts at the Shubert Theater in New Haven, Connecticut, on April 3, 1965, then moving to Boston's Colonial Theater on April 14, *Flora, the Red Menace* opened at Broadway's Alvin Theater on May 11, 1965. The critics' response was nearly unanimous about the musical's star (if not for the show itself).

"Liza Minnelli is a performer of arresting presence who does not merely occupy the stage, but fills it." **—*Time* magazine**

"[Liza] is the most promising youngster that has come along in years. She can belt a tune or whisper it, give it sizzling coalition of sex and/or scorn, or make it so tender you want to cry with her. . . . She knows how to breathe—in the professional sense that all good singers must have—and she knows that you don't parrot lyrics, you make them poetry and give them life. . . . Liza Minnelli is a winner, a fine singer, an excellent singer, and she can control her voice in a remarkable way for one so young and not yet richly experienced.
—Whitney Bolton, *The Morning Telegraph*, June 3, 1965 (This was a return visit by the critic, who obviously liked the show so much that he went to see it again.)

"Liza is a wonder and a magic and a doll."
—*Newsday*

At age nineteen, Minnelli also became the youngest artist to date to win the coveted Tony Award for Best Actress in a Musical. This was not enough to keep a musical involving Communism open, however. *Flora, the Red Menace* closed on July 24, 1965, having played eighty-seven performances on Broadway; of its $400,000 investment, it lost $381,000. Despite this, Liza mentioned in December 1965 that Kander and Ebb were writing a new Broadway musical for her called *Tomato Pie*. This show was never completed.

Components of Liza's performance in *Flora, the Red Menace* have been preserved, along with an audio tape made in the audience during the show's pre-Broadway run in Hartford. There is a surviving black-and-white videotape of two *Flora* numbers Liza performed on *The Ed Sullivan Show* (May 23,

On the left, Liza backstage at the Alvin Theatre before the first night of *Flora*, wearing the traditional "gypsy robe" that is passed from show to show on opening night. On the right, Liza signing autographs for fans attending a *Flora* performance, July 1965.

1965)—"All I Need Is One Good Break," and her solo "Sing Happy." Minnelli recorded those songs and two others from the score as pop singles for Capitol Records. There was also the original Broadway cast album for RCA Records, which was released on CD by RCA/BMG in 1993 and remains in print. Talks about producing a movie version of the show began circa 1972, followed by reports of taping a TV production of *Flora, the Red Menace* early in 1975, although neither happened.

It would be nearly ten years before Liza returned to Broadway or anywhere else in a book show. (Minnelli did perform her live act at the Winter Garden Theatre in January 1974—see Chapters Twelve, "For the Record," and Thirteen, Liza Live, for more information about that engagement). It was not because she wasn't wanted. Minnelli was offered the female lead in the 1968 Bachrach-David Broadway musical *Promises, Promises*, but turned it down so that she could instead star in the movie *The Sterile Cuckoo*. In the spring of 1972 there were rumors that Liza might star in an upcoming contemporary rock version of *Peter Pan* on Broadway, but this never happened (reports would arise again a decade later that she would be *Peter Pan* in New York City).

The Pajama Game (1966)

Liza starred as the female lead in this month-long tour of the 1950s Broadway musical. The tour ran throughout the East Coast, August into September 1966, including a stop at the Westbury Music Fair in Long Island, New York. It also played that circuit's Valley Forge Music Fair in Devon, Pennsylvania, the Camden County Music Fair in New Jersey, and the Storrowtown Music Fair in Springfield, Massachusetts, where it appeared the week of August 8, 1966.

Chicago
(1975)

During the initial 1975 Broadway run of the musical *Chicago*, star Gwen Verdon needed to have surgery on her vocal cords to remove polyps. For five weeks, Liza Minnelli spent the little time she had off between making the movies *Lucky Lady* and *A Matter of Time*, to help out friends in need.

The score from *Chicago* had been crafted by the team that wrote *Cabaret*, Kander and Ebb; the director was Bob Fosse; and the show's co-star was Chita Rivera. "I was just kinda hanging around L.A.," Minnelli mentioned in 1977, "and I thought, 'Wouldn't it be swell if I just whipped in and did that show for five weeks?' So, I called up and I asked if it would be all right, and they said, 'Sure.' So I got to do that show for five weeks, and let me tell you, I never had a better time, ever." Part of this joy may have come from having just completed the time-consuming shoot of *Lucky Lady*. "I needed *something* after being on a boat for six months!" Liza said. After only one week of rehearsals, Minnelli debuted as "Roxie Hart" on August 8, 1975, at the 46th Street Theater/St. James Theater. "Whipping in" without any official publicity, she sold out the show through September 13, 1975. The musical was modified somewhat for its new star, with the closing song for Act One—"My Own Best Friend"—changed to a solo for Liza, instead of being a duet with Chita.

Liza backstage in her dressing room, September 1975, after a performance of *Chicago*. Sammy Davis Jr. came back to offer his congratulations.

Liza and costar Chita Rivera take their *Chicago* bows on Broadway, August 8–September 13, 1975.

As with most of Liza's other Broadway shows, there are various audio and video elements that preserve Minnelli's *Chicago* work. There are at least two performances existing on audio in private collections (one recorded through the sound system and one from the audience), and there are even brief snippets of silent color film. Liza recorded four of the show's songs for her label, Columbia Records, in order to help promote *Chicago*. "All That Jazz," backed with "I Am My Own Best Friend" was released as a single; "Razzle Dazzle" remains unreleased, while "Me and My Baby" is included on *The Best of Liza Minnelli*, a fall 2004 Columbia Records/Sony Legacy CD. Minnelli also sang "All That Jazz" on TV twice in the fall of 1975: first on the syndicated show *Dinah!*, and then she lip-synched to her single of the song on *The Mac Davis Special*. On a fall 1975 episode of the syndicated TV series *Sammy and Company*, Liza sang

At a September 13, 1975, party at the St. Regis Hotel, following her closing night in *Chicago*, Liza sang with her costar Chita Rivera, and performed solo.

"My Own Best Friend," which would remain a part of her concert catalog for many years. The 1980 CBS TV special with Goldie Hawn—*Goldie and Liza: Together*—had the pair dueting on "All That Jazz," and Minnelli used that song as the opener of her solo set for the 1988–1990 *Ultimate Event* tour with Frank Sinatra and Sammy Davis Jr. (broadcast on Showtime and available briefly on VHS).

The Act
(1977–1978)

The Act is often called a "book" musical without the book. Of Liza's book shows (all the shows in this chapter), *The Act* is the only one that has never had a revival anywhere since the day it closed on Broadway. Perhaps that may be due to the fact it was a true Liza Minnelli star vehicle—her only book show that was such a project—and thus became so identified with Minnelli.

Much of the creative team for Liza's new Broadway show was assembled from the same company she'd just worked with on the movie *New York, New York*: Kander and Ebb for the songs (although Marvin Hamlisch had suggested he and Fred Ebb write the score for *The Act*, or at least collaborate on just the show's second act); Theodora Van Runkle for the costumes; and the most surprising credit of all: Martin Scorsese as director. The star's contract gave her final approval on the credit, and while Scorsese was an Academy Award winner, with many movies on his resume (including *Taxi Driver*), he had never directed for Broadway.

Early publicity photo of Liza with her leading man in *The Act*, Barry Nelson. LM is shown here in an outfit and hairstyle she was no longer wearing by the time the show made it to Broadway.

The Act was about "Michelle Craig," a former Hollywood *movie* musical star of the 1960s, who was now making a comeback by debuting her first nightclub act ever, in Las Vegas. Between onstage numbers of *The Act*, Liza's character would recall moments from her past (sometimes in song),

focusing mainly on her ex-husband. Before coming to Broadway, *The Act* began out-of-town tryouts in three major cities, following rehearsals that started in March 1977. At the time of its first performance, the musical was called *In Person* before being renamed *Shine It On*, and then, finally, *The Act*. The reviews in Chicago (where it opened at the Shubert on July 4 for two weeks), San Francisco (four weeks at the Orpheum Theater, starting July 27), and Los Angeles (at the Dorothy Chandler Pavilion, August 30–October 15) were mixed. (Denver had been canceled as the tour's opener.) For New York, costume changes were made, with Halston now on board. Esteemed Broadway musical director Gower Champion (*Hello, Dolly!*) was brought in to be the show's "doctor" at the end of September, although Scorsese retained billing as director (Champion would also play Liza's leading man for two weeks, later in the run on Broadway). Six new songs were put in the show during the tryout tour as well: "Turning"; "Hollywood, California"; "The Money Tree"; "City Lights"; "There When I Need Him"; and "Hot Enough for You." They replaced the songs "Good Thing Going"; "The Princess"; "Love Songs"; "Please, Sir"; "Walking Papers"; and "The Only Game in Town." "Walking Papers" would later be returned to *The Act*, and "Hollywood, California" dropped.

The revamped musical opened at Broadway's Majestic Theatre on October 29, 1977. (Liza's reported salary was estimated at $30,000 per week, which producers could afford: advance ticket sales were $2 million.) The reviews were moderate raves—most critics loved Liza, but decided it wasn't much of a book show, it was really a concert:

"The Act *displays the breathtaking presence of Liza Minnelli exercising a gift far beyond talent—quite dazzling. Liza is not first among equals; she is first of her kind.*" **—Richard Eder, *New York Times***

Liza wearing Theodora Van Runkle's costumes—and longer hair—before *The Act* changed its name, costumes, and the leading lady's hairstyle.

"Minnelli gives an almost unbelievably dynamic performance. A personal triumph. The star is impressive, even awesome in the versatility, concentrated intensity and sustained energy of her singing, dancing, and acting. The sheer physical expenditure leaves the audience limp, though repeatedly responsive, with applause, cheers, and, at the end, a genuine ovation. It's hard to conceive of The Act *without her, when her 39-week contract runs out."* **—Hobe, *Variety***

"Liza Minnelli is fantastic. See her and stock up an experience to tell your grandchildren about." **—Clive Barnes, WQXR, *New York Times Radio***

"The show they built—and rebuilt—for Liza Minnelli has hit Broadway with gale force. It is called The Act, *although 'Hurricane Liza' would have been more apt, and it is the knockout entertainment of the season. With the nerve of a high-wire artist, Miss Minnelli gives an incredibly sustained and spellbinding performance."* **—William B. Collins, *Philadelphia Inquirer***

Sheet music for Liza's "11:00 Number," the next-to-closing song "My Own Space," a haunting Kander and Ebb ballad.

The Act had to deal with many controversies surrounding it. The main "scandals" that got into the legitimate press concerned ticket prices and lip-synching. The musical had a top ticket price of $25.00 for Saturday nights, when most shows were then in the $17–19 range, which outraged many thea-tergoers. They were further enraged when seeing Liza lip-synch on two numbers that involved prolonged, strenuous dancing. (She wasn't able to sing properly after the dancing sections of the numbers were completed, thus the need for the prerecordings.) None of this affected attendance, however, as *The* Act played to sold-out crowds. Due to Liza catching the flu, the show had to be shut down for a total of three weeks' worth of shows, between November and the end of January. Yet from January 30 through the show's clos-

Liza performing in *The Act* on Broadway, including the showstoppers "City Lights," "Hot Enough for You?" and "The Money Tree."

ing six months later, she didn't miss any additional shows. Many Minnelli fans feel she did some of her finest work in *The Act*, and the Broadway theatre community felt the same—awarding her that year's Tony for Best Actress in a Musical. Liza gave her final performance of *The Act* less than a month later, when her one-year contract expired (and concerts were being booked across the country for fall 1978). The show closed on July 1, 1978, after a total of 239 performances on Broadway. Closing night, the star encored with a reprise of the show's "My Own Space," with John Kander at the piano.

The audio and video elements that remain from *The Act* include performances that were preserved professionally on film. (Some of this was included in a 1997 PBS-TV special on Kander and Ebb.) There are also silent, color home movies filmed in the audience, and audio tapes recorded, including shows on February 16, June 21, and July 1, 1978. Also, Liza's showstopping second act opener—"City Lights"—was performed on the 1978 Tony Awards show telecast. Finally, although she was not in peak vocal form the day she did the recording, the original Broadway cast album is still available on CD from DRG Records.

The Owl and the Pussycat (1978)

The same week *The Act* was giving its final performances, Liza also worked with the esteemed Martha Graham Dance Company. With her short hair slicked back (in a becoming style she would duplicate occasionally during the 1979–1980 period), and dressed all in purple, the star served as the narrator of *The Owl and the Pussycat* (an original Graham dance set to the poem). Minnelli performed the piece first at Lincoln Center's Metropolitan Opera, for one performance, June 26, 1978; then again at London's Convent Gardens, July 23—August 4, 1979; then one final engagement, again at the Met, April 22 to May 3, 1980.

Critic Clive Barnes stated in the June 27, 1978, *New York Post*: "There is a storyteller for the piece—taken most charmingly by Liza Minnelli. She has been choreographed into the work, and the pure delight of her performance is an equal tribute to the adroit manner in which Graham has used her." Bill Zakariasen said in the *New York Daily News* that "Liza Minnelli not only delivered the Lear lyrics with crystalline relish, her supple movements likewise held their own in that august company." Anna Kisselgoff, reviewing for the *New York Times* agreed that "Miss Minnelli is tops."

Audiotape of an August 1979 performance and still photographs are the only known surviving elements. (Photo on previous page is from London, 1979).

Are You Now, or Have You Ever Been?
(1979)

Six months after closing in *The Act*, Liza was back on the boards, this time in the off-Broadway drama *Are You Now, or Have You Ever Been?* As a favor to co-producer/fiancé Mark Gero, Liza stepped into the role of Lillian Hellman. In the show, Minnelli delivered Hellman's famous letter to the House Un-American Activities Committee, in which she refuses to testify. (Liza's weekly paycheck was $187.50, and she donated it back to the production.) While Minnelli was appearing in the play at New York City's Promenade Theater for three weeks' worth of performances only (January 9–29, 1979), *Are You Now. . . ?* was videotaped for broadcast on cable TV, and was available at one time on home video by the film developing company Fotomat.

It would be five years before Liza was able to make a return to the stage in any type of play, although there were rumors that she would be doing other shows, which never materialized. In the summer of 1980 *Peter Pan* was again considered for Broadway fare. In the summer of 1981 there was a report that Liza would star as the waitress "Cherry," opposite Joe Namath as the cowboy "Beau" in a Broadway musical version of William Inge's *Bus Stop*, directed by Bob Fosse. And in April–May 1982, Minnelli was this close to signing on to star as "Mama Rose" in a revival of the musical *Gypsy*. The beloved classic would have begun performances in December 1982, with three months in Los Angeles, three months in San Francisco, "then, possibly, New York." Another Broadway musical about legendary female singers from the 1920s through the 1950s, costarring Linda Hopkins and Dorothy Donegan, was also considered. Producer Joseph Papp announced in June 1983 that he wanted Liza to star in a pop version of the opera *Don Pasquale*—renamed *Non Pasquale*—at the outdoor theater Delacorte in Central Park. Liza, however, turned down his offer, and signed on for another Kander-Ebb musical.

The Rink
(1984)

August 30, 1983 brought the announcement from the *New York Times* that Minnelli had just signed a contract to costar with Chita Rivera in the new 2.5-million-dollar Kander-Ebb musical *The Rink*. The show dealt with the relationship of an estranged mother and daughter, who battle over ownership of the family's fading roller rink and relive moments from their past. Liza was reported as getting the same high salary as Chita (not disclosed), plus a portion of the box office—as high as 15 percent. "Her deal is unprecedented," one source said. "It's unlike any deal for any other star. The total of her ownership is very impressive." Liza was cast as Chita's rebellious hippie daughter "Angel;" Rivera's own daughter, singer-actress Lisa Mordente, had initially been considered to play the part. Rehearsals started on September 6, 1983, and the fall was spent work-shopping the show. It was reported in various press outlets that *The Rink* might actually first play a smaller off-Broadway theater for six weeks. It was soon apparent, however, that the draw of Minnelli—reteamed with her *Chicago* costar Chita—would require a larger house, on Broadway. Ultimately, *The Rink* opened at the Martin Beck Theater on February 9, 1984. The reviews were mixed, but critics praised Liza and Chita's ability:

"These two performances will live in Broadway legend, transcending and perhaps obliterating the memory of the musical they served. Miss Minnelli, cuddly and vulnerable, moist-eyed and hot-voiced, tough as calico and yet as soft as candy floss and corny as popcorn, is sublime. . . . They are quite a team." **—Clive Barnes, *New York Post***

"Minnelli lets that lusty voice ride high when she isn't simply being terribly appealing in a waif-like role. . . . And all that talent—for what? A mishmash." **—Douglas Watt, *New York Daily News***

Liza in *The Rink,* belting out the end of Act One's powerhouse finale, "Angel's Rink and Social Center," February 1984.

"Miss Minnelli is convincing in the thankless role of the unkempt daughter." **—Frank Rich, *New York Times***

"For the record, be it noted that Miss Minnelli receives a rare double opening ovation: applause when the lights go on, revealing her from behind, and more applause when she turns to face the audience. It is nice when your back hand is as strong as your fore hand." **—John Simon, *New York* magazine**

"While Liza has the smaller role, she does the kind of calm, fine work seen in her Sterile Cuckoo *days."* **—Linda Winer, *USA Today***

Both Liza and Chita were nominated for Tony Awards for Best Actress in a Musical, and Minnelli threw a party honoring Chita's win—in advance of the actual event. Liza's instincts were correct: Chita did win her first Tony.

Liza was scheduled to leave the show July 14, 1984—a few weeks earlier than the producers would have liked, but she wanted to do a concert tour in Europe with Charles Aznavour at the end of the summer. Liza never made it overseas, though. On July 16, columnist Liz Smith—Minnelli's main media supporter, and friend—made the announcement that Liza had left *The Rink* (her last performance had been midweek, the week before), and had checked into the Betty Ford Center in Rancho Mirage, California, on Friday, July 13, 1984. Liza was determined to take steps to get her health back on track, stating "I have a problem and I'm going to deal with it." Stockard Channing was set to replace Liza in *The Rink*, and stepped in earlier than originally announced. Without Minnelli's box-office pull, *The Rink* closed soon after, within weeks (despite Chita still being in the show).

There are several audiovisual elements that remain of Liza's *Rink* run. A poor-quality videotape exists of the entire show, shot from the balcony by a fan's camcorder, but there are professionally preserved video moments as well: Liza and Chita performed their "The Apple Doesn't Fall" duet on a PBS-TV *Gala of Stars*, and another duet, "Wallflower," was presented on the June 1984 Tony Awards. The original Broadway cast recording is available on a remastered CD edition from JAY Records.

It would be another ten years before Liza would again appear in any play or book show. There were rumors in 1992 and 1993 that she might appear in Kander and Ebb's *Kiss of the Spider Woman* musical, replacing Chita Rivera after her run ended, but this never happened. Nor did a rumored version of *Damn Yankees* with Minnelli, choreographed by Susan Strohman.

Love Letters
(1994)

Liza starred in one performance of this play by A. R. Gurney—about two lifelong friends who write letters to each other over a forty-year period, ultimately discovering how much in love they are. The event was on April 18, 1994, at Miami's Coconut Grove Playhouse, as a benefit for the theater. Desi Arnaz Jr. was her costar in this two-person play. (The stars had been a couple in the early 1970s, although they never married.) After the performance, Liza and Desi were named Florida's "Ambassadors of the Arts."

Playwright Jonathan Harvey (*Beautiful Thing*) was reported to be working on a "musical" with the Pet Shop Boys in 1996. (They had produced Liza's 1989 album *Results*.) That group's Neil Tennant told Harvey "we could get Liza Minnelli, but then it would turn into a monster, so I think maybe we shouldn't have a big star involved."

Victor/Victoria
(1997)

On October 3, 1996, at Sardi's in New York City, Minnelli and her friend Julie Andrews held a press conference. They announced that Liza would be taking over Julie's lead role in the Broadway musical *Victor/Victoria* while Andrews was on vacation for one month. (The show was running at the 1,601-seat Marquis Theater, with ticket prices at a $75.00 top price.) It was an important moment. This would be Liza's return to the Broadway boards after a twelve-year-plus absence, and she'd be filling in for thirty-two performances, from January 7 through February 2, 1997. The musical was based on the hit 1982 Andrews movie about an entertainer in Paris: a woman pretending to be a man, pretending to be a woman.

Minnelli's run in *Victor/Victoria* remains one of the largest "Liza legends" in the star's life and career, with the emphasis on the negative. The positive aspects of the engagement have never

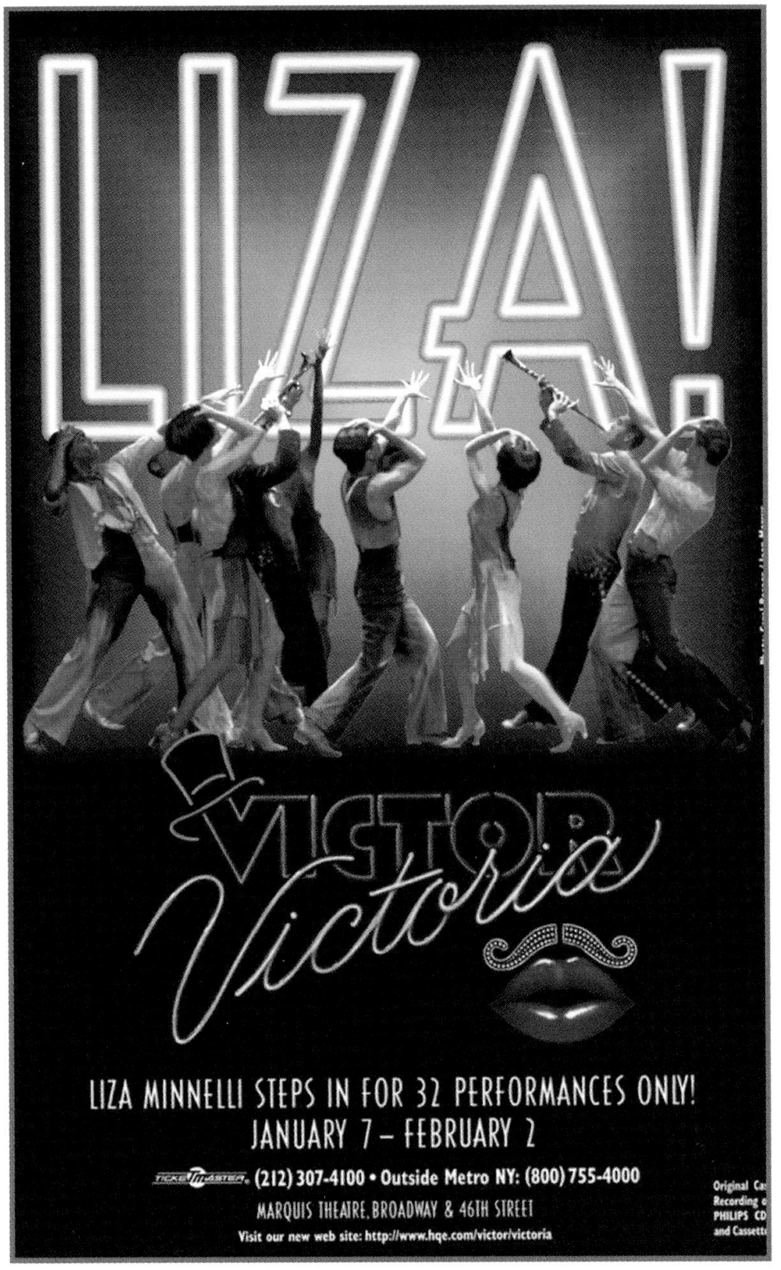

Variety (Greg Evans), January 20–26, 1997:

"Minnelli [infuses] the show with her trademark panache. . . . A new song, 'Who Can I Tell?' (replacing Andrews' 'Crazy World') gives Minnelli a standard pop ballad so suitable to her talents that the song likely will take a spot in Minnelli's concert repertoire for years to come. Her performance of the song here virtually justifies the entire star-replacement gambit. . . . As for Minnelli's much-reported-on hip surgery, audiences will see no evidence in the star's performance."

been reported till now. In most of the press surrounding Liza's *Victor/Victoria* run, it usually is not reported that the star only had a limited number of rehearsals for the show. Minnelli was out on the road doing concerts constantly throughout the fall of 1996—even up through the last week of December. Although the official press opening was not until mid-January 1997, Liza gave her first performance in *Victor/Victoria* on January 7, 1997. The next day, the media was full of raves, which only multiplied with the "official" opening. The consensus was that Minnelli had another triumph:

Variety reported the first week's gross (January 7–12) at $727,822, up $111,724 from the week before, when Julie had been starring. This was the only show on Broadway that saw an *increase* in ticket sales from the proceeding week during the usually slow winter period. Blake Edwards and producer Tony Adams were thus reportedly in talks with Liza to return in the summer of 1997 (rumors were they enticed her by offering to star Minnelli in both a future Edwards show *and* a movie tailor-made for Liza, if she agreed to come back to *Victor/Victoria*). *The Hollywood Reporter* announced on February 4, 1997 that Minnelli's manager stated Liza indeed wished to return to the show in the summer, after Julie Andrews was scheduled to leave.

This success didn't last long in the media's coverage. It quoted costar Tony Roberts' anger over Liza getting one line wrong once—instead of saying, "I'm a hopeless hoofer," she stated, "I'm a hopeless *hooker*." This "drama" became front-page news. Little known, however, is that Julie Andrews was furious that her friend Liza had been subjected to Roberts' wrath, and it was reported she was seeking to replace him. Roberts then tried to turn things around by saying Minnelli was the most talented person he'd worked with. These off-stage events didn't help another problem Liza was facing: the star was battling increasing loss of her singing voice as each week passed with its grueling eight-show schedule. By her

Three scenes from Liza's Broadway performance in *Victor/Victoria*, January 1997: In pajamas; in her closing gown; and two photos from her sizzling show-stopper "Le Jazz Hot."

fourth and final week, Minnelli's doctors were insisting she not appear, and Liza went onstage to apologize to the audience two nights in a row. She was able to get through one more show before her doctors stated that any more singing might permanently damage her voice; the final five shows again featured the show's understudy. The tidal wave of bad publicity continued to erupt, but what was frequently missing from the reporting was the fact that Minnelli's magic was always obvious onstage, no matter what was happening off. Also missing was the most important factor: Liza's presence made *Victor/Victoria* the highest grossing show on Broadway for that month—representing a total gross of just under 3 million dollars for her engagement ($2,916,437, according to *Variety*).

While there never was an album made with Liza covering the *Victor/Victoria* songs, there are various audio-video elements that have preserved her work in the show. Amateur videotapings shot by fans in the audience remain, and audio tapes as well (including the January 17 and 18 shows). There is also professional media video coverage of rehearsals and of that very first January 7 show, which aired on such outlets as CNN, *Entertainment Tonight*, etc. Liza also sang her newly added solo, "Who Can I Tell?" on a December 1996 edition of the syndicated *Live with Regis and Kathy Lee* morning TV talk show.

Victor/Victoria remains Liza Minnelli's last Broadway musical and stage role to date, although there are currently rumors that the star could take over the lead role of "Mama Rose" in the revival of *Gypsy* starring Bernadette Peters, either on Broadway or on tour. From 1997 through 1999, Liza spoke about a book musical that would tell the story of three generations of a show-business family; one source had a title for the show—*Curtains*—but this has yet to transpire. In 2003 it was stated that a script was being fashioned for a new Broadway show to star Liza and Chita Rivera, and there was also talk that Minnelli might star in Tennessee Williams' *The Rose Tattoo* in London's West End. With Liza Minnelli being a Broadway baby at heart—and a potent box office draw—it wouldn't be surprising to see the star tackle yet another role in a show (even a nonmusical play) at some point in the future.

Publicity portrait of 2½-year-old Liza Minnelli on the set of her first film, *In the Good Old Summertime* (1949).

CHAPTER TEN

Minnelli's Movies—Liza on Film

Liza Minnelli would ultimately make her mark in movies and become an Academy Award–winning actress, with a reported total box office gross of $254,398,539 for her films.

Liza grew up on the MGM lot, and actually made her film debut at Metro-Goldwyn-Mayer.

In the Good Old Summertime (1949)

The Judy Garland-Van Johnson movie *In the Good Old Summertime* was in production from October 11, 1948, through January 27, 1949; it was released by MGM in August 1949. During its final moment, the leads are seen strolling in the park with their baby daughter. This is Liza Minnelli's first appearance in a film, at age 2½. The part was non-speaking, unbilled, and lasted only several seconds—the camera zooms in for a closeup when Johnson picks up the child. Liza would later recall that in the excitement of getting ready to appear in front of the camera, her underpants were missing—which might explain the somewhat uncomfortable expression on Miss Minnelli's face.

In the Good Old Summertime grossed $3.4 million at the box office, and has appeared numerous times on TV over the years—lately as an exclusive on the TCM (Turner Classic Movies) cable network. The VHS videotape is still available from MGM/UA/Warner Brothers/Time Warner (although not in a remastered version), and the film was available on laser disc. A DVD from Warner Home Video was released in April 2004. (Liza's scene is included in the 1974 film tribute to MGM musicals, *That's Entertainment!*)

Journey Back to Oz (a.k.a. Return to Oz) (1974; recorded in 1962)

In 1962, Liza was the same age her mom had been while filming *The Wizard of Oz*, so it's ironic that Minnelli was sweet 16 when she played the role that made Mama a star. In the late fall of that year, Liza recorded the singing and speaking voice of "Dorothy" for the animated feature *Journey Back to Oz* (the cartoon followed "Dorothy" returning to Oz to help her friends battle a new witch, voiced by Ethel Merman). Fellow cast members who also recorded vocals included some of Judy's MGM costars, such as Mickey Rooney, Peter Lawford, and even the "Wicked Witch" of *The Wizard of Oz*, Margaret Hamilton, who was now voicing "Auntie Em." Liza's work was full of conviction and sensitivity, and her solos reveal a lovely, melodic voice—especially in her ballads "There's a Faraway Land," and "That Feeling for Home."

Although her work was recorded in 1962, the film would not be released in theaters by Filmation Studios until 1974 and 1975, after making its debut on closed-circuit TV at New Jersey's Mount Laurel-Moorestown Holiday Inn at the end of 1973.

The movie has appeared on TV numerous times, including one that featured Bill Cosby as host. There have also been several low-budget VHS

home videos released, now difficult to find, and even two soundtrack albums. (See Chapter Twelve, "For the Record," for more information.)

Charlie Bubbles
(1968)

Charlie Bubbles marked Minnelli's first film role. Playing the supporting part of a secretary to a famous author (played by Albert Finney), Liza strayed far from the type of part casting directors might have envisioned for "Dorothy's daughter." (Minnelli was being offered mostly Disney musicals, the parts that Lesley Ann Warren ultimately played.) *Bubbles* called for a love scene with costar and director Finney. Although the scene would be edited, and her screen time somewhat brief overall, Minnelli makes a wonderful impression in *Bubbles*.

Filmed entirely in England, shooting began on October 14, 1966, and continued into early 1967. It was released by Regional Films and Universal in 1968. *Charlie Bubbles* has been shown on TV numerous times, but has yet to appear on home video.

The Sterile Cuckoo (1969)

In 1968, Liza had to decide between two projects: starring in the new Bachrach-David-Simon Broadway musical *Promises, Promises*, or her first leading role in a film. Minnelli opted for the movie, for which Paramount paid her a noted $25,000 (following a reported March 1968 screen test; the studio had originally sought Patty Duke or Elizabeth Hartman as the star). *The Sterile Cuckoo* offered Liza an emotionally devastating role playing "Pookie Adams," a dysfunctional girl dealing with her first relationship as she starts college. The challenge was made no easier when rain ruined an outdoor location shoot the very first day of filming (shooting began in late September on location in upstate New York, followed by studio work on the west coast). Minnelli was asked to do one of the movie's most heart-wrenching scenes instead—the telephone scene, where "Pookie's" boyfriend

(Wendell Burton) tries to end their relationship, and the young girl convinces him to give them another chance. It was perhaps this scene that won Liza Minnelli her first Academy Award nomination for Best Actress. She didn't win, losing to Maggie Smith for *The Pride of Miss Jean Brody* in 1970, but the reviews were all any actress could wish for, including:

"The Sterile Cuckoo *is a kook named 'Pookie,' a wacky, wisecracking, motherless, outrageously adorable, collegiate gamin (from a*

*novel by Jack Nichols) who comes on like gangbusters. Liza Minnelli plays the role, and her fragile, funny, freshman love affair with an undergraduate entomologist (Wendell Burton in his first screen role) is in a class by itself. . . . It is Minnelli's one-woman show." **—Hollywood Reporter***

The Sterile Cuckoo grossed $13,982,357, has appeared on TV numerous times (including its U.S. debut on ABC, January 13, 1975), and is available on VHS. It was issued on laser disc, but has not appeared on DVD to date. There was a soundtrack album issued, but Liza doesn't sing on it. She did record *Cuckoo*'s Oscar-nominated Best Song, "Come Saturday Morning," as the title of her 1970 album on A&M; her version of this song is on the *Ultimate Collection* compilation CD.

Liza on location at Hamilton College, October 1968. Leading man Wendell Burton can be seen in the background.

Tell Me That You Love Me, Junie Moon (1970)

Based on the novel by Marjorie Kellogg, *Tell Me That You Love Me, Junie Moon* told the story of three "misfits" who band together. (Liza's character, "Junie Moon," is disfigured when a man she is on a date with turns on her, beats her, and then pours acid on her face.) As the three deal with life's struggles, Liza's and Ken Howard's characters fall in love.

The movie was made on location in Massachusetts, Florida, and California while Liza was grieving over the loss of her mother (work had begun on Garland's birthday, June 10, 1969; Judy passed away on June 22, in London). It was unfortunate that the shooting schedule called for filming the scene where "Junie" is nude in a cemetery (shot at an actual upstate New York cemetery), not long after Judy Garland's passing. There was some minor public and press finger-wagging toward Liza, when certainly the media should have realized she had agreed to make the movie—and film *all* its scenes—long before her mother passed away. The star got no real comfort from the director, Otto Preminger, who gave her little direction. Fortunately, Paramount paid Minnelli her asking price ($50,000, double what she received for *Sterile Cuckoo*), and Liza's godmother, Kay Thompson, was cast in a supporting role. (Thompson was best known as the author of the *Eloise* children's books series, but had also starred in the film *Funny Face*

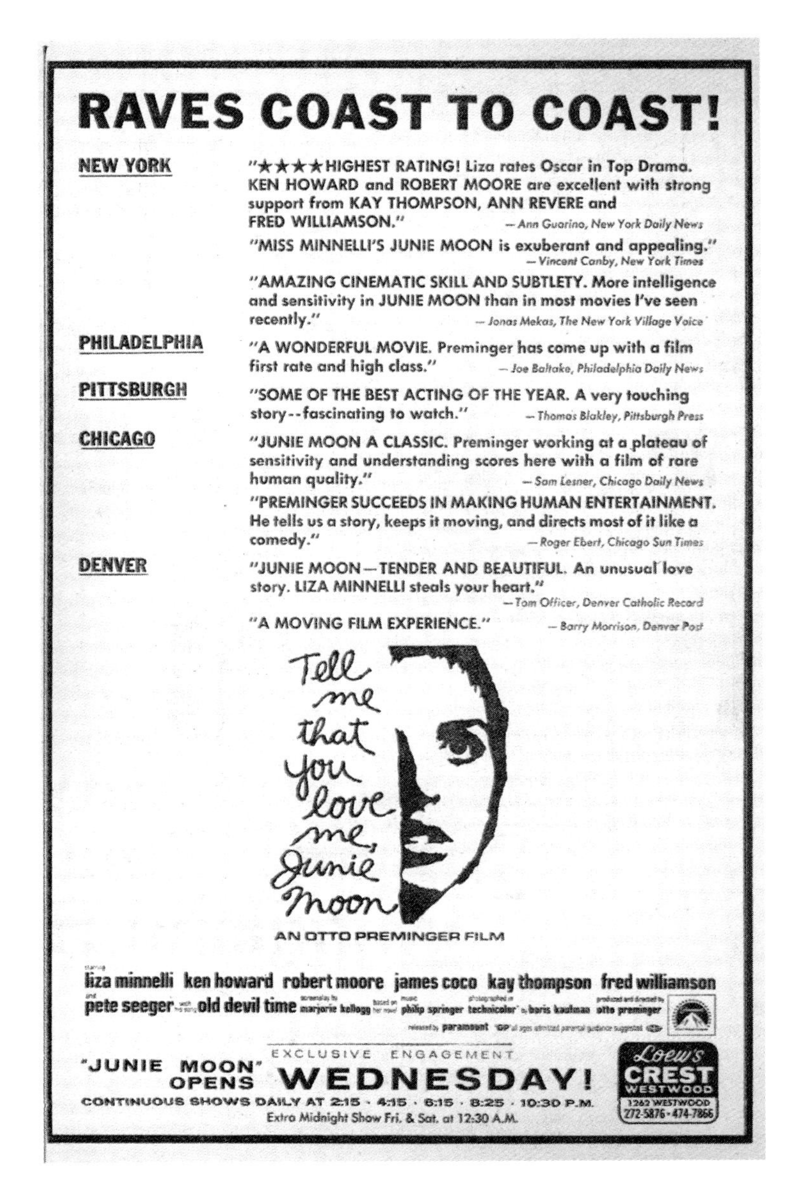

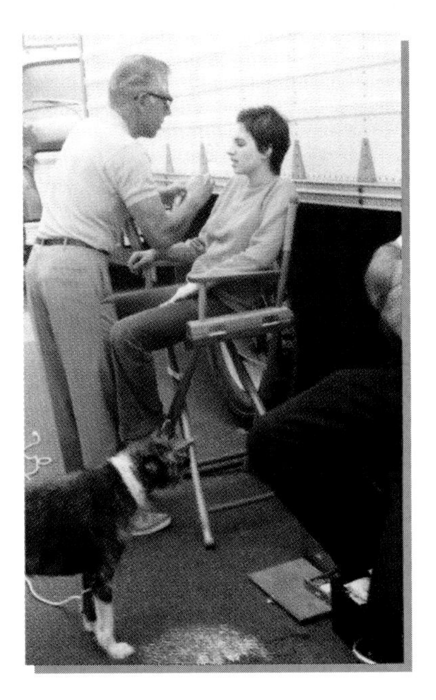

Liza being made up on the set of *Junie Moon*, in Gloucester, Massachusetts, August 1969. Also seen here is her beloved dog Ocho. Minnelli's makeup man is Charlie Schram, who did Judy's make up at MGM circa 1937–1941, except for *Oz*, when he toiled over Burt Lahr as the "Lion."

with Fred Astaire and Audrey Hepburn, and had been a huge influence as an arranger-vocal coach to Judy Garland, starting in the mid-1940s.)

The intense and unusual subject matter of *Junie Moon* kept it from being a mainstream hit, but Minnelli again garnered raves for her work:

"Liza Minnelli's struggle gives this film a perverse appeal that is both grotesque and touching." **—Joseph Gelmis, *Newsday***

*"Liza rates an Oscar in this four-star drama."***—Ann Guardino, *New York Daily News***

Tell Me That You Love Me, Junie Moon has been shown numerous times on TV—including its TV debut, Tuesday, July 10, 1979, on a CBS prime-time broadcast—but it has not yet been released on home video. There was a soundtrack album of the score released by Columbia Records, but Liza didn't do any singing in the movie, nor for the album.

Cabaret
(1972)

Cabaret is considered by many to be the highlight of Liza Minnelli's career—her finest film, the performance of her career in the role of her career, and one of the most memorable movies of all time.

Based on both the John Van Druten play *I Am a Camera*, and the Christopher Isherwood tales of Berlin, *Cabaret* opened as a celebrated Broadway musical in 1966. The show went on to play 1,165 performances and won eight Tony Awards, including one for the score by Minnelli's champions, Kander and Ebb. Liza longed for the leading role of "Sally Bowles," an eccentric girl singing in a nightclub in 1930s Germany, against the backdrop of the turbulent times of Nazism. Auditioning a

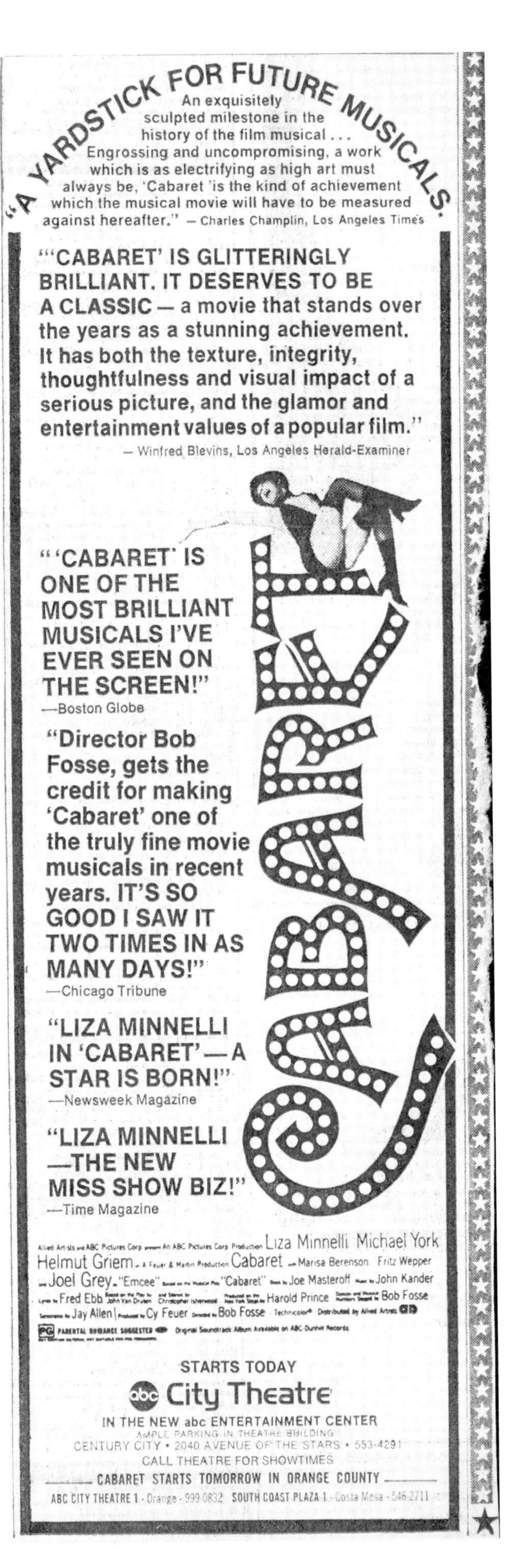

reported twenty times, Minnelli was passed over for the part on Broadway, which made her campaign even more aggressively for the film version. Liza began singing the title song in her nightclub act, as well as on TV, including appearances on *The Tonight Show* and *The Hollywood Palace*. During the time the movie version was being planned, its producer, Cy Feuer, came to see Minnelli perform at the Olympia in Paris in December 1969. It was her rendition of "Cabaret" during this engagement that convinced him Liza had to be the film's "Sally," and Minnelli was hired for a $250,000 fee.

Liza on the set with her *Cabaret* director, Bob Fosse.

Cabaret was filmed on location in Germany. Rehearsals began on February 22, 1971, in Munich, and shooting concluded on July 9, 1971. (There were "looping/dubbing numbers"—where certain audio retakes were required to perfect the film's sound—done in Paris, starting on November 24, 1971.) An acclaimed cast and crew had been assembled. The movie's costars included actors who would remain Liza's friends: Michael York, Marisa Berenson, and Joel Grey, repeating his Tony Award–winning role as the "Emcee" from the stage production. (Minnelli and Grey would reteam for occasional concert appearances over the years, including a major tour in 1981.) Guiding the on-camera talent was a man known more for his choreography of Broadway musicals than for making movies. Bob Fosse had only directed one film

prior to *Cabaret*, the movie version of *Sweet Charity*, which failed at the box office, but he had been in show business all his life. It's even possible his path may have crossed with Liza's when she was a youngster, as Fosse was a featured actor-dancer in several MGM musicals in the early and mid-1950s, including *Kiss Me Kate*. Fosse developed a unique style of dancing, with signature moves that became his trademarks. He forged a close professional relationship with Liza, one that would extend beyond the filming of *Cabaret*.

The effect that *Cabaret* had upon its opening cannot be overstated. It was a complete phenomenon, coloring everything Liza Minnelli would do from then on. The public became convinced Liza actually was like the "divinely decadent" "Sally" off-stage. (The truth is that while Liza and "Sally" may share an energy level and a love of celebration, Minnelli is actually much quieter and, surprisingly, more of a student and a nester than anyone ever mentions. Yet so powerful is the star's acting ability that she is a master at making an audience believe she is anyone—perhaps because she believes it herself, the mark of any great artist.) From the moment *Cabaret* was released by Allied Artists—its world premiere at Manhattan's Ziegeld Theater on February 13, 1972, aired as a 30-minute TV special on WOR-TV in New York City six days later—life would never be the same for Liza Minnelli. She was now officially an international superstar, one who made history by becoming the first star to make the covers of both *Time* and *Newsweek* magazines the very same week, as *Cabaret* was opening across the country.

All the reviews for *Cabaret* were raves, including the following:

"The film version of the 1966 John Kander–Fred Ebb Broadway musical Cabaret *is most unusual: it is literate, bawdy, sophisticated, sensual, cynical, heartwarming, and disturbingly thought-provoking. Liza Minnelli heads a strong cast. Bob Fosse's generally excellent direction re-creates the milieu of Germany some 40 years ago."*
—Variety

Close-up of Liza singing the title song in the movie *Cabaret*.

"A cause for rejoicing. Liza Minnelli defines the word 'star!'" **—Rex Reed, *New York Daily News***

Profiled and publicized like never before, Liza Minnelli was the hottest and biggest star in the world.

The 45th annual Oscar ceremony of March 27, 1973, found Liza in the running for Best Actress. Minnelli's manicurist that day told her she should be prepared to lose. "'I got two words for ya, honey,'" Liza quoted the lady laboring over her nails. "'*Diana Ross!*' To my *face* the woman said this. What do you answer to that? 'Skip the polish?' I kept saying to myself that day that 'It's a thrill just to be nominated.' To be nominated is *plenty*. [I kept saying] 'It doesn't matter. It doesn't matter.' But I'll tell you [when the envelope with the winner's name is opened] at that moment—it *matters*!" Liza was announced the winner ("my father screamed so *loudly* in my ear I think I went *deaf* for a while"), and during her speech she said, "Thank you so much for giving *me* this award. You've made *me* very happy." This was her way of dispelling the myth that she was given the award because of the loss of her mom. If that theory had merit, Minnelli would have been given the award three years earlier in 1970, for *The Sterile Cuckoo*—less than a year after Judy Garland's passing. Liza Minnelli won her Oscar because of her brilliant acting ability. Think of the scene where she returns home from having waited all day for her father to arrive for a visit that never happened. Or the scene after her character has an abortion. A role of a lifetime and the talent to back that up got Minnelli her Academy Award—and a room full of other trophies for her work in the film, including the Golden Globe.

Cabaret grossed $41,326,446 (including a noted $18 million in North America alone) on an investment of only $4 million to make the movie. It has appeared on TV frequently, including a July 31, 1979, broadcast on ABC. The film has been issued on laser disc, and was released in a deluxe "25th Anniversary" home video VHS and DVD edition by Warner Home Video. (The VHS offers a superior print and transfer, surprisingly. The DVD does have a longer interview with Minnelli as one of the disc's extra features, and was issued again in 2003, with only the packaging changed. The disc is exactly the same as the 1997 release.) The soundtrack album was issued on LP by ABC Records and certified gold in August 1973. It is available on CD by Hip-O Records/Universal Music.

That's Entertainment!
(1974)

In this all-star tribute to MGM musicals (from 1929 through 1958), Liza hosts the segment devoted to the undisputed queen of Metro's musicals, Judy Garland. The narration and on-camera dialogue were all scripted of course, and offered no real personal remembrances, just lead-ins to the various film clips of "Over the Rainbow," "Get Happy," etc. One line at the end of Liza's scene did say something so important about film: "Thank God for film. It can capture a performance and hold it right there, forever. And if anybody ever says to you who was he, or who was she, I think a piece of film answers that question better than any words I know of." Minnelli filmed her segment in 1973, and the movie was released by MGM on May 18, 1974. Its premiere at the Ziegfeld Theater in New York was followed by its London premiere October 2, 1974; it then debuted in Paris the first week in January 1975. *That's Entertainment!* became the 6th highest-grossing film of 1974. (*Variety* shows its box office total as $26,890,200.)

That's Entertainment! has appeared on TV many times, including its debut as a CBS primetime telecast, Tuesday, November 18, 1975 (for which the network paid $2.5 million). Other CBS airings were Sunday, January 9, 1977, and Saturday, September 1, 1979. It is currently available on VHS from Warner Home Video. Two different deluxe laser disc box sets were issued as well, and the movie's release on DVD was October 12, 2004. There have been numerous soundtrack versions issued on LP, cassette, and CD, but Liza does not sing in the movie.

Lucky Lady
(1975)

Liza's first film since *Cabaret* (aside from her brief cameo in *That's Entertainment!*) was Stanley Donen's madcap 1930s comedy *Lucky Lady*. Minnelli starred as red-haired "Claire Dobie," a low-rent cabaret singer who is looking to make big bucks by teaming with fellow superstars Gene

Ad for *Lucky Lady* from Japan.

Hackman and Burt Reynolds (as down-on-their-luck con men). The trio begin a major bootlegging project as rumrunners aboard the *Lucky Lady* ship.

Liza was the first to sign on for the movie, and was paid the lowest fee—a reported $350,000 (plus a percentage of profits). George Segal had originally been signed to play Gene Hackman's role, but a leg injury kept him from making the movie. Segal's agent, Guy McIlwaine (who was Judy's agent for a period in the mid 1960s), told columnist Joyce Haber she was "a little low" on the amount Haber mentioned as Minnelli's fee. Reynolds was second to sign and got $500,000; Segal got $750,000 (so Hackman must have been paid close to $1 million, if not $1 million, for stepping in at the last minute).

Liza flew to Guaymas, Mexico, on February 3, 1975, for costume tests. Rehearsals began on February 12, with filming commencing on February 17; it continued through July 1975. *Lucky Lady* was seemingly anything but lucky—weather and technical problems made the budget—and thus tensions—soar (the film featured many explosions of various boats and ships, among other expensive and extensive special effects). Liza admitted she was happy to be back on dry land when filming finished, "after being on a *boat* for six months."

High points of the film are the two new Kander-Ebb songs, "Get While the Getting Is Good" (filmed April 14 through the 19), and the title song. Yet many of Liza's best moments and several of her scenes were cut during the final editing. It seems Twentieth Century-Fox decided it wanted a happy ending for *Lucky Lady*. The original version had

Rare—if blurry—on-set candid, shot during the filming of the alternate *Lucky Lady* ending, with Gene's, Liza's, and Burt's characters still together, years later.

Hackman and Reynolds die in a shooting, during a run gone wrong; Liza was then shown a decade later (minus the red hair, having married her rich boyfriend shown in the film, and having had a son), remembering Burt and Gene. (Some of the footage of Liza reacting to their death was shown in the 1979 Fox-TV syndicated series *That's Hollywood.*) In November 1975—a mere month before the movie's premiere—Reynolds and Hackman joined Liza in Rome (where she was making *A Matter of Time* with her father) to shoot a new ending for *Lady.* This ending was a happy one, showing the trio still together many years later. A public feud soon developed, with Liza and Burt on one side, versus director Donen and studio Fox on the other. The latter camp favored the happy ending; Liza and Burt wanted the shootout/death scene to remain. The stars lost the argument. Donen actually fashioned a last-minute replacement ending for the final released version. Showing the trio still young, happy, and together, it was culled from a scene made during the film's original shooting period, but it had never been intended as the movie's closing moment.

Despite their disappointment over the ending, the stars still attended the huge gala premiere on December 11, 1975, at the Ziegfeld in New York City. The movie was released by 20th Century-Fox on Christmas Day 1975 (the originally planned

December 13 opening was canceled immediately after the premiere). The reviews were raves for Liza, if mixed for the film itself:

"Minnelli is a born performer and a natural star. In Lucky Lady, *she's better than she was in* Cabaret, *giving a tighter, harder, funnier, more knowing performance, without giving up her quality of yearning vulnerability. . . . Minnelli creates one of the most sheerly enjoyable female characters in years. . . . Minnelli becomes the thinking man's Betty Boop. She makes even the more studied cracks of a wisecracking script work."* **—Jack Kroll, *Newsweek***

"It provides a dazzling showcase for Liza Minnelli's dazzling talents . . . star quality triumphs." ***—TV Guide***

"Minnelli, flashing the best pair of legs since Dietrich, speaks in the voice of Mae West, but has the vulnerability of a street urchin, which no audience can resist." ***—New York Daily News***

Despite large grosses at the box office—as high as $24,441,725 according to one report—the movie was not able to turn a profit due to its huge budget, noted as $12.6 million. Liza was also nominated for a Golden Globe award.

Lucky Lady has been shown on TV many times—including its Saturday, September 22, 1979, debut on CBS—but it has not been released on home video to date. The soundtrack LP was released by Arista Records in February 1976, but hasn't yet appeared on CD. The movie was released overseas in PAL format, with a 1989 copyright, from CBS/Fox Video (South Pacific) Pty Ltd (incorporated in NSW, Australia). Not released in U.S.

Silent Movie
(1976)

This Mel Brooks movie features a brief cameo appearance by Liza. The movie concerned a planned comeback of silent movies, with filmmaker "Mel Funn"—played by Brooks—attempting to sign major stars to appear in his opus. Minnelli plays herself, greeting fans who surround her at a studio cafeteria. Liza filmed her short part right after getting back from making *A Matter of Time* in Italy, the first week in March 1976. *Silent Movie* was released on June 30, 1976.

Silent Movie grossed $36,145,695, and is available on VHS, but has not been released on DVD to date.

A Matter of Time
(1976)

What was supposed to be a dream come true for Liza—being directed by her father—turned out to be a disappointment for all concerned. *A Matter of Time* was based on the novella *Film of Memory*, and the movie was initially known by that title, then by *Search For Beauty* (in June 1973), then *Carmella*, then *Nina*, then finally *A Matter of Time*. Liza played the lead role (renamed from "Carmella" to "Nina"), a young chambermaid who was living her life through the memories of an elderly "Contessa" (Ingrid Bergman), who was now poor and staying in the third-rate hotel where "Nina"

worked. "Nina" devoted herself to the "Contessa," whose memories made "Nina" aspire for a better life; the chambermaid would ultimately become a famous film star. In June 1973, Katharine Hepburn was considered an early candidate for the role of the "Contessa" by the two Minnellis, who spent years planning a joint project. Liza had longed to work with her father on a film, and the seventy-six-year-old Vincente Minnelli was signed to direct his daughter. Production started in Rome on October 8, 1975 (the first day of filming was October 28, 1975), and continued through early February 1976, at a final cost of $5 million (the filming had been previously announced as starting in April 1974). American International was looking to make more mainstream films, a change from the thrillers it was known for (*I Was A Teenage Werewolf*, etc.). The studio thus allowed a large budget for scenery and costumes, and hired Kander and Ebb to supply the star with two new songs, "The Me I Haven't Met Yet," and the title number. Yet AMI insisted the film be shot entirely in Italy, in order to save on labor and other expenses. Tensions on the set between the foreign and American crews were noted, and the Technicolor film lab in Italy ruined six days' worth of shooting, which had to be redone. Then the studio took the film out of the director's hands when shooting was completed. Their subsequent final edit was disowned by Mr. Minnelli and Liza. They (along with thirty-three directors) took out an ad in the trade papers, signing their names to a protest that their vision had been violated: "The film is a reedited, revised, altered, and distorted form that has nothing to do with the original content. We are concerned here with principles and ethics. An artist must be allowed his view, and those who back him must support that view after the fact, as well as before it." The signatures offering support included Otto Preminger, Gene Kelly, Elia Kazan, Woody Allen, and Billy Wilder. While the film has numerous flaws—most notably the poor dubbing of the foreign cast members with voices of American actors—it still has many assets. Liza delivers an ernest performance, with a couple of good moments, including the film's highlight: a smokey, jazz-tinged rendition of the standard "Do It Again." Liza looks lovely and gets to wear a multitude of elaborate costumes, one of Vincente's trademark touches. Many of the sets and much of the cinematography are also testaments to the senior Minnelli's still vast gifts, in what turned out to be his final film.

A Matter of Time opened Thursday, October 7, 1976, at New York City's Radio City Music Hall, where Vincente had enjoyed some of his earliest successes forty years before, directing and producing shows there. The movie failed to draw an audience at the box office, given the poor-to-fair reviews:

"If you can imagine a feature film equivalent to a Radio City Music Hall stage show, it might look very much like Vincente Minnelli's A Matter of Time. . . . *It is full of glittery costumes and spectacular props . . . moments of real visual beauty."* **—Vincent Canby, *New York Times***

"The film's only entertaining scene is a simple rendition by Liza of George Gershwin's 'Do It Again.'" **—Ernest Schier, *Philadelphia Evening Bulletin***

A Matter of Time has appeared on TV, and was released on VHS, but is long out of print. There was a small foreign pressing of a soundtrack recording on LP, renamed *Nina*, which has never appeared on CD. The VHS cut "Do It Again."

Will Rogers Fund Trailer (1976)

In the late spring/early summer of 1976, Liza filmed a trailer (commercial/fund-raiser) for the Will Rogers Fund, which was available to theaters on July 1, 1976.

New York, New York (1977)

New York, New York was the third of three movies Liza signed contracts for in 1974 to 1975 (with various studios). The financial failures of *Lucky Lady* and *A Matter of Time* put added pressure on this final film. In the movie, set from 1945 to approximately 1953, Liza played "Francine Evans," a big band singer who would become a major movie, recording, and concert star by the film's end. Her saxaphone-playing husband, however, would struggle before finally achieving his own success after the end of their relationship. Fellow Academy Award–winner Robert De Niro was cast as

Liza's husband, and the film was directed by Oscar winner Martin Scorsese. Minnelli's musical mainstays Kander and Ebb crafted four new songs for the film. Of these, "'But the World Goes 'Round"

Liza in her mom's old dressing room at MGM, during filming of *New York, New York*. Note the photos of Judy and Vincente behind her.

Liza singing her second signature song (following "Cabaret"), the standard "New York, New York," in its first and finest version.

would become a frequent Liza concert stable, and the title song—"Theme from 'New York, New York'" (its official name)—would rank as the second of Minnelli's signature songs (along with "Cabaret").

New York, New York became the first movie musical Minnelli made in Hollywood. It was like coming home for her, since it was filmed mostly at MGM, aside from some scenes shot at Fox, and the United Recording Studios for "'But the World Goes 'Round." Rehearsals started for *New York, New York* in May 1976. Filming began on June 14, and didn't wrap until November 4, 1976. Liza was treated like royalty by the crew at MGM, since some remembered her as a kid from twenty years earlier. She was given the use of what had been her mother's dressing room, and her hair styles were done by the man who'd supervised Garland's at Metro, Sydney Guiloff. Vincente Minnelli was photographed visiting the set, and Liza's father-in-law, Jack Haley, was given a cameo in the lavish "Happy Endings" production number. Word was that the film would be a huge hit.

Director Scorsese was using a unique technique in making *New York, New York*: much of the movie was improvised. The rehearsals were videotaped, and the final film was reportedly a mix of script and what the actors improvised on the set. When Scorsese began editing work, he thus found there was over four hours of footage to meld into a movie. Gone were many sequences that had added substantially to the budget—including most of the lavish movie-within-a-movie, "Happy Endings"—so that the film's running time could be brought down to a still hefty 150 minutes. (Another number cut was Liza's rendition of "South America, Take It Away," which still exists.)

At a total cost of a noted $8.5 million, *New York, New York* premiered *in* New York, New York, at the Ziegfeld, on June 22, 1977, in New York City, and United Artists released it nationwide on June 29. The reviews were mostly ecstatic, especially for the performances of Liza and Robert, and for the period costumes and sets.

"Liza Minnelli at her most charismatic."
—TV Guide

"The movie of the year is here. . . . Scorsese's movie boasts two performances—by Liza Minnelli and Robert DeNiro—immeasurably superior to any of the acting in the year's other top movies. . . . The film really belongs to Liza, whose depiction of yearning is almost orgasmic. . . . There's a measured, orchestral surge to her performance. . . . New York, New York *emerges as a towering achievement that lights up the 1977 movie year like a colossal, flaming beacon. It doesn't open here until Wednesday, but I'd suggest you start forming a line at the Mark One today."* **—Joe Baltake, *Philadelphia Daily News***

Liza admitted to the *Village Voice* that she was hoping the film would be a hit, since "you're not allowed three bad pictures (flops) in a row in Hollywood." The film's high budget kept it from earning a profit, although it grossed a total box office of $16,400,000 according to *Variety*, an amount any other movie would have been happy with in 1977

Vincente Minnelli visited Liza—and director Scorsese—on the set of *New York, New York* during shooting for the ending of the "Happy Endings" production number.

(this figure probably includes the film's reissue, with a reported original take of $13,800,000 still being a respectable amount). The "three strikes, you're out" rule seemed to apply to Minnelli's movie career, as it would be three years before she would make another movie, and thirteen before she would be the star "carrying" a film. (There were reports that Liza had signed a two-picture contract with United Artists circa 1975, but this was the only film she made for the studio.) Liza was nominated for a Golden Globe Award for her performance.

New York, New York was re-released in New York City on Friday, June 19, 1981, with nearly a half hour of the footage that had been cut added back, including the entire twelve-minute "Happy Endings" production-within-a-production musical number. Liza was quoted as saying "Now it makes sense," and the reviews were even more rapturous than they had been four years earlier.

The original version of *New York, New York* had its network TV premiere Friday, May 14, 1982, on CBS, and the extended, restored version is still shown (usually on TCM). This longer version was issued on VHS; it was released in a deluxe laser disc box set with extras and outtakes, but has yet to appear on DVD. The original soundtrack recording was released on a two-LP set by United Artists Records in 1977, and was issued on CD (the two LPs on one disc) in the late 1980s by EMI, and remains in print.

Arthur
(1981)

In June 1980, Liza stepped in front of the movie cameras for the first time since completing *New York, New York* over three years earlier. The comedy *Arthur* starred Dudley Moore as rich, heavy-drinking playboy "Arthur Bach," who risks losing his 750-million-dollar inheritance when he falls in love with aspiring actress/waitress "Linda Marolla." Liza played "Linda," and, as the movie was made in New York, was able to live at home during the filming. (Weeks before the movie's 1981 premiere, Liza had to refilm the final scene outside the church; Minnelli was also the reason the movie was allowed to continue production in the late summer/fall of 1980, during a movie strike—Liza was due to start a new concert tour on October 1, 1980, and had to have the film completed by that time.) Director Stephen Gordon stated how amazed he was by the attention Minnelli received on location. "People just want to touch her, as if some of the magic will rub off." And it did

on-screen with critics, upon its July 17, 1981, release by Orion:

"Minnelli's vivacious personality and appealing kookiness are perfect for the role."
—Hollywood Reporter

"Miss Minnelli is more subdued than is her custom, but she is just right as Linda."
—Atlanta Journal

"Miss Minnelli hasn't been seen to such good advantage on film since Cabaret, *and though she never gets a chance to sing in* Arthur, *her performance is so richly comic and assured, that the film is one of those unusual comedies in which you come to believe that the romantic leads were actually made for each other. Miss Minnelli and Mr. Moore play together with the kind of energizing verve that one sees more frequently in the legitimate theater than on film."*
—Vincent Canby, *New York Times*

Arthur went on to gross an astounding $95,461,682 in the U.S. alone, making it one of the biggest hits of the year (the film played in theaters through March 19, 1982). Moore may have been the star of the movie—as was John Gielgud as the main character's beloved valet. Yet Minnelli was still profiled and hyped at another peak level of media attention (including magazine covers and

appearances on TV's *The Tonight Show*, *Good Morning America*, etc.), which quelled a Liza "legend" later started, saying she couldn't be counted on to do PR for the film. Ultimately, Minnelli was nominated for a Golden Globe award, but lost to Bernadette Peters for *Pennies from Heaven*.

Arthur has been on TV numerous times, and has appeared on all home video formats (including laser disc). It is currently available on DVD and VHS from Warner Home Video. There was a soundtrack album available on Warner Brothers Records, but Liza does not sing in the movie, nor on the LP. ("Arthur's Theme" won the Oscar for Best Song, and was written by Burt Bacharach, Carol Bayer-Seger-Bacharach, Christopher Cross and Liza's first husband, Peter Allen; Allen had contributed the line about getting "caught between the moon and New York City," after being stuck on a plane that couldn't land.)

King of Comedy
(1983)

In 1981, Liza filmed a cameo as herself, in which she appeared on a talk show hosted by Jerry Lewis; she also sang "New York, New York." *The King of Comedy* dealt with a talentless comic who becomes famous by kidnapping a talk show host. *Comedy* was directed by Martin Scorsese, who had also helmed *New York, New York*, and costarred Liza's leading man from that film, Robert De Niro. Oddly, the entire sequence Minnelli filmed would be deleted before Columbia released the movie on February 18, 1983. All that remains of Liza in the final film is a life-size cardboard cutout of her from the sequence Minnelli shot, used for a scene where DeNiro's character stages his own talk show in his house.

The King of Comedy grossed $2.5 million at the box office, has appeared on TV, and is available on VHS and DVD, but there are no outtakes of Liza's deleted sequence included with the movie's home video releases.

The Muppets Take Manhattan
(1984)

Liza filmed another cameo as herself, in October 1983, on location at Sardi's in New York City. The movie dealt with the Muppets trying to succeed in show business while in New York City. Minnelli's brief part consisted of entering the famed restaurant, and noticing her portrait had been replaced by one of Kermit the Frog (Kermit had made the switch himself, in a bid for attention). Liza calls over a Sardi's staff member and says her one line while pointing to the portrait: "Vincent . . . a *frog*?!!" (implying that she was upset over being replaced by a frog; other stars making cameos included Linda Lavin and Joan Rivers).

The Muppets Take Manhattan was released by 20th Century Fox on July 13, 1984. It did fairly well at the box office, grossing $25,534,703, and lasted through September 14, 1984, before premiering in Germany on March 22, 1985, according to *Variety*. The film has been shown on TV, and has been released on every home video format (including laser disc). It is currently available on DVD and VHS. In 2003, the DVD was even included inside select boxes of General Mills' "Golden Grahams" cereal.

That's Dancing!
(1985)

Another cameo for Liza came in this documentary tribute to dancing in films, produced by Jack Haley, Jr. as a follow-up to *That's Entertainment!* and *That's Entertainment, Part 2*. Filmed December 1–2, 1983, in an on-location shoot overlooking Times Square in Manhattan, Minnelli hosted a segment regarding the dancing in film versions of Broadway musicals such as *Sweet Charity* and *Oklahoma!* Other stars making cameos in *That's Dancing!* included Mikhail Baryishnikov, Ray Bolger, and Sammy Davis Jr. The movie was released by MGM on January 18, 1985, and Liza appeared on NBC's *Today* show to promote the film. It lasted in theaters until February 8, 1985, and grossed $4,210,938, according to *Variety*.

That's Dancing! has appeared on TV, and has been released on VHS and laser disc (including a deluxe edition), but has not yet been issued on DVD.

Rent-a-Cop
(1987)

In the fall of 1986, Liza answered a call from friend and former costar Burt Reynolds, to come to Rome and act in a new film with him. (Shooting lasted through December 1986, finishing in Chicago just before the holidays, with some dialogue relooping done in California in July 1987.) *Rent-a-Cop* starred Reynolds as a former policeman hired by a one-time hooker named "Della Roberts" (Minnelli). He is to protect her after she has witnessed a crazed killer in action. Liza wears some stunning Halstons, and has one heartwarming moment with Burt after they realize their feelings for each other. Otherwise, *Rent-a-Cop* plays like a made-for-TV film.

The movie was released in Germany on November 26, 1987 (where it played until December 17), and in the U.S. on January 15, 1988, by Kings Road Entertainment. It was universally panned, although *Variety* said "Minnelli is a lot of fun as the flamboyant prostie."

The film generated only $295,000 in revenue at the box office, according to *Variety*. One wonders why the film was made at all, or why Minnelli felt she had to say yes to Burt's request she be his costar. Did she wish a chance to try to erase the memory of their *Lucky Lady*? In an interview a few years later, Liza made one brief comment about the flop *Cop*: after stating how much she loved her latest film *Stepping Out*, she noted, "I didn't say that about *Rent-a-Cop*!"

Rent-a-Cop has been on TV, and has appeared on all home video formats including laser disc. It is currently available on DVD and VHS. There was a soundtrack album of the background score—by the late Jerry Goldsmith—on LP and CD, but Liza does not sing in the movie nor on the album.

Arthur 2: On the Rocks (1988)

Six years after *Arthur* created such a sensation, Dudley and Liza were back in front of the cameras to make a sequel. This time out, "Arthur's" family was being blackmailed into cutting him off from the family fortune. The blackmailer was the father of the woman "Arthur" had left to marry "Linda," Liza's character. "Arthur" doesn't do well without his fortune, even separating from "Linda," who goes back to being a waitress and living with her father. Eventually, "Arthur" beats his enemy at his own game—with the help of John Gielgud's butler, back as a ghost only Dudley can see—and "Arthur," his millions, "Linda," and an adopted baby are all happily reunited at the film's end. Filming began the last week of November 1987 in New York City, for a month's shooting, before switching to Warner Brothers' studio in Burbank. Production wrapped there on February 16, 1988.

Times had changed in terms of laughing at alcoholics, and when the movie was released by Warner Brothers on July 8, 1988, the reviews were not kind. The movie was simply not very good, with a leaden, far-fetched script. Liza's performance and appearance (she looked even younger and fresher than she had back in 1980 when she made the original) could do nothing to keep the film from sinking at the box office. It only lasted in theaters until August 5, 1988, and grossed a disappointing $14,681,192 in the U.S., and another $2,296,103 upon its February 10, 1989, opening in the U.K.

Arthur 2 has been on TV, and has been issued on VHS and laser disc, but not DVD.

Liza in a scene from *Arthur 2: On the Rocks* (1988).

Stepping Out
(1991)

"It's Liza-as-you-love-her in Stepping Out, *a modest heartwarmer . . . Minnelli's lost none of her pizzazz. Looking as fresh-faced and gamin as ever, and in good voice and shape, she provides the pic's emotional highs in a solo dance spot and the finale's John Kander–Fred Ebb title song."* **—Variety**

The summer of 1990 marked thirteen years since Liza Minnelli had acted and sung in a movie, or been the leading character and star of a theatrical film. That period ended when she began work in July 1990 on *Stepping Out.* Based on the play about a group of misfits who are in a dance class, Liza played their instructor, "Mavis Travis," a former Broadway dancer now in an unhealthy relationship with an unsupportive former pop music star. The movie was described as *Rocky* meets *A Chorus Line* (blending underdogs who ultimately succeed, with a show business slant). Liza sang the only two songs in the movie, a country-tinged version of "Mean to Me," and the title tune, a new song by Kander and Ebb.

Following a three-week rehearsal period in New York and Toronto, the movie started its twelve-week Toronto shoot on August 27, 1990, and completed filming on November 16. Plans were to release the film in conjunction with Minnelli's new stage show, *Liza Stepping Out at Radio City Music Hall*, in April 1991. At the last moment, the studio underwent some internal personnel changes and the new executives wound up putting *Stepping Out* on the shelf until the fall. Paramount scheduled the London premiere for September 19, 1991, followed by the September 23, 1991, U.S. premiere at the Cineplex Odeon Cinemas in New York City—held as a benefit for Broadway Cares/Equity Fights AIDS. The L.A. premiere was a week later—tied-in with Liza getting her star on Hollywood's "Walk of Fame" on September 30 (an event organized by the star's official "Limelight on Liza" fan club, and its president, Suzan Meyer). The film began engagements in London on September 20, and in the U.S. on October 4, 1991. The reviews were mostly raves, especially for Minnelli:

"There is Minnelli, the wondrous, lustrous Minnelli, who unexpectedly dances here more than she sings—and dances wonderfully. In a couple of numbers choreographed for her by Daniel Daniels, she shows precisely the glamour and pizzazz that should have made her a Hollywood diva. Stepping Out*—there is even a neatly sassy new title song by John*

Liza singing the opening portion of the title song to the movie *Stepping Out*, one of Kander and Ebb's best tunes.

Kander and Fred Ebb—reminds us of what we have lost." **—Clive Barnes**

"Liza gives an appealingly low-key performance—even though it's difficult to believe she's stuck singing in a Buffalo dive. It's been a long time since Minnelli has appeared on the big screen. It's so nice to have her back. . . . Liza is lookin' good and she has a solo dance that's more touching and riveting than the high-kicking show-stopping finale." **—Kathleen Caroll, *New York Daily News***

"Liza Minnelli breaks new ground as a mature and multidimensional actress of depth and range. . . . With synchronized intensity, a tony coordination, a svelte new body, and an absence of girlish shtick, Liza is certainly the central force that keeps this charming movie on its feet." **—Rex Reed**

Paramount, however, made a conscious decision not to make enough prints of the film for a full nationwide release. Its president and chief operating officer, Stanley R. Jaffe, addressed this concern in an October 31, 1991, letter from his New York office:

> [I] wish to clear up the misconception that Paramount is walking away from the release of this picture.
>
> Like any business, there are certain indications that one must heed, or ultimately throw money down a bottomless pit. In the case of *Stepping Out*, as proud as we are of the picture, our faith was not met with audience enthusiasm that would have meant a successful release.
>
> We adore Liza and know her to be a true star and a trooper, but even all of her efforts could not have changed the outcome of *Stepping Out*.

What "faith" was shown by the studio making merely eight prints of the film, so it could only play a few select cities at a time? It opened on October 4, 1991, in New York, Los Angeles, San Francisco, and Toronto, Canada—a total of seven theaters. Liza appeared on *Arsenio Hall*, *Phil Donahue*, *Joan Rivers*, and other TV shows in an effort to promote the film (even singing the movie's title song in a specially recorded version for these TV plugs). Since audiences watching these appearances were not even able to see *Stepping Out* in most cities, the film was not a financial success, grossing only $246,000 here in the

U.S. (where it only played through November 1, 1991). It did better during its U.K. engagements, making $3,167,999 from September 20 through November 22, 1991.

Liza delivers a warm and genuine portrayal, looks lovely, and has moments that would have to be included among the finest work of her movie career, such as her performance of the title song, and her amazing dance sequence in front of mirrors. *Stepping Out* is both an excellent star vehicle *and* ensemble film, in which both Minnelli and her supporting cast (including Shelley Winters, Julie Walters, and Ellen Greene) all have a chance to shine. It remains Liza's last theatrical film to date—and one of her most enjoyable.

Stepping Out has been shown on TV, and was released on VHS and laser disc on March 26, 1992, but has not appeared on DVD to date. (The VHS is still in print). The soundtrack CD was released in 1991 by Milan Records. At one point it was widely available at a "Sound Saver" lower price, but is now out of print.

Films Liza *Almost* Appeared In

Easter Parade (1948). Liza was to appear in this MGM musical with her mom, at the age of 1½.

Annie Get Your Gun (1949). Liza was rumored to be cast as a baby sister to "Annie Oakley," Judy's part (before Garland was replaced by Betty Hutton).

The Long, Long, Trailer (1954). Liza made minor appearances in some family scenes that were ultimately cut.

How to Succeed in Business Without Really Trying (1967). Liza had meetings in 1965 about starring in this film (Michelle Lee eventually made the movie version of the 1961 Broadway musical).

The Happiest Millionaire (1967) and *The One and Only Original Family Band* (1968). Liza was offered both movies—Lesley Ann Warren wound up starring in these Disney musicals.

Valley of the Dolls (1967). The author of the best-selling book, Jacqueline Susann, had been quoted that Liza was her first choice to play the role of troubled singer-movie star "Neely O'Hara." Patty Duke played the role in the final film. ("O'Hara" was supposedly based on Minnelli's mom, who had actually been contracted to play Broadway musical comedy star "Helen Lawson." Liza tried to talk Judy out of participating in the project, but she needn't have worried: Garland was ultimately replaced by Susan Hayward.)

The Young Girls of Rochefort (1968). Liza reportedly recorded the voice of a girl singing "On The Good Ship Lollipop," yet this song is not heard in the film, now out on DVD.

I Never Promised You a Rose Garden. Liza was to star in this film in the fall of 1970, but it was shelved at that time. Patty Duke had also been in the running for the role of a young woman dealing with her schizophrenia (based on the novel), but Kathleen Quinlan played the part when the movie was finally made in 1977.

Unnamed Script. In December 1970, Liza enthusiastically told her fan club president, Nancy Barr, about a film script by the writers of TV's *Family Affair*. It dealt with a Joan Baez–type girl who gets marooned in a desolate area with a Barry Goldwater–type man as the result of a plane crash. Ultimately, they're drawn together.

Zelda, or *The Last Flapper* (Summer 1971). Liza wanted to play F. Scott Fitzgerald's wife in either of these films, which her father would have directed. Robert Redford would have starred as F. Scott.

Movie about the life of singer Edith Piaf (1971).

How the World of Rock and Roll was Won (1971) by Roger Corman, with pop star Rick Springfield as costar.

An "out-and-out comedy" as Liza called it, directed by Vincente Minnelli, as a back-up plan if either Fitzgerald movie didn't happen (February 1972).

Film with director Robert Altman (fall of 1972; Liza said she was considering seven movie offers at that time).

The Judy Garland Story (1972). *Photoplay* magazine insisted Liza was going to play her mother in this movie, directed by Vincente. Father and daughter both repeatedly said they would never do such a thing.

Camille (May 1973). Director Franco Zefferelli announced he wanted Liza to play the Greta Garbo role in this remake.

The Optimists (1973). Liza was to sing the title song, written by Lionel Bart.

Dance Land (1973). About the Danceland Club in Los Angeles, California. The movie would have been produced by Tony Bill.

Rain (1974). In this remake, Liza would have played Sadie Thompson.

Rainbow Road (1974). Liza rejected the script to what became the 1976 remake of *A Star Is Born*, starring Barbra Streisand.

How to Marry a Millionaire (September 1974). Remake of 1955 film, which would have starred Liza, Goldie Hawn, and Raquel Welch.

Ring Them Bells (September 1974). A movie based on Liza's beloved Kander-Ebb song about a girl who goes to Yugoslavia to meet the guy next door.

The Great Gatsby. Liza was apparently offered the starring role, which her friend Mia Farrow then accepted.

Chicago. Media reports started circulating in 1975–76, again in 1977 (with Liza, Fred Ebb, and John Kander asking Martin Scorsese to direct), and by 1979–1980 were full-force that Liza would be starring as "Velma Kelly" opposite Goldie Hawn as "Roxie Hart" in the movie version of the Broadway musical. A January 1979 press article stated the film would be made by The Producers Circle and Allan Carr, and that it would feature Sinatra as the lawyer, Carol Channing and Ann Miller as competing newspaper reporters, plus Nancy Walker as "Mama," the prison matron role. In the fall of 1991, Liza's *Stepping Out* director, Lewis Gilbert, reportedly was going to direct *Chicago*, and asked Liza to play "Roxie." Shooting was to start in February 1992 for eight months. In December 1994, Harvey Weinstein of Miramax told Army Archer he wanted Michelle Pfeiffer, Liza, or Goldie Hawn teamed with Madonna; then the first week in January 1995, Archer said Weinstein promised Liza that she would star in it. The film was released in 2002 with Catherine Zeta-Jones and Renee Zellweger. Renee was nominated for Best Actress, while Catherine won the Oscar for Best Supporting Actress, in the part Liza was promised to play. (There were also rumors in 2001 that Minnelli was considered for the role of "Mama Morton" in the movie, which was played by Queen Latifah, who was also Oscar-nominated.)

Lili Marlene (March 1976) with Jack Nicholson, featuring a screenplay by Henry Craig.

Family Plot (1976). Universal wanted Liza for box-office insurance in this Alfred Hitchcock film, but Barbara Harris ultimately played the part.

It was reportedly noted (circa 1978) that Liza was wanted as the star of a film on the life of British movie star Jessie Matthews, to be called "Evergreen," "Dancing On the Ceiling," or "Over My Shoulder."

Much Ado About Nothing (Summer 1979). In London, Liza told the press she would be starring as "Beatrice" in Franco Zeffirelli's nonmusical version of Shakespeare's classic. It was to be filmed in Rio de Janeiro, Brazil, in 1980 at carnival time. The project reportedly caused Zeffirelli to cancel his theater production of *Hamlet* with Richard Gere and film bio of Maria Callas with Irene Papas.

Strictly Business (Summer-Fall 1979). It was reported around the time of Liza's Carnegie Hall Concerts that she was to replace Farrah Fawcett in this movie.

A February 1980 report had Liza "conferring with Claude Lelouche, the director of *A Man and a Woman*, about his next project, a three-generation epic."

Dot and Santa Claus (October 1981). Forbidding visiting artists to perform in two mediums, Australian Actors Equity prevented Liza from recording two songs for this children's animated movie while she was appearing in concert in that country. The songs were "It's So Easy to Be Alone in a Crowd," and "I Love to Walk Around New York."

Gina (Fall 1981). A romantic comedy about an "ordinary woman" (who was an Italian-American housewife) living in Chicago. The film was being planned with Rock Brynner (Yul Brynner's son).

Bad News Bears type of comedy (December 1981). While performing in Vegas at the end of 1981, Liza was reading a script that was similar to that film series.

Road Show (1982). A "Semi-musical" produced by David Merrick. Liza would have played an understudy in a road production of the musical *Seesaw*. Michael Bennett wrote the script, and Australia's Fred Schepesi was to direct. Christopher Walken would have been Liza's costar (he had worked with Minnelli in "Best Foot Forward"). The film was supposedly curtailed when Merrick suffered a heart attack.

Evita (Summer 1982). Liza screen-tested for the film version of the Andrew Lloyd Webber–Tim Rice musical. (Among other scenes, she filmed the one featuring the song "Don't Cry for Me, Argentina.") Director Ken Russell describes her test in this way: "Waves of electricity, waves of power, swept through the studio, waves of sound, waves of sex. And when she reached her climax with an orgasmic 'I'm coming,' so was everyone else in the place—man, woman, and dog. At the eleventh hour, it seemed we had found our Evita." Those who have seen the footage admit Liza is dazzling. Filming was to start that fall, but Paramount reneged, and the Robert Stigwood producers group wanted Elaine Page, who'd originated the role in London. Russell refused to make the movie with anyone other than Liza. The film wouldn't appear until 1996 with Madonna in the role, directed by Allan Jay Parker.

Pipeline (December 1982). This film was to have been financed by Prince Dodi Fayed and shot near the Anchorage oil fields, starting around June 1983. It was said that "Liza's brother-in-law, Christopher Gero, is writing the screenplay, which is about a madam who lives in a tent and runs the best little you-know-what in Alaska." Dodi wanted Koo Stark to costar, and there were also mentions of Lorna Luft appearing in the film with her sister; both would have played two of Liza's "girls."

Jazz and Peachy (1982). In a 1982 appearance on *Good Morning America*, Liza mentioned she'd be starring in this movie, but she didn't give any further details. It was never made.

Hang-Ups (1982, 1983). Liza also mentioned this semi-musical comedy on the above noted *Good Morning America* as one of two new films she'd be making. Based on the book dealing with psychiatry, the movie was to costar Elton John (in a non-singing comedy role), and be directed by Blake Edwards, with songs by Leslie Bricusse. The story concerned "a woman over thirty-five, not particularly beautiful, who's facing the rest of her life. All the songs are overlaid, like the songs in *The Graduate*. Showcases subtle, small, funny side [of Liza]." The movie was to be made in New York in September 1983, followed by filming in Acapulco. Leslie Bricusse had apparently sent his screenplay to Bob Fosse, in hopes of Fosse again directing Liza in a film. A copy of the script is in Fosse's personal archives at the Library of Congress.

The Great Wind Cometh (1982–84). In this drama, Liza would have played Hanna Senesh, a young Jewish freedom fighter during World War II in Hungary. The film was finally made in 1988 as *Hanna's War*. (Maruschka Detmers played Hanna, and Ellen Burstyn costarred as her mother.) Liza never signed a contract, but Cannon jumped the gun (pun *intended*) by running the ad shown.

West Side Waltz (1983). Liza was wanted to play the young, hippie part in this drama about a group of women who become friends. Minnelli's costars were mentioned as Katharine Hepburn and Doris

Day (or Elizabeth Taylor), in the film version of this Broadway play. When finally made as a 1995 CBS TV-movie, Liza played the Day-Taylor part of the violinist (with Jennifer Grey playing the hippie and Shirley MacLaine playing the Hepburn part).

A 1983 report stated that Liza "will play Mrs. James Cagney opposite Martin Sheen in a movie based on the life of the Hollywood great." This never happened.

The Enchanted Cottage (1983). Film columnist Marilyn Beck insisted Liza would star with Tom Selleck in a remake of the 1945 film, which starred Dorothy MacGuire and Robert Young. It never happened.

Once Upon a Time in America (1984). There were rumors Liza had screen-tested for a part in this drama, and was in the running with Claudia Cardinale and Geena Davis, before Elizabeth McGovern was cast, opposite Robert De Niro.

Pinnochio and the Emperor of the Night animated film (1987). Liza did no work for this film, available on VHS, but is often mistakenly billed as having recorded a voice in the film—so "buyer beware."

Sing (1989). Lorraine Bracco wound up playing the role Liza was apparently offered in this drama.

Windmill Theatre (1989–90; 1992–93). A musica-drama about a World War II musical theater was crafted to star Liza. The screenplay was by Peter Stone, with a score by Kander and Ebb. The project was finally rejected by Warner Brothers circa 1992–1993, after the failure of Bette Midler's similarly themed *For the Boys*.

(Fall 1991) A project to costar Charles Aznavour. At this same time, Liza stated on TV that she'd be doing a "French film" with Claude Lelouch. This could have been the Aznavour project, or a different film.

Liza-Streisand-Shirley MacLaine Project (1992–93). There were talks about a film with the trio; Streisand would direct, and possibly play a role in it.

Follies. There were also talks of the Sondheim show being made into a movie starring Liza and Barbra Streisand.

In 1993, Liza mentioned she had two films in development at Miramax, a musical and a comedy, and that the comedy would go into production that fall.

Vamp (Summer 1994). A comedy costarring Jim Belushi, in which Liza would have become a vampire. Directed by Linda Yellen (Liza's 1994 *Parallel Lives* TV-movie.)

Title Not Known (Spring 1997). Liza would have played a TV soap star who goes back to her old neighborhood after becoming famous. The movie would have been made in London.

Michael Jackson movie musical about two performers struggling to become successful (2002).

A film by the makers of the *Four Weddings and a Funeral* movie (2002).

Andrew Lloyd Webber promised Liza she would star in the film version of his musical *Sunset Blvd.* (2002).

Perhaps the most unusual of all film properties that Liza never did was *The Carmen Miranda Story*, which *People* magazine once stated a South American investor wanted to make, starring Minnelli as Miranda. Liza had actually done an impression of Carmen on her first U.S. TV special, *Liza*, in 1970.

Liza has made three TV movies to date, in 1985, 1993, and 1995, covered in this book's chapter on her TV career. There were three other TV movies that Minnelli didn't make but that had been mentioned for her: *The Libby Holman Story*, a biopic about the singer; *The Lillian Roth Story*, another film about a famous singer; and *Face of a Stranger*, about a homeless woman and a society matron to have been played by Liza and Lee Remick. Tyne Daly and Gena Rowlands wound up starring in this 1991 TV movie.

In the fall of 2003 there were reports of Liza meeting with movie executives, and with the advent of movie musicals making a comeback, don't be surprised if Liza wins roles in either the new *Guys and Dolls* (as "Miss Adelaide," who sings "A Person Could Develop a Cold"), or *Damn Yankees* (as the reporter who sings the showstopper "Shoeless Joe"—this last role was touted for Liza by columnist Liz Smith). There were also rumors of a cameo in the new *Catwoman* movie, and a part in an upcoming film with Robert De Niro.

In March 2004, Liza announced she'd be working with Craig Zadan and Neil Meron on an upcoming project. Then in April 2004, Liza was talking about a new movie she was planning, where she would play the owner of a nightclub—which would allow her to sing some songs in the film. At the end of the movie, Minnelli's character would be happily surrounded by her "friends and her music . . . but NOT a man!"

Hollywood loves a good comeback, so it's time for a return to the big screen—and maybe another Oscar—for Liza Minnelli.

CHAPTER ELEVEN

Liza on TV

Television gave Liza her first work and exposure while she was still a youngster—and, ultimately, its greatest reward: the Emmy. As she pursued a career in the theater in early 1963, TV let America know she was starring in an off-Broadway hit, *Best Foot Forward*, and showcased her 1965 move to Broadway in *Flora the Red Menace*. By the early 1970s, Liza was starring in a string of successful specials, including one of the best and most acclaimed solo specials of all time, 1972's *Liza with a Z*. She continued to make specials in the 1980s and 1990s, (including *Baryshnikov on Broadway* and *Liza Live: Stepping Out at Radio City Music Hall*). During the 2002–2003 season, she almost had her own TV series, and during the 2003-2004 season she made her critically acclaimed sitcom and TV series debut on the Fox network's comedy *Arrested Development*.

The following are highlights of Liza's vast TV career. In the most extensive listing of her TV work to date, we'll look at the major appearances and specials she has made from 1955 into 2004.

Art Linkletter's Hollywood (December 1954 or early 1955, both dates have been noted). Eight-year-old Liza was interviewed along with three other school kids. Minnelli was asked if she wanted her expectant mother to have a girl or a boy. She answered "a girl . . . 'cause boys are messy!" It has been noted that Liza sang "Swanee." Another Linkletter show from around this period was filmed outdoors, catching Liza out trick-or-treating at Halloween. (Art asked Minnelli if her mama was with her, obviously hoping to get Judy on his show.) This latter footage still survives and was shown on a recent Discovery channel TV special on the history of Halloween.

The Wizard of Oz (CBS—November 3, 1956). Liza co-hosted the TV premiere of her mother's movie with Bert Lahr, who played the "Cowardly Lion" in the film.

Jack Paar Show (NBC—November 14, 1958). No other information is known about this appearance.

Star Parade Presents The Gene Kelly Show (Variety special, CBS—April 24, 1959). Liza and Gene performed "For Me and My Gal," the title song of Kelly's movie debut (made with Minnelli's mom).

The Hedda Hopper Showcase (NBC—January 10, 1960). Liza sang "Over the Rainbow," her only known complete public performance of the song to date.

The Joe Franklin Show (1963). Liza was just about to open in *Best Foot Forward* when she appeared on this program.

The Jack Paar Show (NBC—March 15, 1963). Liza appeared with a cast on her leg, and was billed as "Dyju Langard" (using the letters of Judy Garland), the "Armenian discovery." Her true identity was not revealed until after she sang "They Can't Take That Away from Me."

The Ed Sullivan Show (CBS—April 21, 1963). Liza sang "Somebody Loves Me," and performed "Just a Little Joint with a Jukebox" from her recent off-Broadway debut in *Best Foot Forward*. This was

Above: Liza with her host on the April 21, 1963, *Ed Sullivan Show*. *Right:* With Judy, on her November 17, 1963, show.

Liza's first of many appearances on Sullivan's show.

The Tonight Show (NBC—June 3 1963). Guest hosted by Arthur Godfrey, from New York City. Liza was the last guest, at 12:45 AM.

Talent Scouts with Merv Griffin (CBS—July 2, 1963).

The Keefe Brasselle Show (CBS—July 23, 1963).

April in Paris Ball (NBC—October 27, 1963).

The Judy Garland Show (CBS—November 17, 1963). Videotaped July 16, 1963, at Studio 43, CBS Television City in Hollywood. This was the first official professional pairing of mother and daughter. Liza's solo was "You Are for Loving" (her hit single from *Best Foot Forward*), and she duetted with Judy on "Together"; "We Could Make Such Beautiful Music Together"/"The Best Is Yet to Come"/"Bye-Bye Baby"; "Bob White," and (in tramp costumes) "Two Lost Souls." (Available on DVD: *The Judy Garland Show—Volume One.*)

Arthur Godfrey Thanksgiving Day Special (NBC—November 28, 1963).

The Judy Garland Christmas Show (CBS—Sunday, December 22, 1963). Videotaped at Studio 43, CBS Television City in Hollywood on December 6, 1963. Liza's solo was "Alice Blue Gown." She also duetted with current beau (and Garland series dancer) Tracy Everett on "Steam Heat," and participated in medleys of holiday songs with Jack Jones, et al. (Available on DVD: *The Judy Garland Show—Volume Three, The Christmas Show.*)

The Ed Sullivan Show (CBS—May 24, 1964). Liza sang "Together" and an "Alabamy" traveling medley with two chorus boys.

The Cliff Richard Show, ITV network (British TV)—June 18, 1964 (also noted as July 1964). Starring Richard and his backup group, the Shadows. Liza sang "Meantime" (a song she recorded during this same time period, June 1964, for her first solo LP, *Liza! Liza!*), and duetted with Cliff on "A Swinging Affair" and "A Wonderful Life." This was billed as Liza's first UK TV appearance.

Mr. Broadway (NBC—October 24, 1964). Liza played "Minnie," a young opera singer with connections to the mafia, on this episode called "Nightingale for Sale."

Juke Box Jury (British TV—November 21, 1964). Liza was part of a panel that rated records.

Judy Garland and Liza Minnelli Live at the London Palladium (ITC British Television—December 1964). Fifty-five minutes of the Sunday, November 15, 1964, concert at the London Palladium. Available on DVD and VHS.

The Ed Sullivan Show (CBS—January 3, 1965).

Hullabaloo (January 19, 1965, second episode of the series). Liza appeared with Paul Anka and Dionne Warwick on this 1960s pop variety show. Her songs included: "Gypsy in My Soul," "Together" (with dancers), and Minnelli also lip-synched to Louis Armstrong's recording of "Hello, Dolly!"

The June Havoc Show (early 1965). There was a short film shown of Liza dancing at Il Mio, a discotheque in NYC's Hotel Delmonico. The club was run by Liza's best friend Tanya and her brother Timmy Everett.

The Ed Sullivan Show (CBS—March 31, 1965). Liza sang one song, and her second one—"The Middle of the Street"—was cut due to lack of time. She later recorded "Street," released as a single for Capitol. Peter Allen, Liza's husband, wrote the song.

Interview (April 1965). Local Boston show. Liza was interviewed about her first Broadway show, *Flora, the Red Menace*, which was playing in Boston at the time.

What's My Line? (CBS—May 16, 1965). Liza was the "Mystery Guest."

The Today Show (NBC—May 18, 1965). Liza's first interview with Barbara Walters.

The Ed Sullivan Show (CBS—May 23, 1965). Liza performed two songs from her Broadway debut, *Flora, the Red Menace*—"One Good Break" with cast, and "Sing Happy." After this appearance, Liza signed a contract for six more appearances on Sullivan's show, over a three-year period.

I've Got a Secret (CBS—May 31, 1965). Liza appeared in her first act *Flora* costume, since she had to go directly from this live broadcast to *Flora* (her attire was explained on the show this way).

The Tony Awards (local New York City broadcast—June 13, 1965). Liza was given her first Tony Award [for Best Actress in a Musical, for *Flora*] by presenter Carol Channing and Bert Lahr—he had played the Cowardly Lion in mama's *Oz*. Liza wore a dress belonging to her agent and thanked "the five men in my life": *Flora*'s producer, Hal Prince, its director, George Abbott, her leading man, Bob Dishy, and Kander and Ebb for the score.

Fanfare (a.k.a. *The Al Hirt Show*; CBS—August 14, 1965). Liza appeared on Al Hirt's summer show to "sing, dance, and be accompanied by Mr. Hirt's trumpet."

The Ed Sullivan Show (CBS—October 31, 1965). Liza sang "Who's Sorry Now?"

The Mike Douglas Show (syndicated—November 5, 1965). Liza sang two solos, chatted with Mike and guests, and performed "Bill Bailey" while Mike sang "Around the World." Clip of this duet was used on a Douglas retrospective circa 1975.

Sinatra (CBS—November 16, 1965). Brief film clip of Liza at a party with Sinatra, at Jillys. This special was shown again on CBS after Sinatra's passing in 1998.

The Dangerous Christmas of Red Riding Hood (ABC—November 28, 1965). Videotaped in color the week of October 11, 1965. Musical version of the famous fairy tale, this time from the wolf's point of view. Liza played "Red Riding Hood." (soundtrack LP issued; see Chapter Twelve, "For the Record," for more info.)

Ice Capades (CBS—December 1, 1965). Liza was hostess of this color special, videotaped in Atlantic City in September, 1965.

The Hollywood Reporter of December 2, 1965 stated that Liza would star in her own special in the fall of 1966 for CBS, and that the network wanted Judy Garland to be Liza's guest. That special never happened.

Danny Kaye Show (CBS—January 5, 1966).

The Hollywood Palace (ABC—February 5, 1966, this episode was rerun on May 24, 1969). Liza sang "Cabaret," "I will Wait for You," and joined hosts Van Johnson and Mickey Rooney in performing a musical sketch "Let's Make a Movie."

The Hollywood Palace (ABC—videotaped January 27, 1966, in Los Angeles, at the Hollywood Palace Theater—as all episodes of this series were). Liza performed two songs from her first nightclub act (1965–66): "There Is a Time" solo, followed by "Where Did You Learn to Dance?" with the dancers from her act, Bob Fitch and Neil J. Schwartz. Liza also duetted with host Vincent Edwards on "Everything I've Got," by Rogers and Hart.

The Tonight Show (NBC)—videotaped February 5, 1966. Aired February 6 on the West Coast, and on February 17, 1966, in the rest of the country.

To Tell the Truth (February 10, 1966). Liza tried to fool the panel and keep her identity "under her hat."

Perry Como Easter Special (NBC—March 28, 1966). Videotaped at NBC in Brooklyn, N.Y., on March 20. (The day before the taping, Liza had her hair cut for the first time in the short signature style she's known for.)

Academy Awards (April 18, 1966). Liza sang the nominated "What's New, Pussycat?"

Hippodrome (CBS—August 2, 1966; aired September 29, 1966, in the UK on ITV). Merv Griffin was the host.

Liza had auditioned for and desperately wanted the lead role in the 1966 TV version of *The Diary of Anne Frank*, which she had played in high school in 1961. Sadly, she was not cast.

The Mike Douglas Show (syndicated—1967). Liza with Peter Allen.

The Hollywood Palace (ABC—1967). Liza sang "Cabaret" on the same show as the Beatles "Strawberry Fields" video.

The Hollywood Palace (ABC). Liza appeared with Bobby Darin. Videotaped in early February 1967 (Liza left New York City on January 31, 1967, to tape the show in California).

The Tonight Show (NBC—March 23, 1967). Woody Allen subbed for Johnny Carson. Liza talked about her first real movie role, which she'd just finished, in *Charlie Bubbles*, and sang "Cabaret."

The Match Game (NBC—April 3–7, 1967).

The Mike Douglas Show (syndicated—June 27, 1967). Videotaped in Philadelphia.

Liza's First Solo TV Special—filmed in Sydney, Australia, summer 1967.

The Carol Burnett Show (CBS—September 18, 1967). (This was the second episode of Carol's legendary comedy-variety show.) Liza and Sid Caesar were the guests. Minnelli was to sing "I Wanna be Loved by You," but instead sang "The Debutante's Ball," from her first A&M album, which she was recording at this time. Liza and Carol duetted on a "Time" medley, including the song "Just in Time."

The Tonight Show (NBC—fall 1967). Liza sang "I Wanna Be Loved by You."

Kraft Music Hall: Give My Regards to Broadway (NBC—October 4, 1967).

Hollywood Palace (ABC—videotaped approximately December 9, 1967). Liza sang "Married/You Better Sit Down Kids" with Peter Allen; she would keep this song in her act over the years.

Hollywood Palace (ABC—December 21, 1967; airdate has also been noted as December 12, 1967). Herb Alpert hosted.

The Kraft Music Hall: Woody Allen Looks at 1967 (NBC—December 27, 1967). Liza appeared in a "Bonnie and Clyde" spoof with Allen, and a sketch about miniskirts. The sketches were videotaped December 4, 1967; musical numbers taped December 13, in New York.

Comedy Is King (1968).

The Today Show (NBC—January 2, 1968).

The Tonight Show (NBC—January 9, 1968).

The Hollywood Palace (ABC—January 20, 1968; rerun August 20, 1968). With Jack Benny.

Grammy Awards (1968).

The Carol Burnett Show (CBS—February 5, 1968. Videotaped September/October 1967). Liza's two solos: "Butterfly McHeart"; "The Happy Time"; and she performed "Big Beautiful Ball" with Burnett (both as clowns). Minnelli had wanted to sing "Feelin' Groovy," but Gwen Verdon had just performed it on a recent episode.

The Ed Sullivan Show (CBS—March 10th, 1968; rerun on September 22, 1968). Liza sang "You Better Sit Down Kids" and later did "The Life of the Party/It's Today" as a lavish production number

with a chorus. This episode of the Sullivan show was broadcast from Las Vegas, while Liza was appearing there.

The Hollywood Palace (ABC—March 30, 1968; videotaped February 1968). Liza performed with host Jimmy Durante (see photo below).

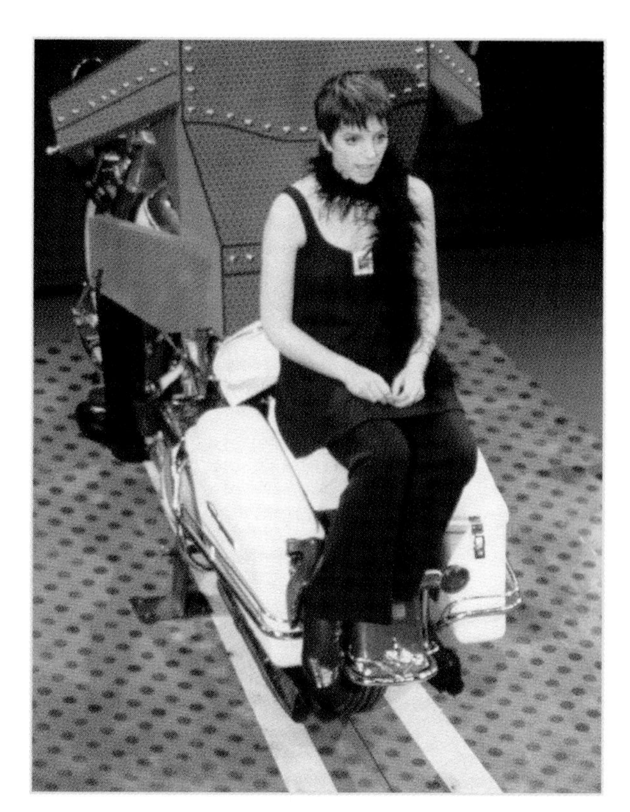

Liza singing "Frank Mills," on *Ed Sullivan*.

The Best on Record (NBC—May 8, 1968).

The 1968 Tony Awards (Bette Midler can also be seen, appearing in a number from *Fiddler on the Roof*).

The Ed Sullivan Show (CBS—December 8, 1968). Liza sang "Sweet Blindness" with two male dancers, and Peter Allen's "Simon" (which had been prerecorded, and included a filmed montage of Liza, similar to today's music videos).

That's Life (ABC—December 17, 1968).

The Ed Sullivan Show (CBS—January 19, 1969). Liza sang "Frank Mills."

The Glen Campbell Goodtime Hour (CBS—April 30, 1969). Liza sang "L.A. Breakdown," then duetted with Glen on "The More I See You" and "I'd Like to Get to Know You."

The Ed Sullivan Show (CBS—May 18, 1969). Liza sang "You Made Me So Very Happy" and "Didn't We?"/ "McArthur Park."

The Ed Sullivan Show (CBS—October 26, 1969, rerun September 6, 1970). Liza sang "Come Saturday Morning," from her film *The Sterile Cuckoo*.

The Mike Douglas Show (week of December 22–26, 1969; videotaped November 17, 1969). Liza co-hosted the show that entire week. Kay Thompson appeared on one episode, and duetted with Liza on "Breezin' Along (with the Breeze)."

The Pearl Bailey Show (1970).

Movin' (CBS—March 1970). Liza appeared with The Bojangles on this TV special.

The Ed Sullivan Show (CBS—March 22, 1970). Liza sang "Simon," written by Peter Allen.

42 Annual Academy Awards (April 7, 1970). This was the year Liza was nominated for *The Sterile Cuckoo.*

Liza (NBC—Monday, June 29, 1970). Minnelli's first network TV special in the U.S. (following a 1967 show in Australia). This new NBC special had just been videotaped May-June, in L.A. It was postponed from the spring, when she suffered injuries from a motorcycle accident. Liza's guests: Anthony Newley (his solos were "Very Soft Shoes" and "A Certain Smile"), Michael J. Pollard, and songwriters Jimmy Webb (his solo was "Careless Weed") and Randy Newman (his solo was "Love Story"). Highlights included Liza duetting with Anthony and Michael on "Singin' in the Rain," "New York, New York (A Helluva Town)," "I Won't Dance," and "That's Entertainment." Liza also performed a Carmen Miranda impression, and her solos included: "Tradition," "Let Me Sing and I'm Happy," "Let the Sunshine In," "Cabaret," "Sing Happy," "Maybe This Time," "Makin' Whoopee," "Can't Help Lovin' That Man," and a moving version of "You Made Me Love You," identified with Liza's beloved mama, of course.

The Johnny Cash Show (CBS—September 23, 1970). Videotaped summer 1970 in Nashville, Liza's

Publicity photo for the 1970 TV special *Liza.*

first time there. Guests were Ray Charles, Arlo Guthrie, and Minnelli. She sang "Lazy Bones" and Stormy Weather," both from her *New Feelin'* album. (Cash said she'd "just recorded a new album with a folk-country beat.") This was the first show of the new season, and featured Liza with permed hair.

This Is Tom Jones (ABC—Friday, October 23, 1970).

The Ed Sullivan Show (CBS—Fall 1970). Liza sang "You've Made Me So Very Happy."

Laugh-In (NBC—November 8, 1971; rerun on April 16, 1972; videotaped September 1971). In various sketches, Liza played a French maid, a Southern belle, and a circus-act knife-thower. She also sang in a production number, "Bring Back the Thirties."

The David Frost Show—Videotaped February 8, 1972, in New York City.

The Dick Cavett Show—Videotaped February 10, 1972, in New York City.

Premiere of Cabaret (WOR-TV, NYC, February 19, 1972). Thirty-minute special on the premiere of *Cabaret*; videotaped February 13.

Anthony Newley Special (February 20, 1972; rehearsed and videotaped January 3–8, 1971, in L.A.). Liza sang "I Wonder Where My Easy Rider's Gone" (from her A&M album *New Feelin'*), and a medley with Newley and Diahann Carroll.

Rona Barrett Special: Sex Symbols (February 29, 1972).

44 Annual Academy Awards (April 10th, 1972). Liza presented the award for Best Song of 1971.

Liza with a "Z" (NBC—September 10th, 1972; repeated on March 9, 1973, and again in September 1973). Filmed in New York City on May 31, 1972 (following five weeks of rehearsals), with eight different 16mm cameras planted throughout the theater. In one magazine interview, Liza was

Publicity photo for the TV special *Liza with a "Z"* (1972).

reported as explaining there was a hair caught in the lens of the main camera, and that the whole special was refilmed with paid extras in the audience. (The special was originally set to be filmed during the time Liza was at the Greek Theater the previous fall, September 20–26, 1971.) Liza won an Emmy Award, as *Liza with a "Z"* was named Best Variety Special of 1972. (Soundtrack album available on CD; a bootleg VHS was issued in 1980 by a firm called All-Star Video in Long Island, New York. Liza has mentioned this special is being restored/remastered for DVD and possible theatrical release, but nothing has appeared since it was first mentioned in the early-to-mid-1990s.) This was a monumental Minnelli moment in Liza's life and career, and is perhaps her most cherished and successful TV appearance.

Men Who Made the Movies (1973). Liza appeared in the segment on her father.

A Royal Gala Variety Performance in the Presence of Her Majesty the Queen (ABC—January 3, 1973). Liza was Emmy-nominated for her performance in this show, in the category of Outstanding Supporting Performer on a Music or Variety Program. She lost to Tim Conway of *The Carol Burnett Show*, but this was the year/TV season she shared in the victory of *Liza with a "Z"* as Outstanding Variety/Music Program—she was give a statuette by the TV academy for being the show's star.

Entertainer of the Year Awards (CBS—Tuesday, January 23, 1973). Videotaped in Las Vegas the first week of January 1973. Liza won as Entertainer of the Year, and was presented the award by sister Lorna Luft.

The Merv Griffin Show (January 26, 1973). Videotaped and aired that same day.

Jack Paar. Videotaped February 6, 1973, in New York City.

45th Annual Academy Awards (NBC—March 27, 1973). Liza won as Best Actress, for *Cabaret*.

Today (NBC-1973). Barbara Walters interview.

The Dick Cavett Show (December 20th, 1973). Pretaped.

46th Annual Academy Awards (April 2, 1974). Liza sang "Oscar." Vocal prerecorded at Glen-Glen Sound on Paramount's lot.

The 1974 Tony Awards (ABC—April 21, 1974).

Love from A to Z (NBC—April 30th, 1974). Joint concert with Charles Aznavour. Filmed mid-late October 1973, at London's Rainbow Theater. Liza's songs: "My Romance"; "La, La, La," "And I in My Chair"; "You've Let Yourself Go"; "Liza with a 'Z'" sung in French; "I Have Lived" (duet); "There Is a Time" (duet).

The Tonight Show (NBC—May 14, 1974). With Fred Astaire. (This appearance was canceled.)

The Merv Griffin Show (May 16, 1974).

That's Entertainment: Fifty Years of MGM (ABC—May 29, 1974).

Kup's Show (Summer 1974). From Chicago. Host Irv Kupcinet. Liza appeared on two episodes, one with Jack Haley Jr.

The Tonight Show (NBC—August 30th, 1974). With Jack Haley Jr. and Vincente Minnelli, promoting *That's Entertainment!*

The Merv Griffin Show (syndicated—summer/fall 1974). Appearance to promote *That's Entertainment!* Liza said the funniest thing she'd ever read about herself in the tabloids was that "I'd run away . . . to Bali. . . with Henry Kissinger!"

The Tonight Show (NBC—September 1974). Sammy Davis Jr. as host. Liza sang "I'm One of the Smart Ones."

The Merv Griffin Show (syndicated—September 23, 1974). Videotaped early September. Tribute to Vincente, with Liza, Sammy Davis Jr., and Leslie Caron. Liza sang "Our Love Is Here to Stay."

Wide World of Entertainment (ABC—Wednesday, September 25, 1974). World Premiere Party for

That's Entertainment! Liza was interviewed by George Hamilton (to be in the DVD box).

Dinah! (syndicated—February 28, 1975). Videotaped mid-January (approximately January 20), at CBS Television City. Guests were Liza, Jessica Walter, Roy Clark, and Earl Holliman. Liza sang "All That Jazz," which she recorded in New York City (The star mentioned it was "the name of a new album I'm doing," but she only recorded this and three other songs from the score of the Kander-Ebb Broadway musical *Chicago*. Recording dates have been mentioned as either January, February 5, or the first week in March 1975. No further recording would be done for this alleged album). Minnelli also talked about *New York, New York* for the first time, which she'd just signed to do.

The Mike Douglas Show (syndicated—1975). Filmed interview on the set of *Lucky Lady* in Guimas, with Liza and her *LL* costars, Gene Hackman and Burt Reynolds.

Rona Looks at Raquel, Liza, Cher and Ann-Margret (CBS—May 28, 1975). Daytime special. This interview with Liza was videotaped at her home.

60 Minutes (CBS—Sunday, August 3, 1975; rerun in an abridged form on Sunday, December 25, 1977). Retrospective on Judy's life and career. Liza was interviewed from Mexico, while filming *Lucky Lady*.

The Dick Cavett Special (CBS—August 16, 1975).

Sammy and Co (syndicated—November 1, 1975; taped in New York City, August or September 1975). Chita Rivera and Stephanie Mills also appeared on this show. Liza sang "My Own Best Friend."

Dinah! (syndicated—Friday, November 7, 1975; videotaped at CBS TV City, Hollywood, fall 1975). Kander and Ebb tribute. Liza sang "A Quiet Thing"; "Lucky Lady"; "Sing Happy" (with Dinah and Fred Ebb; John Kander on piano); "Nowadays" (with Chita Rivera, who surprised Liza by appearing on the show during this song); "Maybe This Time"; "Money, Money" (with Fred); "Cabaret" (with all).

Mac Davis Special (NBC—Thursday, November 13, 1975). Liza sang "All That Jazz" (lip-synched to her Columbia Records single), and "I Believe In Music" with Mac.

The Tonight Show (NBC—Monday, December 15, 1975). Burt Reynolds hosted; Liza and Gene Hackman were his guests, to promote their new *Lucky Lady* movie. Liza sang "Lucky Lady" and "Don't Let Me Be Lonely Tonight."

Bell Telephone Jubilee (NBC—Friday, March 26, 1976; repeated on September 8, 1976. Liza hosted this special with Bing Crosby, and sang: "The Way We Were/Yesterdays" and "What a Swell Party It Was" (with Bing); *Cabaret* medley (with Joel Grey); "If You Could Read My Mind/Come Back to Me" (with Marvin Hamlisch at piano); medley (with Joel Grey and Ben Vereen), which included Liza singing "I Don't Know How to Love Him," from the musical *Jesus Christ, Superstar*, which Vereen had appeared in.

People magazine special (NBC—Saturday, August 28, 1976). Liza was interviewed with Jack Haley Jr. Minnelli appeared in costume for the movie she was filming, *New York, New York*.

Life Goes to the Movies (NBC—October 31, 1976). Liza hosted this show (along with Henry Fonda and Shirley MacLaine), which included her tribute to Marilyn Monroe. Jack Haley Jr. produced the three-hour show.

Golden Globe Awards (January 1977).

Who's Who (CBS—February 1977).

The American Film Institute Tribute to Bette Davis (CBS—March 21, 1977).

The Mike Douglas Show (syndicated—July 15, 1977). To promote *New York, New York* Liza lip-synched to "New York, New York," then sang "World Goes 'Round" with the Bernie Herman Band.

The Merv Griffin Show (syndicated—July 25, 1977). Liza lip-synched to "New York, New York."

Today (NBC—February 15, 1978). Interview with Gene Shalit about her Broadway show *The Act.*

Gene Kelly: An American in Pasadena (CBS—March 13, 1978). Liza and Gene talked about the first time they worked together, and a clip was shown from that 1959 program. This 1978 special is available on an import DVD.

The 1978 Tony Awards (CBS—June 4, 1978). Liza sang "City Lights" from her Broadway musical *The Act*, and won her third Tony Award, for her performance in that show.

Superstar Profile (Aired in U.S. and in France in December 1978). French TV, thirty-minute Interview show. Filmed while Liza was in rehearsals in August 1978. Minnelli is seen performing two numbers that would be cut from a later HBO videotaping of this concert: "Everybody Gets the Blues," and "Twelve Fellas."

That's Hollywood (syndicated TV series, 20th Century-Fox—1979). Show had an outtake from *Lucky Lady*—the alternate ending where the Hackman and Reynolds characters die. Tom Bosley (*Happy Days*) was host of this series.

In June 1979 it was announced that John Travolta was planning a TV special to "be taped next year," and that his costars would be Liza and Lily Tomlin. It never happened.

Good Morning America (ABC—August 29, 1979). Liza plugged upcoming Carnegie Hall concert and was interviewed by David Hartman.

Muscular Dystrophy Association Telethon (Jerry Lewis)—September 2–3, 1979. Syndicated.

The Muppet Show (syndicated—November 15, 1979; videotaped in London on July 31, 1979). The series was Emmy-nominated for Outstanding Variety or Music Program, and Liza's episode (a musical murder mystery in which she played singing actress "Liza O'Shaugnessy") was up for Outstanding Directing in a Variety or Music Program (Peter Harris), and Best Video Tape Editing for a Series (John Hawkins); also nominated by the Writers Guild of America for outstanding achievement in a television show, variety, musical, or comedy. Liza's songs: "Copacabana"; "A Quiet Thing" (with Kermit the Frog); and "Everything's Coming Up Roses." Available on DVD from Time-Life.com

20/20 (ABC—January 24, 1980). Geraldo Rivera Interview. Included footage of the closing night of Liza's 1978–1979 concert tour, in New Orleans, November 25, 1979.

Goldie and Liza: Together (CBS—February 19, 1980; repeated May 31, 1980). Videotaped (mostly at ABC, with opening scene shot at CBS) September 18–30, 1979; September 30 was the closing sequence taping, at ABC. The special received an Emmy nomination for "Outstanding Variety or Music Program" of 1980 (Liza shared the nomination with costar Goldie Hawn, and producers George Schlatter, Don Mischer, and Fred Ebb).

Variety raved in their February 20 issue: "Variety comes back with a bang . . . Minnelli is done up in a becoming hairstyle she should consider more often [in the drama scene, Liza's hair was upswept in a style she wore on occasion in 1979–1980]. . . . Together or solo, Minnelli and Hawn are a class act." Lee Winfrey wrote for the *Philadelphia Inquirer*, "When Liza Minnelli appears, the show is really special. Liza is so superior to most entertainers who star in television specials that it is always a treat to see her reappear. Tonight is no exception to that rule. Watch first one and then the other of the women, the energy and the artistry that each puts into the number, and you will understand better why Miss Minnelli is a star, while Miss Hawn is still basically a walk-on act. There is an incandescence about Liza that justifies every glance of attention the public has ever cast her way." The special did not do well in the ratings, coming in at number 47 out of 51 shows, with a skimpy 15 rating, due to the Winter Olympics on ABC and a Burt Reynolds movie, *The End*, on NBC.

Standing Room Only (HBO concert series—March 9, 13, 17, 19, 21, 25, and 29, 1980). Videotaped Saturday, November 24, 1979 (both shows that night) in New Orleans, during the penultimate night of Liza's 1978–1979 fifteen-month tour. *Video Review* magazine's Roy Hemming wrote, "To the surprise of many of us, Liza Minnelli has developed into the best pop singer in America today. She does it with a combination of rhythmic incisiveness, complete involvement with the lyrics whether she's projecting them with soft understatement or with riveting dramatic intensity, a lightheartedly comic and even ironic touch where appropriate, a wide range of vocal colors, and sheer physical energy. She's always in complete control, whatever the tempo, but never with any loss in projecting the personal warmth that makes you feel she absolutely loves every note she's singing."

The Tonight Show (NBC—April 11, 1980). Liza sang "I'm Old Fashioned."

Academy Awards (ABC—April 14, 1980). Liza was a presenter, with Walter Matthau.

Baryshnikov on Broadway (ABC—April 24, 1980; repeated June 6, 1981. Videotaped first few weeks of January 1980, in Hollywood, opening scenes taped in New York City). Liza played "tour guide," guiding us and Baryshnikov through Broadway musical history for this very popular and successful special. Liza's solo was "The Music That Makes Me Dance," and she performed numerous numbers with the show's star. The special was number 17 in the Nielson ratings for that week, and won four Emmy Awards—Best Variety or Music Program; Best Directing in a Variety or Music Program; Art Direction, Variety or Music Program; Achievement in Musical Direction.

Muscular Dystrophy Association Telethon, Jerry Lewis (September 1, 1980). Liza sang a medley of love songs ("Just You, Just Me," "His Is the Only Music That Makes Me Dance," "Our Love Is Here to Stay," "Slap that Bass," "My Funny Valentine," "Come Rain or Shine") and "'But the World Goes 'Round."

Today (NBC—December 25, 1980). Liza read "'Twas the Night Before Christmas." Videotaped at Liza's Lake Tahoe home, and aired again in 1981 and 1982 on Christmas morning.

Marvin Hamlisch Special (Showtime—taped and aired early 1981). Liza sang "If You Could Read My

Mind/Come Back to Me," "My Funny Valentine," and "Oscar" (with Hamlisch), and talked with Marvin about their starting their careers together in the early 1960s.

Gala of Stars (PBS—March 22, 1981; videotaped at Carnegie Hall, February 1981). Liza sang "'But the World Goes Round," and "New York, New York."

Good Morning America (ABC—May 26, 1981; videotaped while Liza was appearing at the Executive Inn in Owensboro, Kentucky, May 15 and 16, 1981).

The Tonight Show (NBC—May 26, 1981). Liza promoted her concert engagement at the Greek Theater in L.A., and her new movie, *Arthur* (clip shown). She also sang "New York, New York."

Good Morning America (ABC; May 27, 1981). Second of two-parter profile. Liza was interviewed by Tom Sullivan and shown rehearsing "Some People" around a piano.

Tomorrow Coast-to-Coast with Tom Snyder (NBC—June 2, 1981). Videotaped interview with Rona Barrett.

11th Annual Entertainer of the Year Awards (syndicated; aired in markets between June 22 and August 9, 1981. Videotaped May 29 and 30, 1981).

Today (NBC—July 23, 1981). Interview about *Arthur* and the reissue of *New York, New York*.

Good Morning America (ABC—August 12, 1981). Interviewed by David Hartman. Liza promoted *Arthur* and the *New York, New York* reissue.

Telethon (not the MDA). (Late in 1981; videotaped in Las Vegas from her onstage act.) Liza sang her "It's a Miracle" opening, another number, then asked that people pledge: "Just give a dollar. Now the *rich* people, that's another story!"

Night of 100 Stars (ABC—March 8, 1982). Videotaped February 14, 1982, at Radio City Music Hall, New York City. Liza sang "New York, New York" with baseball players.

Bloopers and Outtakes special (NBC—1982). Liza was seen in outtakes from Arthur.

Merv Griffin (syndicated—August 1982). Liza with a curl (permed hair), received an award.

Good Morning America (ABC—November 5, 1982). Report on Liza's concert at the Moulin Rouge in Paris, France, the night before, with clips. Liza was then on the show live a week or so later, where she mentioned two upcoming films—"Well, one is called *Jazz and Peachy* and one is called *Hang-Ups*." They never were made.

55th Annual Academy Awards (ABC—April 11th, 1983). Liza as cohost, along with Dudley Moore, Richard Pryor, and Walter Matthau. This was the highest-rated show in Oscar history until the 1998 Awards (that garnered a 34.9 rating and 55 share).

The President's Command Performance (syndicated special—May 29, 1983; videotaped September 25, 1982). Liza with curls (perm), sang "Yes," "My Ship/The Man I Love," "Some People," and "New York, New York" (reportedly, she also sang "Rose's Turn," but that was cut from the broadcast).

Hour Magazine (syndicated—May 30th, 1983). Video clips from Liza's latest concert "By Myself," appearance in L.A. the month before.

The Best of Everything (NBC—November 1983). Liza sang the Kander–Ebb title song of this TV special, over its opening and closing, off camera. Recorded in a New York City studio, September 1983—photo in the *New York Post* of recording session.

Entertainment Tonight (syndicated). Press day/rehearsals for workshop of *The Rink*—late 1983.

American Music Awards (ABC— January 1984). Liza taped a message in New York City to Michael Jackson, who was getting a special tribute.

Gala of Stars (PBS—January 1984). Liza and Chita (in red Halstons) sang "The Apple Doesn't Fall" from their Broadway show *The Rink*.

I Love New York (TV commercial—February 1984). Filmed November—December 1983.

Live at 5 (local New York City NBC station—early February, 1984). Liz Smith interviewed Liza and Chita Rivera about their new Broadway musical, *The Rink*. (There were also two TV commercials filmed for *The Rink*.)

Entertainment Tonight (syndicated—February 1984). Interview with Liza about *The Rink*.

Live at 5 (local New York City NBC station—March 5, 1984). Interview by Liz Smith; Liza and Chita Rivera returned to talk about *The Rink*.

56th Annual Academy Awards (ABC—April 9, 1984). Liza presented award with Rock Hudson.

Good Morning America (ABC—Spring, 1984). Host David Hartman interviewed Liza and Chita. Liza said she would be returning to films following *The Rink*.

Faerie Tale Theater (Showtime—April 16, 1984). Liza starred in *Princess and the Pea* (videotaped in L.A., August 1983). Out on VHS and laser.

Today (NBC—January 14, 1985). Liza promoted her *That's Dancing!* movie, opening at that time. She was interviewed by Gene Shalit.

Golden Globe Awards (January 26, 1985). Liza presented the Cecil B. DeMille Award to Elizabeth Taylor.

Entertainment Tonight (syndicated, hourlong weekend show, February 1985; videotaped January 1985). Barbara Hower interviewed Liza, who sang one song at the show's conclusion.

Entertainment Tonight (syndicated—June, 1985). Covering Liza's concert tour "comeback" / opening of tour.

The Tonight Show (NBC—October 22, 1985). Liza as a blonde, sang "Boys and Girls Like You and Me," and promoted her *A Time to Live* TV movie.

A Time to Live (TV movie, NBC—October 28, 1985; filmed August 13–September 3, 1985, in Montreal). The original title was *Intensive Care*, based on the true story of Mary-Lou Weisman, the mother of a young boy who was dying from muscular dystrophy. The quick filming was due to Liza's concert schedule having been booked, thus there were many twelve-to-sixteen-hour days on the set, six days a week. The *New York Post*'s review said, "So much does she take this role to her heart that it is impossible to imagine any other actress—even those who routinely do such dramatic roles on television and in the movies—in her shoes." The movie ranked number 28 for the week in the ratings and Liza won a Golden Globe award for her performance. Was on VHS.

Golden Globe Awards (January 1986). Liza won for Best Performance in a Made-for-TV Movie or Miniseries, for *A Time to Live*.

London morning talk show (March 1986). Liza's sister, Lorna Luft, was co-hosting a week of a British AM talk show, and on one episode, Liza appeared as a surprise to Lorna. The sisters also chatted with actor Harvey Fierstein (*Torch Song Trilogy, Hairspray*).

Standing Room Only (HBO concert series—May 1986). *Liza in London*, videotaped week of March 19, 1986. (There had been talks back in the summer of 1985 about either HBO or Showtime videotaping her in concert.)

TV promo/commercial for The Animal Peace Plantation, in Walton, New York. Filmed March-April 1986.

Salute to Lady Liberty (July 4 special, ABC—1986). From Giants Stadium. Liza sang "New York, New York," admidst thousands of people chanting "Li-za, Li-za, Li-za, Li-za," during their ovation.

60 Minutes (CBS—September 28, 1986). Filmed during London Concert tour, March 1986

American Music at the White House (PBS—March 25, 1987; videotaped March 8, 1987). In superb voice, Liza sang "Ten Cents a Dance," "Boys and Girls Like You and Me," and her "New York, New York."

Minnelli on Minnelli: Liza Remembers Vincente (PBS—March 1987; videotaped the week between Christmas and New Years, 1986, in L.A.) Liza hosted this clip-filled tribute, featuring scenes from her father's films. (During 1999 and 2000, she mounted a revue-concert tribute to the music from her father's movies for Broadway and a brief tour, which was also titled *Minnelli on Minnelli*.)

Happy Birthday, Hollywood (ABC—May 1987; videotaped in L.A. April 26, 1987). Liza did a Charlie Chaplin impression and sang "Love Makes the World Go 'Round."

Metropolis (TV commercial for this Estee Lauder men's cologne—Fall/November 1987). "Wear it, and you own the world" was Liza's tag-line/slogan. Minnelli sang "City Lights" during the commercial. The spot was filmed around New York City in the middle of September 1987. Liza also made in-store appearances in November. She was paid $1 million for her work. (Around this same time, she also did a print ad for Revlon's "The Most Unforgettable Women in the World Wear Revlon" campaign, and donated her $200,000 fee to AIDS research.)

Entertainment Tonight (January 1988). Piece on *Rent-a-Cop* and Liza.

Academy Awards (ABC—April 11, 1988). Liza introduced the nominees for Best Song (with Dudley Moore).

Liza Minnelli: Triple Play (Sam Found Out) (ABC—May 31, 1988; filmed in and around New

Publicity photo for *Triple Play* (1988).

York City during ten days in March–April 1988). This unique special featured Liza performing in three individual comedy-drama segments (in which she played a hooker, a dance instructor, and a woman torn between a man and her dog). Costars were Ryan O'Neal, Lou Gosset Jr., and Howard Rubenstein. Liza also sang the new Kander–Ebb songs "Triple Play" and "Tomorrow Is Another Day."

Late Nite with David Letterman (NBC—July 7, 1988). Liza promoted *Arthur 2*, and sang "God Bless the Child."

Oprah (syndicated—summer 1988). Liza and Dudley Moore appeared to promote *Arthur 2*.

American Film Institute Salute to Gregory Peck (CBS—1989).

Frank, Liza and Sammy: The Ultimate Event (Pay-per-view—February 1989; videotaped during Detroit engagement at the Fox Theater, December 2, 3, and 4, 1988). The TV show was also stereo simulcast on nationwide radio. A VHS was released in the U.S. in September 1989, on Kodak Home Video, following a successful European release. It has yet to appear on DVD, although Liza did record an audio commentary for the disc in November 2001, in New York City.

Variety Club Telethon (March 11 and 12, 1989). From St. Louis, Missouri.

Songwriter's Hall of Fame 20th Anniversary (June 22, 1989; videotaped on May 11, 1989, at Radio City Music Hall). (Liza had just returned from Italy that same day.) Minnelli sang "A New Life" (its world premiere), and "New York, New York."

Top of the Pops (BBC—summer–fall 1989). Liza sang "Losing My Mind"—from her new pop album, *Results*—on this British TV show.

Muscular Dystrophy Association Telethon (Jerry Lewis) (September 2 and 3, 1989). Liza sang "Stormy Weather," "When the Sun Comes Out," "Blues in the Night" and "Carolina in the Morning" with Sammy Davis Jr.

Entertainment Tonight (September 1989). Promoted Liza's new *Results* album.

Arsenio Hall (syndicated—November 22, 1989). Liza plugged *Results* by singing "So Sorry I Said" and "Losing My Mind."

Grammy Living Legends (CBS—November 24, 1989; videotaped November 21). Video tribute (clips) to Liza, who was awarded a special Grammy for her body of work. Minnelli sang "But the World Goes 'Round," followed by lip-synching to "Losing My Mind."

50th Anniversary of The Wizard of Oz (CBS—February 1990). Interview with Liza, Lorna, and Joe Luft, videotaped in L.A. in September 1989 (Liza sporting her *Results* mod-punkish hairdo).

Annual Bafta Awards (British TV—February 1990). Liza presented the Best Album by a British Artist to the Fine Young Cannibals.

Top of the Pops (BBC, England—February 1990). Two days after the above appearance, Liza sang "Love Pains," from her *Results* album.

Going Live (England—February 1990). Liza again sang "Love Pains."

Aspel & Co (British TV show, England—February 1990). Yet again, Liza sang "Love Pains." Another guest on this show was actor William Shattner.

Christmas at Rockefeller Center (NBC—December 1, 1990). Liza as host.

Live with Regis and Kathie Lee (syndicated—April 1991). Liza's first appearance on this show. She promoted her *Stepping Out at Radio City* engagement.

Film '91 (London)—British interview with Barry Norman, done at the time of Liza's fall 1991 appearances there.

TV AM (London)—British interview with Mike Morris.

Muscular Dystrophy Association Telethon (Jerry Lewis—September 1991). Liza sang a medley of love songs with her musical arranger, Billy Stritch, and a solo of "Stepping Out."

Also in September 1991, to promote the *Stepping Out* movie, Liza appeared on *Joan Rivers*, *Donahue*, and *Arsenio Hall* (*Hall* was done the day she got her star on the Hollywood Walk of Fame, September 30, 1991). Liza lip-synched on the first two shows, to a "single"-sounding studio version of "Stepping Out." This version has never been released on record.

Live with Regis and Kathie Lee (syndicated—January 20, 1992). Liza promoted her upcoming week-long return to Radio City Music Hall.

Academy Awards (ABC—spring 1992). Liza presented "Best Song" with Shirley MacLaine.

Liza's *Live at Radio City Music Hall* began airings on PBS on December 6, 1992, and resulted in a total of six Emmy Award nominations, including one for Liza herself, for Outstanding Individual Performance in a Variety or Music Program in 1993. Liza lost to comedian Dana Carvey. The special was also nominated for Art Direction, Choreography, Costume Design, and Music and Lyrics for "Sorry I Asked"; Technical Direction (Camera/Video). "Sorry I Asked" won an Emmy for Kander and Ebb as Best Song.

Oprah (syndicated—December 24, 1992). Liza sang a Christmas medley with Tony Bennett, and also performed "Christmas Is an Island" with Billy Stritch.

The Tonight Show (with Jay Leno, NBC—January 1993). Liza promoted her *Live at Radio City* CD and video, and sang "So What?"

Great Performances: Sondheim—A Celebration at Carnegie Hall (PBS—March 3, 1993; videotaped

June 10, 1992. Liza sang "Water Under the Bridge" with Billy Stritch and "Back in Business." (This concert has been released on CD, DVD, and VHS.)

65th Annual Academy Awards (ABC—March 29, 1993). Liza's ninth appearance on an Oscar telecast. Minnelli sang "Ladies' Day" by Kander and Ebb.

The Tony Awards (CBS—June 6, 1993). Liza hosted. She sang an opening number, and a medley with her sister Lorna Luft—the only time they've performed together on TV to date.

Larry King Live (CNN—December 1, 1993). Liza's first of many appearances on this show. This was also the first "World AIDS Day," and there was a clip of Liza at the UN that same day, singing "The Day After That."

The Tonight Show (NBC—January 26, 1994). Liza sang "The Day After That."

The Tony Awards (CBS—June 12, 1994). Liza presented the award for Best Direction of a Musical, and performed with Bernadette Peters.

In a New Light '94 (ABC—July 9, 1994). Barbara Walters hosted. Liza sang "The Day After That" with a choir, in a videotape of her June appearance at "Stonewall 25" from Central Park.

Parallel Lives (Showtime—August 14, 22, and 30, 1994; Liza filmed her role over a ten-day period in Salt Lake City, from September 21 through September 30, 1993). Minnelli played "Stevie (Stephanie) Merrill," a woman who organizes a college fraternity/sorority reunion, which the film centers around. The all-star cast was working only from an outline, and reportedly ad-libbed their lines.

American Movie Classics (October 1, 1994). Liza hosted three of her favorite films, *The Joker Is Wild*, *Funny Face*, and her own movie *The Sterile Cuckoo*.

American Movie Classics (October 21–23, 1994). Film Preservation Festival. Liza appeared in promo spots for this cause, apparently taped in 1993.

Concert of the Americas (syndicated—December 1994; videotaped December 10, 1994). Liza opened the show with "Old Friends," closed it with "New York, New York," then encored with the all-star cast in singing "Freedom."

April 6, 1995—*The Hollywood Reporter* announced that Liza was set to play Helen Morgan in the Krost/Chapin telefilm *Torch* for CBS. The TV movie was never made.

The Tonight Show with Jay Leno (NBC—June 5, 1995). Liza sang "Some People," and promoted her upcoming TV movie *West Side Waltz*.

Muscular Dystrophy Association Telethon (Jerry Lewis—September 4, 1995). Liza's songs included "But the World Goes 'Round." Liza was the "heavy-hitter," called out at the last minute to CBS-TV City in Hollywood to be the final guest on the show.

Liza Live in Japan (September 1995). Concert videotaped during Minnelli's August 22–24 stand. Famed makeup artist Kevyn Aucoin did Minnelli's makeup.

West Side Waltz (CBS—November 23, 1995; filmed in New York City and in L.A., February through mid-late April 1995). Based on the Broadway play about a circle of lonely people who learn to reach out to each other. *Variety*'s Adam Sandler wrote: "Ernest Thompson serves up a well-scripted adaptation of his play, buoyed by strong perfs, good character development and well-crafted dialogue. But telefilm suffers from a lack of uniqueness, with none of the actors stretching far from characters they've played in the past; though the familiarity may be welcomed by some viewers, most are likely to think they're watching a holiday season rerun." The airing didn't pull many people away from their turkey dinners, and ended ranking around 74 out of 100 shows. Out on DVD.

There were talks about a Christmas special being taped in Vienna, Austria, at the end of November 1995, but this did not happen.

Tony Bennett: Here's to the Ladies (CBS—December 1, 1995; videotaped at Pantages Theater in Los Angeles on October 16, 1995). Liza sang "Maybe This Time" with Tony.

CBS This Morning (CBS—May 21, 1996; videotaped in New York City on May 17, 1996). Liza plugged her new *Gently* album by singing "Embraceable You," to Billy Stritch's piano accompaniment.

May–June 1996—Liza did several TV shows to promote her new *Gently* CD, including *Live with Regis and Kathy Lee* and a June 27, 1996, appearance on *Rosie O'Donnell* (it was Liza's first time on *Rosie*).

The Tony Awards (PBS—June 2, 1996). Liza presented an award during first hour of telecast on PBS. She was not seen on CBS' national broadcast (aside from a split-second during "arrivals").

Today (NBC—end of August, 1996). Liza sang songs from *Gently* (including "Some Cats Know") at the studio's outdoor concert, and encored with "New York, New York."

Oprah (syndicated—October 22, 1996; videotaped early October, in Chicago). Liza sang songs from *Gently*.

Live with Regis and Kathy Lee (syndicated—December 27, 1996). Liza sang "Who Can I Tell?" to promote her upcoming appearance in the Broadway musical *Victor/Victoria*.

One of Liza's representatives stated there had recently been an offer (late in 1996 or early in 1997) for a TV series, but no deal transpired at that time.

Grammy Awards (CBS—February 26, 1997). Liza presented an award with Quincy Jones.

Fox After Breakfast (New York City–based Fox show—May 12, 1997). Liza appeared with Billy Stritch to plug the start of her new concert tour, opening that weekend in Atlantic City. Liza and Billy sang "People Magazine."

The Tony Awards (PBS—June 1, 1997). Liza presented the award for Best Score.

Rosie O'Donnell Show (syndicated—June 20, 1997). Videotaped June 10, 1997. Liza sang "The Day After That."

Late, Late Show with Tom Snyder (CBS—July 29, 1997). Liza promoted *Gently*, and her Pantages Theater appearance. She sang "It Had to Be You."

Biography and *E!* (October 1997. Two bios on Mia Farrow. They each used footage from the same interview videotaped around this time, of Liza talking about Mia.

The Gale King Show (syndicated—November 1997; videotaped late October 1997 in Connecticut). Liza appeared with Billy Stritch.

Kander and Ebb: Razzle-Dazzle (PBS—December 3, 1997). Minnelli appeared in a new interview videotaped for this clip-filled tribute.

The Kennedy Center Honors (CBS—December 30, 1998). Videotaped December 5, 1998. Liza sang "New York, New York" at the conclusion of a tribute to honorees Kander and Ebb.

60 Minutes 2 (CBS—January 1999). Segment on Judy Garland's legacy. Liza's interview was videotaped in October-November 1998.

Jackie's Back! (Lifetime—June 14, 1999; this TV movie was filmed February through April 1999). Liza is seen being "interviewed" in this "mockumentary" about her friend "Jackie," a fictitious singer making a comeback. Out on DVD.

AFI 100 Years, 100 Stars (CBS—June 22, 1999). Liza sang "Without You" over the opening credits. The song had been recorded in L.A. earlier in June 1999, and was nominated for an Emmy Award as Best New Song (it was written by Carole Bayer Sager and Marvin Hamlisch).

My Favorite Broadway: The Leading Ladies (PBS—December 1, 1999; videotaped September 28, 1998, at Carnegie Hall). Minnelli sang "Some People"; her "Liza with a 'Z'" intro with Rosie O'Donnell and her "Sing Happy" solo were cut. Liza redubbed her vocal for "Some People" after her voice returned to fuller force in the spring of 1999. Out on DVD and CD.

Press conference (covered on TV news) to announce the new Broadway revue/tribute to her father, *Minnelli on Minnelli*—October 20, 1999. Liza sang "Baubles, Bangles, and Beads" with Billy Stritch.

Army Archer wrote in his December 3, 1999, column that Liza would host a Sid Luft–produced PBS special, *Duets*, featuring clips from Judy's TV series and specials. It never happened.

20/20 (ABC—December 7 and 8, 1999). Cynthia McFadden interviewed Liza to promote the star's comeback in *Minnelli on Minnelli.*

Good Morning America (ABC—December 13, 1999). Promoting *Minnelli on Minnelli.*

Rosie O'Donnell Show (syndicated—December 14, 1999). Liza sang "What Did I Have?" to promote *Minnelli on Minnelli.*

Radio City Music Hall Grand Re-Opening Gala (NBC—December 18, 1999; videotaped October 4, 1999). *Variety*'s review noted "the singer['s] bring-the-house-down finale of 'New York, New York,' accompanied by the Rockettes."

The View (ABC—December 21, 1999). Liza promoted *Minnelli on Minnelli* during her first appearance on this popular daytime series.

Today (NBC—December 22, 1999). Liza promoted *Minnelli on Minnelli.*

QVC (March 28, 2000). Liza appeared on this shop-at-home channel. She sang "What Did I Have?" (using a prerecorded orchestra track) to plug her new *Minnelli on Minnelli* CD, which was being sold during her segment.

CBS This Morning (CBS—May 2000). Liza was interviewed on this Sunday show. She discussed *Minnelli on Minnelli*, and hinted she might pursue other interests outside of entertainment that involved helping children.

Rosie O'Donnell Show (syndicated—September 19, 2001). Liza sang "New York, New York," eight days after 9–11.

Shea Stadium Baseball Game—September 21, 2001. Liza sang "New York, New York."

Larry King Live (CNN—Late September 2001). Interview about singing "New York, New York" at Shea Stadium.

Live from the White House—October 2001: Liza's songs included "Yes," and "New York, New York."

Michael Jackson: 30th Anniversary Celebration (CBS—November 2001; videotaped at Madison Square Garden in New York City, September 7 and 10, 2001). Liza sang "You Are Not Alone," and "Never, Never Land/Over the Rainbow." The second song would be cut for the initial airing; but the little bit of "Rainbow" that she did sing during the taping (the ending "If happy little bluebirds fly . . .") was inserted for subsequent airings on VH-1.

New York at the Movies (A&E—2002). Documentary on movies about New York.

Graham Norton (BBC—February 1, 2002). British talk show. Liza plugged her upcoming *Liza's Back!* concerts at London's Royal Albert Hall.

Larry King Live (CNN—March 20, 2002; repeated May 4, 2002).

Late Show with David Letterman (CBS—May 13, 2002). Liza talked about her upcoming Beacon Theater show, and sang "Some People."

Larry King Live (CNN—May 23, 2002). Liza sang several songs in the second half of this hour-long appearance, including "Maybe This Time," "Cabaret," and "New York, New York," promoting her upcoming *Liza's Back!* concert engagement at the Beacon Theater.

Good Morning America (ABC—May 2002). Liza sang "I Believe You," "Cry," and talked about her upcoming concert at the Beacon Theater.

Dateline (NBC—Spring 2002). Jane Pauley interview (Liza was briefly seen singing at piano).

The View (ABC—May 24, 2002). Liza talked about her upcoming Beacon Theater show and sang "Cry" and "Maybe This Time."

Graham Norton (BBC—July 29, 2002). British talk show.

Liza and David's Wedding (VH-1—October 15, 2002). Included promos for the aborted *Liza and David* series.

The *Liza and David* show was officially announced by Minnelli and Gest at L.A.'s House of Blues on Thursday, July 25, 2002. (The hour-long series was to follow the couple as they lived their daily lives, rehearsing, etc. There would also be a weekly dinner party where Liza would sing, alone and with all-star guests.) The Gests had been

promised $1.25 million for ten episodes, with options of three additional ten-episodes arcs for a total of forty shows. The series taped its first dinner party on October 21, 2002, and had been slated to premier November 30, before being pushed to January. The plug was pulled on October 29, resulting in a twenty-three-million-dollar lawsuit being filed against the network (for stopping production, and damages to their home, etc.), with VH-1 countersuing (claiming that they hadn't been given complete access to Liza, among other charges). Both sides dropped their suits in September 2003, and Liza would ultimately return on her own to VH-1 a year later, on *Best of '03*.

Larry King Live (CNN—November 20, 2002).

The View (ABC—November 29, 2002).

Late Show with David Letterman (CBS—November 29, 2002). Liza sang "What Did I Have?" to promote her new *Liza's Back* CD, and talked about her upcoming Christmas show at Town Hall in New York City.

Late, Late Show with Craig Kilborn (CBS—January 2003; repeated late July 2003). Liza promoted her upcoming concert tour.

Pavarotti and Friends (May 27, 2003). Liza sang "Cabaret," from her hospital bed, as she had just injured her knee while in Italy for this concert.

Entertainment Tonight (syndicated—August 1, 2003). Liza was shown with her MAC Cosmetics line for the first time.

Arrested Development (Fox—November 23, 2003; filmed in L.A. September 22–24, 2003). Episode # 5: "Key Decisions." Liza Minnelli's TV series *and* sitcom debut. This new weekly situation comedy follows a rich dysfunctional family facing fiscal problems. One of the series' producers, Ron Howard, invited his old friend Liza to appear on the show in a "special guest star" capacity. Minnelli's first episode was the fourth show aired. The series debuted November 2. The character of "Lucille Austero"—a wealthy widow who pursues a younger man, "Buster"—was created for Minnelli's multi-episode arc. Originally scheduled for only two episodes, Liza's run was immediately doubled to four, then six. Liza's first show on this comedy featured her character at a posh gala, trading barbs with her neighbor/rival (and also old family friend)—another "Lucille" ("Lucille Bluth," a.k.a. "Lucille 1," played by Jessica Walter), whose husband was in jail on fraud charges. "That's one phone call a day, isn't it?" was one of Liza's great quips toward Walter.

The critical reponse was incredibly strong for Minnelli's contributions to the show:

"It gives Minnelli a part to play that she plays to the hilt, and returns her to TV in a role that viewers are likely to laugh not just at, but with. She's only in a few scenes, but they're strong scenes. And neither she nor her character are out of place—not in a larger-than-life human cartoon comedy." ***—New York Daily News***

"Minnelli adds a daffy sweetness to a character who might otherwise seem utterly pathetic. Her scene in a hospital emergency room, where she's being treated for 'a touch of the dizzies,' is priceless." ***—Boston Herald***

"Looks like our girl Liza Minnelli has been a big help to Fox TV's 'Arrested Development.' Ratings are almost back to its premiere high of 7.7 million viewers—it had been as low as 3 million before Liza came aboard as the rich, ditsy victim of vertigo. Start spreading the news—Liza Minnelli, Oscar-winning actress, is back." ***—Liz Smith***

"Cheers to Liza Minnelli, doing what she does best: performing. Minnelli's winning turn as a society matron on Fox's 'Arrested Development' is all the proof we'll ever need that she should be in front of the cameras, not on the front of the tabloids. Spewing barbs and flirting with younger men, Minnelli's character, Lucille, is a hilarious creation. Let's hope she stays on the show for a while." ***—TV Guide***

It was announced shortly after the airing of Liza's first episode—and the resulting ratings increase—that Fox was ordering a full season of 22 episodes of the series. Minnelli was also in talks about appearing on additional episodes, beyond the six she already filmed.

Arrested Development (Fox—November 30, 2003; filmed in L.A., September 26 and 29, 2003. Episode #6: "Charity Drive." Liza's second "special guest star" appearance as "Lucille Austero." Minnelli was seen continuing her pursuit of "Buster," youngest son of her rival, the other "Lucille." Buster mistakenly places a winning bid on a date with Liza's character at a charity event.

Best of '03 (VH-1—Sunday, November 30, 2003; videotaped in L.A. on November 20, 2003). Liza made a grand entrance as the first guest on the show, being carried out like Cleopatra, on a huge divan, by a multitude of muscular men. Minnelli presented the "Gay Icon" Award to the *Queer Eye for the Straight Guy* cast. Liza mentioned how happy she was to be back on VH-1 (a year after her aborted *Liza and David* series).

Arrested Development (Fox—December 14, 2003; filmed in L.A., the first week in October 2003). Episode #7: "In God We Trust." Liza's third "special guest star" appearance as "Lucille Austero." Minnelli was seen with "Buster," youngest son of her rival, the other "Lucille." This episode featured Liza insisting she and "Buster" take their budding relationship public, and "Buster" reacting to his mother's reaction. "That old lady's done a number on you," was Minnelli's comedic response.

Arrested Development (Fox—December 21, 2003; filmed early-to-mid October 2003). Episode #8: "My Mother the Car." Liza's fourth "special guest star" appearance as "Lucille Austero." Her character was seen playing poker with her friends, and also having her first kiss with "Buster."

Arrested Development (Fox—January 4, 2004; filmed mid-October 2003 in California). Episode #9: "Storming the Castle." Liza's fifth of six guest appearances on this series. One of Liza's funny yet touching lines as "Lucille Austero" was that she would "heal the hole" in the heart of the young man she was seeing, "Buster Bluth."

Arrested Development (Fox—January 11, 2004; filmed mid-October 2003 in California). Episode #10: "Pier Pressure." Storyline: "Buster" believes that marijuana will help cure Lucille 2's" (Liza's) vertigo, and sets about securing some for her. (Minnelli is only seen for a few seconds, gripping a wall for balance.)

Arrested Development (Fox—February 8, 2004). Episode #12: "Marta Complex." Liza's character, "Lucille 2," refuses to allow "Buster" to move in with her after he leaves his mother's apartment next door. (It is hinted that "Lucille 2" has now taken up with actor Carl Weathers, who answers her door when Buster comes knocking.) This was Liza's sixth official appearance on this series (seventh, if you count the January 11 airing where she had no lines at all), and her last scheduled episode to date. The series was renewed for a second season, and a DVD box set of the complete first season had its release in October 2004. In the year-end wrap-up issue of *Entertainment Weekly*, the magazine named Liza the "Best TV Guest Star" of 2003, for her wonderful work on *Arrested Development*.

Dateline (NBC—March 12, 2004). Liza appeared in an interview videotaped in L.A. with her sister, Lorna Luft. This was their first on-camera/major network TV appearance since their June 1993 medley on the Tony Awards. The new interview was taped for inclusion in an upcoming documentary on sisters, for worldwide distribution (although no release/broadcast date was mentioned). The taping was the first time the sisters had seen each other in two years, according to *Dateline*.

The TV Land Awards (TV Land [cable network]—March 17, 2004; videotaped Sunday, March 7, 2004, in L.A.) The second annual tribute to legendary TV shows featured Liza presenting the Future Classic Award to the cast and crew of her own currently acclaimed sitcom *Arrested Development*. Minnelli received a standing ovation from the star-studded crowd.

Biography (A&E [cable network]—June 11, 2004). Liza was profiled in a two-hour episode of this TV series and was interviewed on camera the week of December 16–20, 2003, at her home in New York City. The show made by ITN in the UK. It included rare material, and clips from a current concert (video was shot of portions of the star's January 30, 2004 performance in Arkansas). A DVD-R (and VHS) are available on A&E's website.

Michael Douglas and Friends (ABC—July 18, 2004). Sports-showbiz gala, benefiting the Motion Picture and Television Fund. Videotaped May 1–2, 2004, at Caesar's Palace, Las Vegas. Liza was shown singing a portion of "Sara Lee."

While having achieved great success on television in specials, Liza Minnelli is currently winning new respect and fans via her very first appearances on a TV series, *Arrested Development*. The series has already been sold for airing in England on the BBC, and to Latin America, and is currently nomi-

Liza on her first episode of *Arrested Development*, with the other "Lucille," played by Jessica Walter.

nated for an Emmy as Best Comedy Series. This new exposure has again brought Minnelli to the attention of producers for other projects—including the possibility of playing the title role in a new TV version of the classic Jerry Herman musical *Mame*. At a March 6, 2004 event in Beverly Hills, Liza announced while onstage that she would be working with famed producers Craig Zadan and Neil Meron and their Storyline Entertainment Company—who did the movie musical *Chicago*—on an upcoming project. Most of their projects are for the small screen, but they are also making more theatrical releases. On March 29, 2004, it was reported that Liza would be starring in a new TV series that Zadan was working on for her, with a fall 2004 premiere date—but no official announcement has been made as we went to press. In July 2004, it was reported (and confirmed by this author) that Liza had definitely just been offered two TV series. Liza is savvy enough to know the power of television to connect with her multitude of fans, and will certainly continue to harness that power to great effect.

Exclusive Offer...
Original Soundtrack
Musical Story
Album
Only
$2.00
PLUS
PROOF-OF-PURCHASE
See details below
ORIGINAL SOUNDTRACK
Musical Story Album
JOURNEY BACK TO
OZ
texize
Featuring the
voices of these famous stars:
Liza Minnelli
(AS DOROTHY)
Mickey Rooney
(AS SCARECROW)
Danny Thomas
(AS TINMAN)
Milton Berle
(AS COWARDLY LION)
Paul Lynde
(AS PUMPKINHEAD)
Ethel Merman
(AS MOMBI THE WITCH)
Plus many others
14 SONGS IN ALL
LONG PLAY STEREO
Pine Power
Spray 'n Wash
Spray 'n Wash
Glass Plus
Grease relief
Grease relief
Fantastik
HERE'S HOW TO GET YOUR
ALBUM —
BUY: Any two of these
Texize products.
MAIL: The ounce content statements, plus $2.00 and the completed mail-in offer certificate.
RECEIVE: The "Journey Back to Oz" Musical Story Album by mail.
HURRY: Offer expires July 31, 1980. See the mail-in certificate on the right for complete offer details.

CHAPTER TWELVE

"For the Record": Liza's Recordings

Minnelli has recorded for many labels, but her main associations have been with: Capitol (1963–1966); A&M (1967–1972); Columbia (1972–1977, and again in 1992–1993), Epic (1989–1990), Angel (1995–2000), and J Records (2002 to date).

Many of Minnelli's recordings have been critically praised. Her *There Is a Time* 1966 LP for Capitol was named Album of the Year by *Stereo Review* magazine. She also had a number one single in England ("Losing My Mind" from her 1989 *Results* album). Several of her recordings have sold well (any figures known will be mentioned within each album's entry), with two of the albums being certified gold (the soundtracks to *Cabaret* and her TV special *Liza with a "Z"*).

Liza's first time in a recording studio was around November or December 1961, when the fifteen-year-old recorded two songs as a Christmas gift for her mom with the help of her friend Marvin Hamlisch. One number was "The Travelin' Life," which she would sing on her first solo album. This demo track was played on a 1974 episode of *The Mike Douglas Show* when Marvin co-hosted. (Other demos done with Marvin at this time have been noted as "At the Roxy Music Hall," with the flip side being "It's Just a Matter of Time," which Liza would also record for her first solo album.)

Journey Back to Oz (a.k.a. Return to Oz) (Album)

Soundtrack for animated film; recorded in late fall 1962. Two versions were released on LPs, although they both used the same vocal performances, one used a larger orchestra. The first release was from Japan, on the RFO label. Then the U.S. version was issued in 1980 by Texize cleaning products as a "premium" tie-in with a TV airing of the movie, over the SFM Holiday Network. This version was produced by Norm Scott and Lou Scheimer for Filmation, a TelePrompTer company. It was never sold in stores, and had to be ordered by mail. The Japan version runs a little longer, approximately forty-eight minutes, versus thirty-eight minutes on the U.S. version. The Japanese version also has a smaller-sounding orchestra (it seems as if additional instruments were added later on to prepare the film for its release in 1973–1974), and also has Peter Lawford as the "Scarecrow," whereas the U.S. version features Mickey Rooney doing the vocals for that character. (Rooney obviously replaced Lawford before the film was released.) Both albums are in mono sound, not stereo. Liza, as "Dorothy," has four songs in the film and on the albums, all solos: "A Faraway Land"; "Keep a Happy Thought"; "Return to the Land of Oz"; and "That Feeling for Home." (The Japanese release

features a slightly longer and different vocal by Minnelli on "That Feeling for Home.")

Liza's vocals reveal a beautifully pure, lovely, and touching voice; a truly fine instrument that marks much of her early work (if lacking the polish, pizzazz, and depth that would come in later years). There was also a promo 45 RPM issued—seen here—of two of Minnelli's solos, although it was never available to the public.

"You Are for Loving"/ "What Do You Think I Am?" (Single)

Recorded February 26th, 1963, in New York City, for Cadence Records, single #1436. Included as bonus tracks on the most recently released CD version of Liza's original off-Broadway revival cast recording of *Best Foot Forward*, from Varèse Sarabande Records.

This single was Liza Minnelli's first released record, and her first professional recording session specifically for records. Both songs were from her current project, the 1963 off-Broadway revival of the 1941 musical *Best Foot Forward*. While the cast album featured only twin pianos, this single utilized an orchestra. Though not as strong vocally as she would be a month later for the full cast recording, it remains a fascinating experience to hear Liza Minnelli in her first real recording. The media attention given to Minnelli at the time (magazine articles, TV shows, rave reviews) reportedly resulted in this single selling half a million copies.

Best Foot Forward— Original Off-Broadway Revival Cast Recording (Album)

Recorded March 29, 1963, at Capitol Studios in New York City for Cadence Records. Available on CD from Varèse Sarabande Records (Varèse Vintage), distributed by Universal Music and Video Distribution (UMG/UME). Issued on CD in 2001, number 302 066 221 2. www.varesesarabande.com.

This was the first released album to contain recordings by Liza Minnelli. (Two weeks before making this record, she turned seventeen.) Liza sings the following songs on the album (as she did in the show): "Wish I May" (with cast); "The Three B's" (with Kay Cole and Renee Winters); "Buckle Down Winsocki" (with cast); "What Do You Think I Am?" (with Edmund Gaynes, Kay Cole, and Christopher [Ronald] Walken; "Just a Little Joint with a Juke Box" (with Gene Castle, Don Slaton, and Paul Charles); "You Are for Loving"; and "Finale (Reprise of): Buckle Down Winsocki. "

It is Liza's one solo, "You are for Loving," the

"11 o'clock number" (so called for its show-stopping performance near the end of the play), that really makes this cast album a must-have for any Minnelli fan. The version heard on this album remains one of the high points of Liza Minnelli's career. Her vocal quality is simply breathtakingly pure and devastatingly musical. While the later polish may be missing, and there are no Minnelli "markings" that make one instantly aware they are listening to Liza Minnelli, this is one astonishing singer.

The Varèse Sarabande CD has sold 883 copies, and the earlier version on DRG 1,334, according to SoundScan reports through April 25, 2004.

The success of the *Best Foot Forward* album—and certainly of Liza's "You Are for Loving" single—brought her to the attention of Capitol Records. Capitol began testing the waters slowly, marketing Minnelli toward her own age group with a series of singles (all listed within this chapter in the order they were recorded). (There would be additional singles recorded for Capitol from 1963–1966, some of which were not released; a similar fate would befall album tracks as well.) These singles all have a definite "pop" sensibility.

"One Summer Love" / "How Much Do I Love You?" (Single)

Recorded May 27, 1963, in New York City for Capitol Records; orchestra conducted by Jack Pleis. Produced by Si Rady. Released as single # 4994.

Liza's very first session with Capitol produced this single. Both tracks are basically ballads, with "How Much" having a more haunting feeling, and "Summer" having just a bit more of a beat.

"Together, We Could Make Such Beautiful Music" / "The Best Is Yet to Come"

Recorded live, July 16, 1963, at CBS Television City in Hollywood, Studio 43; Available on the CD *Judy Duets*, released in 1999 by Sid Luft.

Sung with Judy Garland, these numbers were taken from the soundtrack of Garland's 1963–64 CBS musical-variety TV series. This was the first time mother and daughter worked together professionally (in a rehearsed, officially scheduled performance).

"Bob White (Whatcha Gonna Swing Tonight?)"

Recorded live July 16,1963, at CBS Television City in Hollywood, Studio 43; available on the CD *The Judy Garland Show: The Show That Got Away* from Hip-O Records/Universal Music Group; Released 2002.

Another duet between mother and daughter, from the first of two appearances Liza made on Judy's TV series. There is some dialogue lead-in to this song, which became a family favorite.

"Day Dreaming"/"His Woman"
(Single)

Recorded August 15, 1963, in New York City. Arranged and conducted by Mort Garson. Produced by Si Rady. Released as Capitol single # 5103.

Liza's second single for Capitol, "Dreaming" is an upbeat ballad. "Woman" remains one of Minnelli's most "fun" recordings: a latin-influenced novelty song. It is a real hoot to hear Liza singing with a comical accent and an over-the-top chorus backing her. There were two other songs recorded at this session, "My Little Corner (of the World)," and "We'll Be Together," which were not released, which is a shame as they were quite good, especially the latter.

The Judy Garland Christmas Album
(CD)

Recorded live December 6, 1963, at CBS Television City in Hollywood, Studio 43. This CD is an abridged soundtrack album of the Christmas episode of Garland's TV series. Released in 1995 by LaserLight; still available. Liza's "Alice Blue Gown" solo had been issued on a 1969 album of Garland solos culled from the TV series *Judy's Portrait in Song* (Radiant Records). (Liza herself brought this up to me in March 2002, laughing at the label's inability to tell the difference between her voice and Judy's, before proceeding to sing the song to me, still remembering the words nearly forty years later.) Liza's songs on the album are "Consider Yourself" (with Judy, Lorna Luft, and Joe Luft; the ending lines only); "Alice Blue Gown" (solo); "Steam Heat" (with Tracy Everett, Liza's then boyfriend); "Alice Blue Gown"; "Jingle Bells (with Judy, and Jack Jones)/Sleigh Ride (with Jones)/It Happened in Sun Valley (with Jones)/ Jingle Bells" (with entire cast); "It Came Upon a Midnight Clear" (with Everett); "Deck the Halls" (with entire cast)

Liza! Liza!
(Album)

Recorded June 1964. Orchestra arranged and conducted by Peter Matz. Produced by Si Rady. Cover Photo: Sherman Weisburd; Back Jacket Photo: John Engstead. Released by Capitol Records, in September 1964, on LP (#ST 2174). There was an abridged vinyl reissue from Capitol in 1973, renamed *Maybe This Time*, that cut two songs ("I'm All I've Got" and "Blue Moon"). This version of the album was reissued on CD in 1987 and again

in 1996 (it is now out of print). A British import called *Liza Minnelli: The Best of the Capitol Years* was issued in 2001 and contains all the songs from *Liza! Liza!*, but changes the order of the songs from the original LP (see below for songs listed as they appeared on the vinyl release), and added songs from her next two Capitol albums.

Liza's twelve songs: (Side One) "It's Just a Matter of Time"; "If I Were in Your Shoes"; "Meantime"; "Try to Remember"; "I'm All I've Got"; "Maybe Soon"; (Side Two) "Maybe This Time"; "Don't Ever Leave Me"; "The Travelin' Life"; "Together (Wherever We Go)"; "Blue Moon"; "I Knew Him When."

Liza! Liza! was Liza Minnelli's first solo album. Her old friend Marvin Hamlisch helped choose her material, as did her new friends, songwriters John Kander and Fred Ebb. Liza's conductor-arranger, Peter Matz, was also instrumental in selecting the songs. Matz had performed the same chores for Barbra Streisand's early albums (1963–1966), and it seems as if Capitol's A&R executives—and Matz—may have been trying to mold Minnelli into another Streisand , by choosing offbeat tunes, for example. The end result is a superb debut disc, lush and lavish, that showcases the eighteen year old's already spectacular talent. A mix of ballads with more uptempo tunes proves Minnelli could handle all moods, with an evident acting ability. Her vocal quality is lovely, if not quite at the peak level it was on the *Best Foot Forward* album's "You Are for Loving," or as it would be on her second solo album (*It Amazes Me*). Nevertheless, *Liza! Liza!* is still a great achievement, and a highlight of her recording career.

Liza! Liza! spent a total of eight weeks on *Billboard*'s charts. Debuting on November 21, 1964, the album peaked at number 116. The LP reportedly sold out its first pressing in two weeks. The album received some truly superb reviews: "An auspicious debut . . . fine new talent"—*Cashbox*; "Impressive . . . beguiling . . . beautifully varied . . . major singing talent"—*Record World*; "Simply great . . . a gas . . . clarity of tone, genuine feeling, emotion . . . truly great"—*Billboard*. (The album supposedly sold half a million copies within a 2–3 year period, by the end of 1966 or 1967—although it has not been certified Gold to date.)

Judy Garland and Liza Minnelli Live at the London Palladium

(Album)

Recorded November 8 and 15, 1964, at the London Palladium; studio retakes done on November 23, 1964, in England. The Palladium Orchestra was conducted by Harry Robinson and the album was produced by Simon (Si) Rady. Supervised by Norrie Paramor. Released by Capitol Records on August 2, 1965, as a two-LP set (#SWBO-2295), and would later appear as a two-cassette tape set import and a bootleg import on CD. It was issued May 1973 as a single LP. The single LP was issued as an audiophile half-speed master LP circa 1978. The single LP was issued in a further abridged CD, *Judy Garland and Liza Minnelli: Together* by Curb Records, in January 1993. An unreleased song, "Don't Rain on My Parade," was issued on a 1991 Garland box set called *The One and Only*, and another version of this song is on the 2002 two-CD set *Classic Judy Garland: The Capitol Years 1955–1965*. A complete version of the entire fifty-song program was produced by this author in 2001–2002. It was originally scheduled to be issued by Capitol Records on September 17, 2002, but is still awaiting release. This new 24-bit remastered two-CD set also contains rehearsal recordings of

Judy and Liza singing "Together," "When the Saints Go Marching In/Brotherhood of Man," and "He's Got the Whole World in His Hands." (There are also additional rehearsal songs that exist, including one of the lengthy "Hooray for Love" medley mother-daughter perform in the concert, and on the album.)

Liza's twenty-seven songs on the two-LP set (all solos, unless noted; a total of fifteen solos and twelve duets) : "The Travelin' Life"; "Gypsy in My Soul"; "Hello, Dolly!" (duet); "Together (Wherever We Go)" (duet); "We Could Make Such Beautiful Music Together"/"Bob White (Whatcha Gonna Swing Tonight?)" (duet); "Hooray for Love" (duet)/ "By Myself"/"How About You?" (duet)/"Lover Come Back to Me"/"It All Depends on You" (duet); "Who's Sorry Now?"; "How Could You Believe Me When I Said I Love You When You Know I've Been a Liar All My Life?"; ("Mama Medley" tribute to Judy): "Take Me Along"/"If I Could Be with You"/"That's Entertainment"/"Tea for Two"/"They Can't Take That Away from Me"/"By Myself"/"Take Me Along"/"My Mammy"; "Pass That Peace Pipe"; "When the Saints Go Marching In"/"Brotherhood of Man" (duet); "He's Got the Whole World in His Hand" (duet); "Swanee" (duet); "Chicago"; "San Francisco."

The restored/remastered/complete version adds the following eleven Liza songs (solos, unless noted; a total of five solos and six duets): "Maybe This Time" (Liza's first known live version of this Kander-Ebb signature song, later added to the movie version of *Cabaret;* she included it on her first studio album, *Liza! Liza!)*; "Hello, Dolly!" (reprise; duet); "The Best Is Yet to Come" (duet); "Don't Rain on My Parade" (duet); "I Love a Piano" (as part of Liza's "Mama Medley" tribute); "I'm All I've Got"; "It's Just a Matter of Time"; "If I Were in Your Shoes"; "Johnny One Note" (duet); "Get Happy"/"Happy Days Are Here Again" (duet); and "Battle Hymn of the Republic" (duet).

This was the first and only official joint concert with her mother (not including the countless impromptu appearances Minnelli made at Garland concerts from 1956 to 1967), and this was Liza Minnelli's first live album.

So much has been written about the two Judy-Liza Palladium concerts and the album, much of it untrue. While mother and daughter may have been dealing with a mass of complex emotions during the experience, the surviving tapes reveal an overflow of love from both artists. Each seems to be the other's best audience, and the "complete" remastered version reveals just how much they made each other laugh. The album as originally released does leave much to be desired (Judy's *opening song* here is "The Man That Got Away!"), and omits much of the magic of the evening. Entire songs, and even little moments, were mysteriously edited—such as an audience member yelling out, "Good luck, Liza!," to which Minnelli responds "Oh, you know it!" in appreciation, before she begins her first number ("The Travelin' Life"). The album runs approximately seventy-four minutes over two LPs, whereas the restored version adds another full hour of material and is a much more accurate representation of two great artists delivering peak performances (aside from some dryness and roughness Judy is experiencing on her opening set of five songs).

While the "complete/restored" version allows you to hear Liza's performance exactly as it progressed, even the edited original release showcases Minnelli's dazzling ability with a ballad—"Who's Sorry Now?" remains a highlight of her acting and singing careers—or up-tempo tune, such as "How Could You Believe Me When I Said I Loved You When You Know I've Been a Liar All My Life?"

The shortened album received mixed reviews upon its release in 1965 (including a scathing notice from *Stereo Review*), but it sold very well: the album debuted on *Billboard*'s charts on September 4, 1965, and spent a total of fourteen weeks there, peaking at number 41—a great accomplishment for something that wasn't the Beatles or rock in the fall of 1965.

It Amazes Me
(Album)

Recorded December 1964 and January 1965. Orchestra arranged and conducted by Peter Matz. Produced by Si Rady. Released by Capitol Records in March 1965, as # ST-2271. Reissued as an abridged LP by Capitol's Special Markets division, circa 1978–80, which dropped "I Never Has Seen Snow." Album not issued on CD to date.

Liza's eleven songs: (Side One) "Wait Till You See Him"; "My Shining Hour"; "I Like The Likes of You"; "It Amazes Me"; "Looking at You"; "I Never Have Seen Snow"; (Side Two) "Plenty of Time"; "For Every Man There's a Woman"; "Lorelei"; "Shouldn't There Be Light'ning?"; "Nobody Knows You When You're Down and Out." There was one song cut before the album was released, a medley of "Walk Right In"/"How Come You Do Me Like You Do?," recorded on December 19, 1964. Liza "duets" with herself for the first time on this sexy track, years before she would on songs for *The Singer* album (released in 1973) such as "Where Is the Love?" followed by the numbers "All That Jazz" and "Lucky Lady," both recorded in 1975.

Liza's voice is flawless on the *It Amazes Me* album: she still has just a touch of "newness" in her voice, as if she was still in the process of discovering what she could do. Yet she had also developed a great deal in the approximately six months between the time she recorded her first solo album (*Liza! Liza!*) and this *It Amazes Me* disc. Her growth is also felt as an actress: "I Never Has Seen Snow" has incredible feeling, and her "Plenty of Time" is worthy of an Academy Award, and remains one of her finest recordings. There is also an even lusher orchestra here—the success of a first album would certainly make a label willing to spend more on the making of a second LP (also evidenced by the difference between the orchestras used on Streisand's first and second

Capitol Records Club ad for *It Amazes Me.*

albums). A greater sound quality adds even more to the winning mix here. Capitol boasts on the LP jacket, "New Improved, Full Dimensional Stereo" and "sounds better than Stereo has ever sounded before!," and *It Amazes Me* does seem to have a richer, deeper sound quality. The brilliant Peter Matz again supplied the arrangements and they are as stunning as the star's singing. Minnelli and Matz made a winning combination, and Mr. Matz continued working with Liza as late as the spring of 2001 (as her accompanist at an AIDS event where she sang "Maybe This Time"), shortly before his passing. *It Amazes Me* remains a must for Minnelli collectors, and is among the top albums of her career.

Flora, The Red Menace (Original Broadway Cast Recording; Album)

Recorded May 5 or May 9, 1965 (both dates have been noted), at Webster Hall in New York City. Released by RCA Victor Records, as # LSO-1111 in May 1965. Issued on CD (# 09026-60821-2) by RCA Victor-BMG Classics, in 1992; still available. Total playing time: 47:41.

Liza recording the cast album to *Flora, the Red Menace.*

Liza's nine songs (solos, unless noted): "Unafraid" (with chorus); "All I Need Is One Good Break" (with chorus); "Not Every Day of the Week" (with Bob Dishy); "Sign Here" (with Bob Dishy); "A Quiet Thing"; "Hello, Waves" (with Bob Dishy); "Dear Love"; "Sing Happy"; "You Are You"/"Sing Happy" reprise" (with cast).

Minnelli's first Broadway show is *Flora, the Red Menace*, for which she won her first Tony Award, at age nineteen (the youngest to win the Best Actress in a Musical category). This album preserves the explosion that was Minnelli at nineteen. There is no doubt you are listening to someone born for Broadway. One may hear shadows of a Streisand/New York–type of sound in Liza's voice in this recording (*Funny Girl* had opened in New York a year earlier), but that could be just a coincidence, or the fact that "Flora" *is* a New Yorker.

Sparkling sound, and a great supporting cast (including Cathryn Damon from the cult TV hit *Soap*), make this another Minnelli "must-have."

Flora, the Red Menace debuted on *Billboard*'s Top 200 album chart on July 3, 1965, and stayed there for eight weeks, peaking at number 111. This recording has sold 6,410 copies from 1992 through April 25, 2004, according to SoundScan.

"A Quiet Thing" / "All I Need"
(Single)

Recorded March or April, 1965, in New York City (exact date not noted in Capitol's logs). Orchestra arranged and conducted by Peter Matz. Produced by Tom Morgan. Released by Capitol Records as single # 5411.

"Sing Happy" / "Dear Love"
(Single)

Recorded May 20, 1965, in New York City. Orchestra arranged and conducted by Peter Matz. Produced by Tom Morgan. Released by Capitol Records as single # 5473.

These are Liza's "single" versions of four of her songs from *Flora, the Red Menace*, released on the two singles noted above. They certainly differ from their cast album versions, having been made for the "pop" singles market, with different arrangements/orchestrations.

The Dangerous Christmas of Red Riding Hood
(TV Soundtrack: Album)

Recorded October 1965. Released in November 1965 by ABC-Paramount Records, # ABCS 536.

Liza's five songs (solos, unless noted): "My Red Riding Hood"; "I'm Naive"; "Ding-a-Ling, Ding-a-Ling" (with Cyril Ritchard); "Granny" (with Cyril Ritchard); "We Wish the World a Happy Yule" (finale with Vic Damone, Cyril Richard, and cast).

This is the soundtrack recording of Liza's first musical comedy written for TV. Meant to become

an annual holiday tradition, a la *The Wizard of Oz*, *Peter Pan*, and *Cinderella*, the show only aired twice: November 28, 1965, and again in 1966 (according to one source), in color, on ABC. The singing heard on the TV show was done live, with no prerecording. This cast album was recorded in the studio. The score—by the team responsible for the recent smash *Funny Girl* (Jule Styne and Bob Meril)—is quite charming, and Liza is in fine form.

"Imprevu"
(Single) /
"Did I Hurt Your Feelings?"
(Single: #5473)
"I'm Not Laughing" / "Did I Hurt Your Feelings?"
(Single: # not noted)

Recorded October 28, 1965. Released by Capitol Records, "Imprevu" actually served as the music for a well-known TV commercial of the time, but not with Liza's vocal, which is charming and full of fun. At the same session, she recorded two other songs for Capitol: "I'm Not Laughing" and "Did I Hurt Your Feelings?"—two loud, bouncy pop songs, with a heavy chorus. Very interesting, and all very much of the period.

There Is a Time
(Album)

Recorded April–May 2, 1966. Arranged and conducted by Ray Ellis (who also arranged Billie Holiday's classic *Lady in Satin* album). Produced by Marvin Holtzman. Released by Capitol Records, 1966, as # ST-11803; reissued circa 1978–1980 by Capitol's Special Markets in an abridged form, which deleted "One of Those Songs." Album not yet issued on CD.

Liza's eleven songs: "There Is a Time"; "I Who Have Nothing"; "M'Lord"; "Watch What Happens"; "One Of Those Songs"; "The Days of the Waltz"; "Ay Marieke"; "Love at Last You Have Found Me"; "Stairway to Paradise"; "See the Old Man"; "The Parisians." There were other songs recorded at the

same time , but none of them were included on the final release. On April 6, 1966, Liza recorded "The Many Faces of Love" (a fine up-tempo, very sixties tune) ; "At My Age" (a pensive ballad, also very period-sounding); "Middle of the Street" (a wonderful, very "pop" up-tempo tune. This was written by Peter Allen, and was actually released on a single, as the flip-side of "I Who Have Nothing"); and "Everybody Loves My Baby" (a great "swinging" recording, taken just a tad slower than the tempo used when she sang it during her club act in the 1965–66 period; very effective, with a nice chorus backup). Two days later, April 8, 1966, she recorded three more songs for Capitol that would remain unreleased: "Marriage Is for Old Folks" (a slight, throwaway sort of tune); "Come On and Baby Me" (a great, fun song, that sounds right out of the 1920s); and her first recorded version of "Liza With A 'Z'" (listed and known as "Say Liza, L-I-Z-A"; this first version even included the spoken introduction that she used from 1965 on).

There Is a Time was Liza's third and final solo album for Capitol Records. It would be critically lauded, including *Stereo Review*'s proclaiming it "Album of The Year." The singer is in fine form vocally, especially on "Love at Last You Have Found Me," which remains one of the most haunting and moving recordings of Minnelli's career as a recording artist.

"I Who Have Nothing" / "The Middle of the Street"

(See entry for "There Is a Time" album, above, for more information on this single)

Liza Minnelli
(Album)

Recorded from October through December 1967, in Los Angeles. The first song recorded was "Happy Land." Songs to be done for the album, but that didn't appear on the final release were : "Snow"; "No One Ever Hurt So Bad"; and "Hong Kong Blues." Additional, unreleased songs listed on an A&M tape labeled "1968" are: "Four Leaf Clover," "Alicinha," "I'll Never Fall in Love Again," "This Girl's in Love with You," and "For Once in My Life." Producer: Larry Marks. Arrangers: Peter Matz, Nick DeCaro, Bob Thompson, and J. Hill. Photography by Guy Webster. Released Summer 1968 on the A&M label, # SP-4141. Issued on CD only as an overseas hard-to-find import that fetches hundreds of dollars on eBay.

Liza's eleven songs: "The Debutante's Ball";

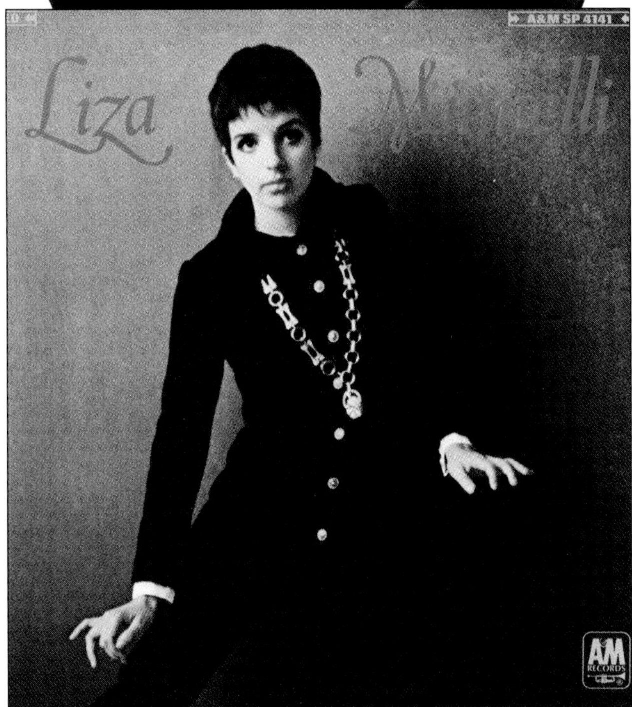

It's Liza with a Z, which A&M Records had to learn the hard way, obviously, via this first pressing of her debut album for the label

"Happyland"; "The Look of Love"; "(The Tragedy of) Butterfly McHeart"; "Waiting for My Friend"; "Married"/"You Better Sit Down, Kids"; "So Long Dad"; "For No One"; "My Mammy"; "The Happy Time."

Moving to a new label in the summer of 1967—Herb Alpert's A&M Records—Liza began recording much more contemporary, "pop" songs, although some Broadway songs were kept in her A&R (artist repertoire) for A&M, including two Kander–Ebb show tunes. Randy Newman gets three of his numbers represented here, and Minnelli even does a John Lennon–Paul McCartney song. *Liza Minnelli* finds Liza Minnelli in absolutely flawless voice.

Frank Mills
(Single)

Recording date of this song from the Broadway musical *Hair* is not known, but Liza sang it on a January 19, 1969, episode of *Ed Sullivan*.

Come Saturday Morning
(Album)

Recorded 1969 (no other information available in the label's logs). Arrangements by Dick Hazzard, Michael Colombier, Bob Thompson, and Peter Matz. Photography by Guy Webster. Produced by Larry Marks. Released 1969 by A&M Records, # SP-4164. Not released on CD.

Liza's eleven songs: "Come Saturday Morning"; "Raggedy Ann & Raggedy Andy"; "Leavin' on a Jet Plane"; "Wailing of the Willow"; "Nevertheless"; "Wherefore and Why"; "Love Story"; "On a Slow Boat to China"; "Don't Let Me Lose This Dream"; "Simon"; "MacArthur Park—Didn't We?"

Named to tie-in for the song from Minnelli's

British release of the *Come Saturday Morning* album

movie the same year—*The Sterile Cuckoo*—The "Come Saturday Morning" LP is an entire album of pop songs from the time, with one "standard" (Frank Loesser's "On a Slow Boat to China"). Among the crop of songwriters showcased: John Denver, Gordon Lightfoot, Jimmy Webb, and Randy Newman. The album also features another song by Peter Allen—"Simon"—the first he wrote on his own. ("Butterfly McHeart" was on Liza's first A&M album, and was co-written with Allen's musical partner, Chris Allen. "Middle of the Street" was also a collaboration.) Highlights of Minnelli's second A&M LP include "Slow Boat to China" and, supremely, Allen's "Simon."

Liza Minnelli Live at the Olympia in Paris
(Album)

Recorded live to half-inch, two-track tape at the Olympia, December 11, 1969. Photography: Guy Webster. Producer: Larry Marks. Released in 1972 by A&M Records, # SP-4345. Not released in U.S. on CD, but was issued briefly overseas as a very expensive compact disc import.

Liza's eleven songs: (Side One) Opening Medley "Consider Yourself" / "Hello, I Love You, Won't You Tell Me Your Name?" / "I Gotta Be Me" / "Consider Yourself (reprise)"; "Everybody's Talking" / "Good Morning Starshine (Medley)"; "God Bless the Child"; "Liza With A 'Z'"; "Married" / "You Better Sit Down,

Kids (Medley)"; (Side Two) "Nous On S'Aimera"; "I Will Wait for You"; "There Is a Time"; "My Mammy"; "Everybody Loves My Baby"; "Cabaret."

Live at the Olympia in Paris was Liza's first *solo* live album. The album sat on the shelf until 1972, and was obviously edited, representing only about thirty-eight minutes from her act. The LP still manages to capture the interaction with and impact on her audience, who are chanting her name by the end of the disc. ("Li-za! Li-za! Li-za! Li-za!") Her act was a hybrid of contemporary tunes mixed with standards, and the album accurately represents that. A must-have for Liza lovers.

New Feelin'
(Album)

Recorded in 1970 at Muscle Shoals, Alabama. Engineers: Mickey Buckins and Sonny Limbo. Album photography: Rex Kramer. Produced and arranged by Rex Kramer. Released fall 1970 by A&M Records, # SP-4272. Never issued on CD, although seven of the album's eleven tracks are on the 2001 career compilation "Liza Minnelli: Ultimate Collection," from Hip-O Records / Universal Music.

Liza's eleven songs: (Side One) "Love for Sale"; "Stormy Weather"; "Come Rain or Come Shine"; "Lazy Bones"; "Can't Help Lovin' That Man of Mine"; (Side Two) "(I Wonder Where My) Easy Rider's Gone"; "The Man I Love"; "How Long Has This Been Going On?"; "God Bless the Child"; "Maybe This Time."

New Feelin' is among Liza's most unique albums. It is also perhaps her poorest album, in both conception and execution. The disc presents standards arranged in a pop-rock-funk-bluegrass-country format. To make matters worse, there are some poor choices made in terms of the vocal arrangements, especially at the end of "Come Rain or Come Shine," where things go a little too over the top. (There's only one track on the album that's completely enjoyable, "Lazy Bones.") Liza was romantically involved with musician Rex Kramer at the time this album was made, and Kramer served as arranger and producer for this album. Perhaps she was judging this project more with her heart than with her head—or more specifically, her ears. Similar to Streisand's *Butterfly* album misfire that her then partner John Peters produced, the project shows that Kramer may have been a better musician than a record producer. If there is one album to avoid, it would be this one. (Oddly enough, Liza was scheduled to record a followup LP at the same recording studio, from January 25–February 13, 1971, immediately before beginning work on the movie *Cabaret*. This must have been canceled at the last minute.) Only for the curious, or the very serious "Minnelli maniacs" who must have everything.

New Feelin' spent three weeks on *Billboard*'s Top 200 charts. Debuting on November 28, 1970, the album peaked at number 158.

Cabaret
(Original Soundtrack Recording)
(Album)

Recorded in 1971 (No other info available from label's logs. The film's production period ran from February 22 through July 9, 1971, with looping/ dubbing numbers in Paris starting November 24 1971.) Musical Director and Orchestrator: Ralph Burns. Album Coordinator: Lee Young. Released 1972 by ABC Records, on LP # ABCD-752.

Issued on CD by Hip-O Records/Universal Music on November 19, 1996, # HIPD-40027.

Liza's four songs (solos, unless noted): "Mein Herr," "Maybe This Time," "Money, Money" (with Joel Grey); "Cabaret."

The original motion picture soundtrack recording to Minnelli's greatest film success. Each of Liza's four numbers are among her most beloved, with "Cabaret" being her signature song. The songs are here in their most famous versions, in sparkling stereo (whereas the movie was released in mono sound). The performance is perfection, as is her voice. A must-have for any Minnelli maniac/Liza lover, or even a more casual fan.

The *Cabaret* soundtrack debuted on *Billboard*'s Top 200 album chart on March 18, 1972, and spent a staggering seventy-two weeks (eighteen months) there, peaking at number 25. The CD has sold 81,120 copies from November 1996 through April 25, 2004, according to SoundScan. The album is perhaps Liza's biggest selling record. It is one of two of her recordings to go gold, representing sales between half a million to one million (sales over a million copies are certified platinum by the RIAA). *Cabaret* was certified gold in August 1973. It's possible that the album has reached platinum status by now (or even multi-platinum), but it's up to the label to seek an updated accounting on older titles (usually the artist must request this). Liza's next album would be her other gold record.

Liza with a "Z" (Original Television Soundtrack Recording) (Album)

Recorded May 31, 1972, live at the Lyceum Theater in New York. Additional studio recording done both before and after the show was filmed. (For example, "Ring Them Bells" was pre-recorded for Liza to lip-synch to—portions of the song are live, including its dialogue. "Bye, Bye, Blackbird" also seems to be pre-recorded and lip-synched, as is "Son of a Preacher Man.") Orchestra conducted by Jack French. Engineering: Phil Ramone and Arthur Kendy. Album produced by Andrew Kazdin. Released by Columbia Records, September 1972, on LP # PC-31762. Issued on CD, August 16, 1988, by Columbia Records/Sony—#CK-31762.

Liza's eleven songs : "Yes"; "God Bless the Child"; "Say Liza (Liza with a 'Z')"; "It Was a Good Time"; "I Gotcha" ; "Ring Them Bells"; "Son of a Preacher Man"; "Bye, Bye, Blackbird"; "You've Let Yourself Go"; "My Mammy"; medley of tunes from *Cabaret*: "Willkommen"/"Married"/"Money, Money"/"Maybe This Time"/"Cabaret."

Another cornerstone of Liza's career, this album represents the complete program of songs from the hour-long NBC-TV special. The CD/LP runs 48:35, and remains one of the most potent of Minnelli's albums, live or studio. The song selection is perfection (again, a mix of current pop and older standards—this was largely her nightclub act), as is the orchestra and sound quality. Minnelli is in perfect voice, and as *Liza with a "Z"* is quintessential Liza, it remains a must-have for all Liza lovers and Minnelli maniacs.

Liza with a "Z" was her first album for Columbia Records. She was signed to the label on March 1, 1972, by the great Clive Davis (who would sign her again in 2002 to his hot new J Records label, now part of the Arista/BMG umbrella of labels). *Liza with a "Z"* likely remains Liza Minnelli's biggest-selling solo album to date, based on information available. It debuted on the Top 40 charts on September 30, 1972, and stayed within the Top 40 for a total of twenty-three weeks (a week shy of six months), peaking at number 19 on *Billboard*'s charts. In December 1999, it was finally certified gold. It remains the only Minnelli Columbia album to have *never* gone out of print. According to SoundScan reports, the CD had sold slightly more than 38,000 copies from 1991—when SoundScans started—through January 25, 2004.

The Singer
(Album)

Recorded September 1972 (and possibly other dates as well. Not all label logs are still available). Recorded at Larrabee Sound Studios. Photography: Alan Pappe. Produced by "Snuff" Garrett for Garrett Music Enterprises. Released by Columbia Records on LP, # KC 32149, in March 1973. There was also a quadraphonic LP, for stereo systems set up with four speakers instead of the typical two. The album was issued on CD, circa 1988, by Columbia/Sony, #CK 32149. This CD has gone out of print, but *The Singer* was issued in 2001 as a two-CD set import from Sony in Australia, *Liza Minnelli: Double Pack*, which also contains the *Liza with a "Z"* album.

Liza's eleven songs: "I Believe In Music"; "Use Me"; "I'd Love You to Want Me"; "Oh, Babe, What Would You Say?"; "You're So Vain"; "Where Is the Love?"; "The Singer"; "Don't Let Me Be Lonely Tonight"; "Dancing in the Moonlight"; "You Are the Sunshine of My Life"; "Baby Don't Get Hooked On Me." (*The Singer* is noted as having been recorded on September 26, 1972, the same date as "You're So Vain," and "Where Is the Love?") 35:58 total playing time.

Liza Minnelli was the biggest, hottest, and "newest" star in the spring and summer of 1972, and her new label obviously decided her second album should reflect this, and her youthful age (twenty-six), in appealing to a younger record-buying public. *The Singer* is a great deal of fun: a light, rhythmic romp through nearly a dozen of early 70s "light pop" hits (AM radio/Top 40). (It has been noted that the "Dancing in the Moonlight" single from this album reached number 22 on the British pop charts.) The only real ballad here is probably the best track: "Don't Let Me Be Lonely Tonight" is thrilling. Liza is in superb voice and form on the entire album (if with a bit less control on the title tune, which may have been a deliberate call, since the song deals with a singer in live performance mode). *The Singer* reportedly sold fairly well; It first joined *Billboard*'s charts on March 24, 1973, and stayed there for twenty weeks, peaking at number 38, the last time to date that a Minnelli solo album would hit the Top 40.

"Singer"/"Mr. Emory"
(Single)

Released by Columbia Records in 1972. Single # Columbia 4-45746. "The Singer" is the album track; no other info available from label's logs. "Mr. Emory" is available on the CD *Liza Minnelli: All That Jazz*, released by Sony Music Special Products in 1999, Release # A 31053. Available from Footlight Records in New York City (Phone 212-533-1572), or try Sony's website: www.smsp.com.

"Mr. Emory" is an up-tempo tunc, aimed at the singles market.

"One More Hurt"
(One song)

Released in 1972. Included as part of a United Artists LP. Up-tempo tune. (On June 6, 1972, there was a report that Liza had brought suit in New York to prevent what she called the intended unauthorized distribution of a number of songs she recently recorded. Minnelli was asking $1.5 million in damages from United Artists Recordings.)

Alice Cooper: Muscle of Love
(Album; Liza sings on two tracks)

Recorded October 3rd, 1973, in NYC. Released in 1973 by Warner Brothers Records. Available as an import CD from Germany, on the same label.

Liza sang backup on two songs: "Man with the Golden Arm" and "Teenage Lament '74." The fact that her singing is in the background—with other singers—makes it very difficult to pinpoint or hear Minnelli's voice clearly.

Liza Minnelli Live at the Winter Garden
(Album)

Recorded January 6–8, 1974, at the Winter Garden Theater, New York City. Remote engineer: Phil Ramone. Remix and Editing Engineer: Don Puluse. Album Produced by Gary Klein. Released by Columbia Records in May 1974, as LP # PC 32854. Album not issued on CD to date. Total playing time: 53:19.

Liza's thirteen songs: (Side One) Overture ("Liza with a 'Z'"/"Ring Them Bells"/"I Can See Clearly Now"/"Maybe This Time"/"Cabaret"); "If You Could Read My Mind"/"Come Back to Me"; "Shine On Harvest Moon"; "Exactly Like Me"; "The Circle"; "More Than You Know"; "I'm One of the Smart Ones"; (Side Two) "Natural Man"; "I Can See Clearly Now"; "And I in My Chair"; "There Is a Time"; "A Quiet Thing"; "Anywhere You Are"/"I Believe You"; "Cabaret"; "Cabaret" (curtain calls/bows).

Recorded during Liza's acclaimed and Tony-awarded engagement (for Best Personal Achievement) at the famed Winter Garden Theater, this album distilled a two-act show into fifty-three minutes of highlights on a single LP. It is sad that Columbia didn't release a two-record set, as they could have documented the entire concert on two LPs. *Live at the Winter Garden* deserves to be heard in its entirety. (See the Winter Garden Theater entry in Chapter Thirteen, Liza Live, on pages 167–68, for the complete program of songs performed at the Winter Garden.)

Liza Minnelli Live at the Winter Garden debuted on *Billboard*'s Top 200 charts on May 18, 1974, and stayed there four weeks, peaking at number 150.

"More Than I Like You"/ "Harbour"
(Single)

Recorded and released by Columbia Records in 1974. No other info available from label's logs. Both songs are on the CD *Liza Minnelli: When It Comes Down to It, 1968–1977.*

There was an October 1974 report—reprinted in Minnelli's fan club journal of February 1975—that Liza had filed suit in L.A.'s Superior Court to cancel her contract with CBS (Columbia) Records. The suit charged the label had failed to release an album "during the first option period," and "that her contract actually expired April 15, 1974." It said "Minnelli also charged that CBS contacted Warner Brothers Records and allegedly threatened action against Warner if they attempted to enter into a contract with Minnelli. CBS also contacted other record companies throughout the United States for purported purposes of interfering with her prospective business relationships in the same manner, the suit also charged." Apparently, there had been the possibility of her leaving Columbia Records and signing with Warner Brothers Records. There was also a report in May 1975 that she was to start work on a new LP "anytime between now and and next year for 20th Century-Fox Records," which never happened—unless this was to be the soundtrack recording of *Lucky Lady*, which surfaced on Arista Records (see *Lucky Lady* entry below). Liza stayed with Columbia through 1977.

"All That Jazz"/ "I Am My Own Best Friend" (Single)

Recorded in 1975—January has been reported as a recording date, although February 5, 1975, is listed in label's logs. No other info available. Released by Columbia Records. Both songs are available on a CD that has superior sonics: *Liza Minnelli: 16 Biggest Hits*, released by Columbia/Legacy/Sony, # CK 53778, in 2000. (There was a mention in the May 1975 issue of Liza's official fan club "Limelight on Liza" that said Minnelli had recorded two other songs from the *Chicago* score: "Razzle Dazzle" remains unreleased, and "Me and My Baby" is included on *The Best of Liza Minnelli*, a fall 2004 Columbia Records/Sony Legacy CD.

"All That Jazz" is one of the best recordings of Liza's career: The perfect marriage of song, performer, and orchestration. The number sizzles, and builds, and the last note on "Jazz" is Minnelli at her most dynamic. (Liza lip-synched to this recording of "All That Jazz" on her fall 1975 appearance on *The Mac Davis Special.*) A must-have.

Lucky Lady (Original Soundtrack Recording) (Album)

Recorded early spring 1975, and fall 1975. Released February 1976 by Arista Records, LP # AL 4069. Album produced, arranged, and conducted by Ralph Burns. Not yet released on CD.

Liza's songs: "(Get) While the Getting Is Good"; "Lucky Lady Montage"; "Lucky Lady" (reprise).

The soundtrack to Liza's 1975 20th Century-Fox film features only three tracks by Minnelli (one a reprise), but "Get While the Getting Is Good" is a longer version here than the one in the film. Both songs are fun, and Liza's in fine form and voice. This LP was one of Arista's early releases.

"A Matter of Time" Soundtrack (Album)

Recorded Fall 1975. Released 1976, in Italy, by Oceania Records. Never released on CD. (There was also reportedly a single with the title track.) The soundtrack album contains two Liza vocals: the title track "A Matter of Time" on the first side of the LP (by Kander and Ebb), and a torchy, jazzy

rendition of the standard "Do It Again" (the highlight of the movie to many). Liza is in fine form and voice. The LP does not contain the other song Minnelli sings in the movie—"The Me I Haven't Met Yet"—but contains twelve tracks in total, ten of them instrumentals. This album remains one of Liza's rarest, often fetching $400 on eBay.

New York, New York
(Original Motion Picture Score)
(Album; two-record set)

Recorded spring through summer 1976 in California (No info from label's logs available). Musical supervisor, arranger, conductor, and album Produced by Ralph Burns. Released May 1977 by United Artists Records as a two-LP set, # UA-LA750-L2. Issued on audio cassette, and still available on CD (a single disc that contains all the tracks found on the two-LP set) from EMI America/EMI-Manhattan: CD # : CDP 7-46090-2. There was a single version of "Theme from New York, New York," which used an alternate vocal take. Total playing time—1:10:07.

Liza's nine songs: "You Brought a New Kind of Love to Me," "Once in a While"; "You Are My Lucky Star"; "The Man I Love"; "Just You, Just Me"; "There Goes the Ball Game"; "Happy Endings"; "'But the World Goes 'Round"; "Theme from *New York, New York*." She also sang "South America, Take It Away," which was cut from the film before release, and does not appear on the album. This soundtrack recording's takes of "Just You, Just Me," "There Goes the Ball Game," and "Once in a While" are longer than they are in the movie. "Once in a While" used a different vocal take for the album than for the movie, and one line in "The Man I Love" is also a different vocal take on the album versus the movie.

The *New York, New York* soundtrack recording is a testament to Liza Minnelli's great versatility. While she may be stamped in the masses' minds as a belter of show tunes—which she does on the title track—the *New York, New York* album shows off her chameleon capability. Here she becomes a 1940s big band singer, who also happens to possess an eerie ability to impersonate Peggy Lee performing Kander and Ebb's "There Goes the Ball Game." (Then the star's character, "Francine Evans," evolves into Liza Minnelli.) Superb sound and Liza in peak vocal form and voice—singing what is still the "ultimate" version of "New York, New York"—make this another must-have for Minnelli maniacs and Liza lovers.

The *New York, New York* soundtrack debuted on the *Billboard* Top 200 album chart on July 16, 1977, and spent fourteen weeks there, peaking at Number 50. The CD has sold 23,011 copies from 1991 through April 25, 2004, according to SoundScan.

Tropical Nights
(Album)

Recorded late January 1977, at Hollywood Sound Recorders and Western Studio One. Photography by Reid Miles. Produced by Rik Pekkonen and Steve March, for Waylentsote Productions. Released July 1977 by Columbia Records, LP # PC 34887. Issued on CD by DRG Records (under license from Sony) in February 2002, # 91469. Distributed by Koch International. Available at Footlight Records, 212-533-1572, or from DRG at www.drgrecords.com Total playing time: 35:18.

Liza's nine songs: "Jimi Jimi"; "When It Comes Down to It"; "I Love Every Little Thing About You"; "Easy"; "I'm Your New Best Friend"; "Tropical Nights (Bali Ha'i)"; "Take Me Through/I Could Come to Love You"; "Come Home Babe"; "A Beautiful Thing."

One of Liza Minnelli's finest albums, features the singer in a genre she's not known for: pop-rock (a 1970s, lighter, "California"-type sound). One of the reasons I admire Minnelli so much is because of the chances she's taken, and the different types of musical material tried over the years. Every song on *Tropical Nights* is a strong one. Liza is in peak form and voice. Yet another must-have, *Tropical Nights* remains one of Minnelli's finest albums.

Variety raved: "Liza Minnelli has a new sparkler. Most of the tunes are bright and uptempo, but she also has a way with a couple of gentle ones that wind the second side. Minnelli, who's at her peak, has a big one here."

Songs Cut from Broadway Musicals
(Album; Liza has one song)

A bootleg LP—never issued on CD—that contains songs cut from Broadway musicals while on the road, etc. One of the album's tracks is "Hollywood, California," cut from *The Act*. This track was obviously recorded from the audience, and has only fair sound quality, but it is a treat to be able to hear the star sing the upbeat Kander and Ebb tune.

The Act
(Original Broadway Cast Album)

Recorded April 1978 during a one-day, eleven-hour-plus session—Liza arrived at 9:30 AM, and the album was completed at 9 PM at A&R Recording Studios, New York City. Orchestrations by Ralph Burns. Produced for records by Hugh Fordin. Issued in May 1978 by DRG Records on LP. Also released on cassette, and still available on DRG's CD: # CDRG 6101. There was also a version issued in Germany on LP, by RCA Records, # FL 42709. The CD has also turned up in a seemingly endless series of versions issued overseas, under titles such as *City Lights*. Total playing time: 47:56. This recording has sold 2,835 copies from 1991 through April 25, 2004, according to SoundScan.

Liza's eleven songs: "Shine It On" (with chorus); "It's the Strangest Thing"; "Bobos"; "Turning (Shaker Hymn)" (with chorus); "Arthur in the Afternoon"; "The Money Tree"; "City Lights" (with chorus); "There When I Need Him"; "Hot Enough for You" (with chorus); "My Own Space" (John Kander at the piano); "Walking Papers/Shine It On reprise."

Liza's Tony Award–winning performance (her third Tony) is preserved on the original cast album. The recording had been scheduled to be done for Liza's label, Columbia Records, with a release number assigned: JS-35072 (S). Minnelli's contract with the label lapsed while she was out of town with this musical, however. DRG Records' Hugh Fordin came to the rescue, mere months

before the show closed. The score is another winner from Kander and Ebb, and Liza is in fine form, but not at a vocal peak: there are tapes that exist in private collections of some of *The Act* performances on Broadway, and the star is in much stronger voice. Misgivings about her vocal quality aside, the album is a thrilling document of a Minnelli musical. (For more information about the making of the album, seek out a copy of Rex Reed's circa 1979 book *From Travolta to Keaton,* which has a chapter on the recording session for *The Act.*)

Liza Minnelli Live at Carnegie Hall (1979 engagement) (Album; two-record set)

Recorded September 1979 at Carnegie Hall. Produced by Hank Cattaneo and Bill LaVorgna. Released in August 1981 by the company that did Liza's sound for her concerts: Altel Sound Systems, Inc., 461 Park Avenue South, New York, New York 10016. Also issued on audio cassette tape, but never issued on CD. Long out of print. Total Playing Time: 1:12:34

Liza's thirteen songs: (Side One) "How Long Has This Been Going On?"/"It's a Miracle"; "My Ship"/"The Man I Love"; "Some People"; "Come In from the Rain"; (Side Two) "London Town"; "New York Medley" ("I Guess the Lord Must Be in New York City"/"Take Me Back to Manhattan"/"Manhattan"/"New York City Rhythm"/"42nd Street"/"Lullaby of Broadway"/"On Broadway"/"New York, New York (It's a Helluva Town)"/"Every Street's a Boulevard"/"Theme from New York, New York"); (Side Three) "Someone to Watch Over Me"; "Twelve Fellas"; "You and I"/"The Honey-

moon Is Over"/"Happy Anniversary"; "City Lights"; (Side Four) "Cabaret"; "Shine on Harvest Moon"; "But the World Goes 'Round"

From September 4–14, 1979, Liza Minnelli gave what was then the longest-running, consecutive number of performances by an artist in the history of Carnegie Hall (eleven shows)—a record that she broke herself in 1987 while performing at the famed hall for three weeks. The singer had worked at this particular venue—one so identified with her beloved mama—only once before, as part of a benefit concert on January 10, 1965. As Liza was not under contract to a record company at the time, she had this 1979 concert recorded and released herself. This album presents Liza Minnelli at an entirely new and greater level as a singer. Her voice is at one of the top vocal periods of her career. Minnelli persevered to get this released, and it took almost exactly two years. The two-record set was finally sold at the star's concerts, starting at the Garden State Arts Center in Holmdel, New Jersey, on August 19, 1981. (The set had been shipped to her Houston, Texas, concerts at the end of June, but it was realized the Warhol cover painting was printed with the wrong hue: Liza's skin was *purple.* The LP jackets were reprinted, and the purple version is not known to have surfaced to date.) The album continued being sold at concerts throughout the fall of 1981, and had limited distribution to stores (I once found the audio cassette version at a Philadelphia Sam Goody's store, for $13.98). We can only hope that someday Liza will have this album released on CD, as this is a milestone in Minnelli's career, and deserves to be heard by everyone. A must-have.

During an interview for an August 10, 1980, article on the making of her new movie *Arthur*, it was revealed that Liza was "getting back to recording . . . she has new management—Philadelphia's Gamble and Huff, the masterminds behind Lou Rawls' disc-shop revival." This association never produced any recordings. There was also a report in *Variety* during the summer of 1981 that stated Liza had signed a recording contract with Criteria Records, based in Florida, and had recorded a single for them. This turned out not to be true, nor was a report in the early 1990s that she would be signing with Hollywood Records. On Friday, August 13, 1982, Liza was quoted as saying in the *New York Daily News* that she was recording a new album: "No name yet. But it's a contemporary album. It's good rock." This album never surfaced. On the 1980 Warner Brothers album *Calling All Girls* by Hilly Michael, the "backing vocalists" are listed as Liza Minnelli, Lorna Luft, Ellen Foley, Karla DeVito, Ellen Bernfeld. Liza can be most clearly heard on the track "U.S. Male."

The Rink (Original Broadway Cast Recording; Album)

All-Digital Recording (DDD). Recorded at RCA Studios in New York City, on May 6, and 8, 1984. Musical director and conductor for the album: Paul Gemignani. Photography: Ken Howard; Executive Producer: John Yap. Produced for records by

Norman Newell. Released July 24, 1984, on LP, audio cassette, and compact disc, by Polydor/PolyGram Records, CD # 823 125-2-Y-1. Newly remastered and produced for records by John Yap in 1999. Released by JAY Records in 1999, on CD, #CDJAY 1328. The remastered recording has sold 2,546 copies from 1999 through April 25, 2004, according to SoundScan.

Liza's songs (solos, unless noted): "Colored Lights"; "Don't Ah Ma Me" (with Chita Rivera); "Under the Roller Coaster" (with Chita); "Angel's Rink and Social Center" (with Chita and cast); "The Apple Doesn't Fall" (with Chita); "Mrs. A" (with Chita and cast); "Wallflower" (with Chita); "All the Children in a Row" (Liza also has lines in "Not Enough Magic," and the final track, "Finale/Coda.")

The last of Liza's book shows to be recorded to date is this 1984 Kander and Ebb musical. This was the second Broadway cast album to be recorded in the new all-Digital format (1983's *On Your Toes* was the first), and Liza talked about how impressed she was with the sound quality. The album does sparkle (even more so on the newly remastered version), and producer John Yap should be proud of his hard work in making this cast recording happen. What prevents the recording from being a complete—and accurate—representation of the score is the fact that Liza was not in her best voice during the album's sessions. Minnelli's two solos were recorded on May 8, two days after the album's original session, and are more successful than the rest of her tracks made two days earlier. Yet even those solos reveal the strain of doing eight shows a week—although she could still astound vocally during this period, such as her performance at a Jule Styne tribute on April 29, 1984. Still, *The Rink* cast album is something one will want to add to their collection. The brilliantly remastered edition on JAY Records remains one of the label's top sellers, a testament to Minnelli's fans.

While in concert a year later (in August 1985), Liza mentioned she planned to record a new album in late September through October 1985. This was not known to have happened, as her concert schedule was too demanding.

Remember: Michael Feinstein Sings Irving Berlin
(Album; Liza is featured on one song)

Recorded in the fall of 1986, at Group 4 Recording Studio, Hollywood, California. Engineer: George Belle. Mastered at Bernie Grundman Mastering. Arrangement and piano accompaniment: Stan Freeman. Album produced by Herb Eiseman. Released by Elektra/Asylum Records; still available on CD: # 9 607744-2. This recording has sold 65,559 copies from 1999 through April 25, 2004.

Liza sings one song: a duet with Feinstein on "Remember"/"Always"/"What'll I Do?," and is in fine voice. This song was recorded during a three-day break Liza had while filming *Rent-a-Cop* in Italy. She had suggested the duet to Michael, and flew in to California from Italy, instead of having Michael fly to her. Yet another testament to Liza's endless generosity. Feinstein picked her up at the airport and had a cassette of the arrangement for her, which she listened to repeatedly. They then rehearsed in the studio for an hour and recorded it in six takes, with the final one used for the album.

Liza Minnelli at Carnegie Hall
(a.k.a. Three Weeks at Carnegie Hall)(1987)
(Two-album set)

All-Digital Recording (DDD). Recorded and mixed live to two-track digital at Carnegie Hall in New York City, during six shows: June 10, 11, 14, 16, 17, and 18, 1987. Recording producers: Larry Marks, Robert Woods. Released by Telarc, September 28, 1987, on two-album sets (in LP, audio cassette, and CD formats). Still available on CD, number: CD-85502. Also issued by Telarc as an abridged, single disc album of "Highlights from Carnegie Hall," on November 15, 1989. Total playing time of the two disc set: 100:16 (an hour and 40 minutes)—Disc One (Act One): 47:38; Disc Two (Act Two): 52:38. (The *Highlights* disc runs 64 minutes.)

Liza's songs: (Disc One/Act One) "I Happen to Like New York" ; "Here I'll Stay"/"Our Love Is Here to Stay"; "Old Friends"; "I Never Have Seen Snow"; "If You Hadn't, But You Did"; "I Don't Want to Know"; "Some People"; "How Deep Is the Ocean?"; "I Can See Clearly Now"/"I Can See It"; "Married"/ "You'd Better Sit Down, Kids"; "Ring Them Bells"; (Disc Two/Act Two) "The Sweetest Sounds"; "Toot Toot Tootsie"; "Buckle Down, Winsocki"; "Alexan-

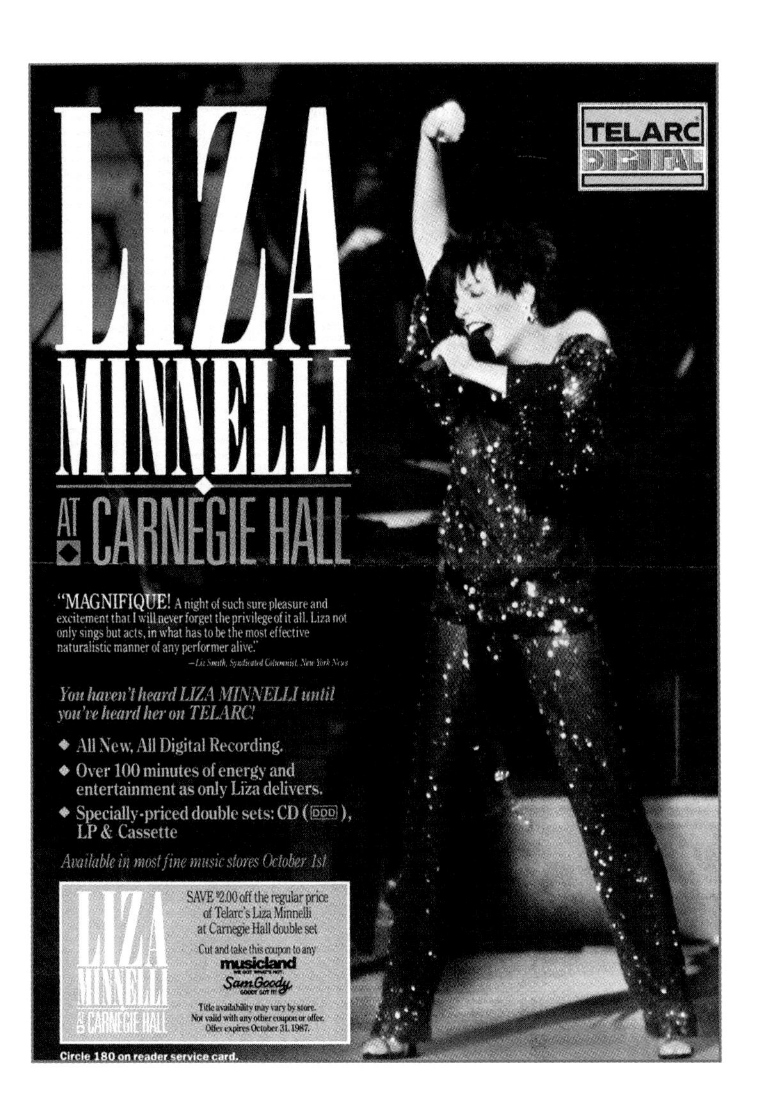

der's Ragtime Band"; "Somewhere Out There"; "Lonely Feet"; "You Can Have Him"/"Time Heals Everything"; Kander and Ebb Medley: "Liza with a 'Z'"/"All I Need Is One Good Break"/"Sing Happy"/"A Quiet Thing"/"Mein Herr"/"Money, Money"/"Maybe This Time"/"Yes"/"City Lights"/"I'm One of the Smart Ones"/"But the World Goes 'Round"/"Cabaret"/"New York, New York."

A monumental moment in Minnelli's career. This engagement marked the longest run at Carnegie Hall by a single performer: seventeen sold-out performances. The star presents one of her finest assembled programs of songs, and is backed by one of her largest and best orchestras—forty-five pieces—presented in a spectacular, all-digital recording that captures every one of Minnelli's songs from this concert. This album also captures Liza in one of her best vocal periods. The singer is in remarkable voice (and form), and offers definitive versions of many of the numbers heard here. Liza's arrangements were transposed into a lower key sometime in 1987, before this concert (and subsequent tour). Although she is in spectacular voice here and beyond, I do have a slight preference for the sound quality on some of her pre-1987 recordings. Some of Minnelli's absolute peak periods vocally were (in chronological order): 1962–1965; 1967–1973; 1975–1979 (1979 was an especially great year for the singer, vocally); 1981; and perhaps my all-time favorite vocal period of Liza as a singer: 1985–1986. Other honorable mentions would be the years 1987–1991; the spring of 1996 through the end of that year; the first two weeks of December 1999; and Liza's current "comeback": 2002–2004.

The 1987 *Liza Minnelli at Carnegie Hall* album *is* arguably the best available commercially released audio representation of the star as a concert artist at a peak period vocally, and also thus can arguably be seen as the one Liza Minnelli CD to get if you're just buying one particular performance.

Liza Minnelli at Carnegie Hall—the two-CD set—debuted November 14, 1987 on *Billboard*'s Top 200 Chart, where it stayed for eight weeks, peaking at number 156. The single disc of "Highlights" had sold 70,944 copies through January 25, 2004, according to SoundScan reports, and the two-CD set has sold 23,777 copies.

The Michael Feinstein Anthology

(Album: Liza sings on one track on this two-CD set)

Liza duets with Michael on the wonderful Kay Thompson song "Violin," a previously unreleased track. This number was taken from privately made tapes recorded through the sound system (in stereo) of a live concert performance from the fall of 1987, when Feinstein was touring with Minnelli.

For You Armenia

(Single)

In 1988, Liza participated in an all-star recording (à la "We Are the World," "That's What Friends Are

For," etc.). This was for relief after the 1988 earthquake disaster in Armenia. Charles Aznavour was born there and conceived this single.

The song "For You Armenia" was recorded and released in 1988 on the Trema/EMI label. (There was a later all-French version, "Pour Toi Armenia," but Liza was not a part of this rendition.) Minnelli has a solo section in the recording, which also featured Irene Cara and Dionne Warwick, among other artists.

Results
(Album)

All-Digital Recording (DDD). Recorded April 18 through April 22, 1989, at Sarm West Studios, London, England. Produced by The Pet Shop Boys and Julian Mendelsohn. Released by Epic Records/CBS Records (Sony), on October 11, 1989, in the U.S., on LP, audio cassette, and CD. CD # EK 45098 still available. Total playing time: 45:26.

Liza's ten songs: "I Want You Now"; "Losing My Mind"; "If There Was Love"; "So Sorry, I Said"; "Don't Drop Bombs"; "Twist in My Sobriety"; "Rent"; "Love Pains"; "Tonight Is Forever"; "I Can't Say Goodnight."

Liza in her first music video, "Losing My Mind," the first single from her *Results* album.

One of Liza Minnelli's greatest achievements for records, or for any other media, *Results* is a masterpiece. Yes, it is as far removed as possible from what one might "expect" from a Liza Minnelli album: it is not a concert album, nor a soundtrack, nor a Broadway cast album. The music is richly textured, and each song tells a story, just like all the best Liza songs do. The arrangements and orchestrations are often majestic, the sound is superb, and to top it off, Liza is in completely flawless voice—among the best of her entire career.

Recorded at midnight sessions during her London engagement with Frank and Sammy—who

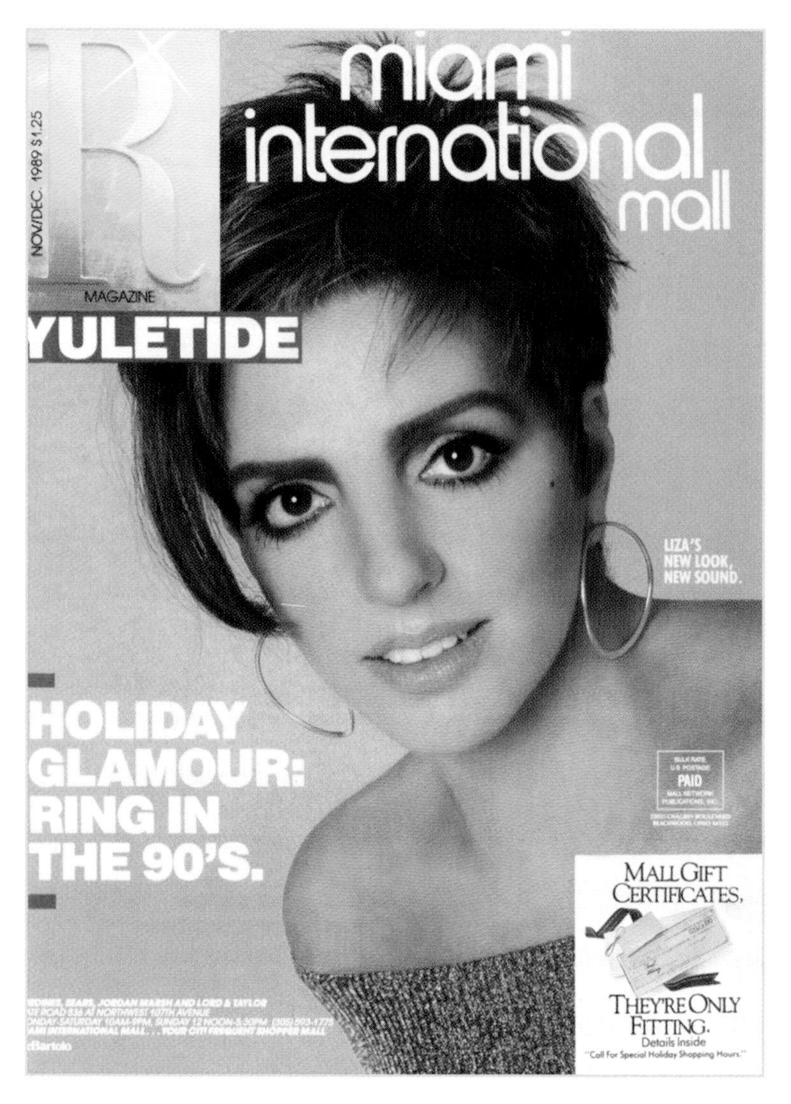

"dug" this disc—*Results* was the result of Minnelli's own musings with rocker Gene Simmons (of Kiss fame) as to why she never had a huge, breakthrough record. Gene thus became her "recording manager." Simmons brought her to Epic Records, who quickly signed her to do this album. The Pet Shop Boys were huge Liza fans, and the star said she liked them "because their music is very good, sort of like poetry set to music." Minnelli thought they wanted something very non-Liza-like when she started recording the album. They stopped her first take when they realized she was trying to be someone else. This is why *Results* works so well—there is no doubt Liza Minnelli is singing, but her *environment* is different than what one would "expect."

It seemed as if *Results* would get them, as the critics praised the disc. The *Guardian's* Adam Sweeting summarized the album as "a canny distillation of modern pop technique steeped in a rich tradition of musical theater. The entire project is both a technical feat and an audacious imaginative leap." The L.A. *Times* gave the album three and a half stars, and raved, "Minnelli has become a Pet Shop Girl—with often dazzling results. Produced and mostly written by the Pet Shop Boys, this album features dark, moody ballads, and dark, moody dance tunes. The Boys' trademark ethereal production liberates Minnelli, who reveals an impressive contemporary-pop dimension. One of the year's most intriguing albums." Neil Tennant of the Pet Shop Boys coproduced the album, and revealed to the *Advocate* in 1996, "I think *Results* was possibly the best album we've ever made."

The public came very close to accepting this very different Liza Minnelli. The album's first single, "Losing My Mind" went to number one in England following its release on July 24, 1989. The album itself reportedly sold over 600,000 copies in Europe for which it has been noted she received a Gold record, although this has never been reported in the media, or verified by the NIRAS or RIAA. Liza filmed a video for "Losing My Mind," and for two other tunes on the album, "So Sorry, I Said," and "Don't Drop Bombs." (All three were released on VHS and laser disc by Sony, titled *Visible Results*, but are out of print.) Liza looked breathtakingly beautiful during this *Results* period, as she launched a media blitz to promote the record.

The singles did fairly well here in the U.S. "Losing My Mind" debuted on *Billboard*'s Top 100 Dance Tracks on September 16, 1989, where it spent fifteen weeks, peaking at number 11, the week of October 21. "Love Pains" spent two weeks on that same singles chart, debuting on April 21, 1990, and peaking at number 40 one week later. Despite reports of a follow-up album being planned, and a single being released from the album months into 1990, the *Results* album peaked at number 128 in the U.S. on *Billboard*'s Top 200 Charts—debuting there on November 11,1989—and staying for a total of ten weeks, selling a reported 160,000 copies in the U.S. by the end of

1989. (SoundScan shows sales of an additional 38,053 copies from 1991 through January 25, 2004.) MTV's sister network, VH-1, rarely played the "Losing My Mind" video, and the idea of Liza Minnelli as a pop star soon faded.

Results has very strong supporters to this day. While it's a close call between this disc and *Tropical Nights* (another album so far removed from an "expected" Liza Minnelli), *Results* may win by a nose. It's hypnotic, a disc easily played repeatedly. While it may not be to everyone's taste, it is a must-have for any Minnelli maniac or Liza lover.

Stepping Out (Music from the Original Soundtrack; Album)

Recorded summer-fall (August–November),1990. Recorded in Toronto, Canada, at Mantra Sound Studios. Arranged and conducted by Peter Matz. Released October 8, 1991, by Milan (Milan Records/Milan America, Inc.). Manufactured and distributed by BMG Music/BMG Distribution, on audio cassette and CD. CD Release # 73138-35606-2. Reduced in price in the mid 1990s as a "Sound Value" release, and then deleted from Milan's catalog. No longer available. Total Playing Time: 42:23. This recording has sold 14,080 copies from 1991 through April 25, 2004, according to SoundScan.

Liza's songs: "Mean to Me"; "Stepping Out."

The soundtrack album to Liza's most recent theatrically released film, *Stepping Out* is a delight. The title song remains a favorite Kander-Ebb tune, and the disc offers many superb background score moments. A bonus here is a slightly longer "Mean to Me" than the version that appears in the film. Minnelli is in superb voice, and this CD is a delight, if it can be found.

Billy Strich (Album; Liza is featured on one song)

Recorded and mixed at Soundtrack New York during September 1991. Produced by Hugh Fordin. Released February 18, 1992, on cassette and CD, by Fordin's label, DRG Records. CD #: 5215. This recording has sold 5,371 copies from 1991 through April 25, 2004, according to SoundScan.

Liza sings one duet with Billy: "Come Rain or Come Shine"/"As Long as I Live." The talented Stritch had supplied vocal arrangements for Minnelli's Radio City Music Hall engagement, and continues to work with Liza to this day. A must-have.

Aznavour-Minnelli: Paris—Palais Des Congrès
(Album; two-CD set)

Concert with Charles Aznavour. Recorded live, November 20–December 15, 1991, in Paris. No album credits listed. Released in 1995 by EMI Holland/EMI France, on CD, # 8324262. Available in the U.S. only as an import—never released domestically. Contact Footlight Records in New York City: Phone: 212-533-1572. This recording has sold 895 copies from 1995 through April 25, 2004, according to SoundScan.

Liza's songs: (Disc One) "Prologue" (duet); "The Sound of Your Name" (duet); (Disc Two) "Pour Faire Une Jam" (with Aznavour, and Billy Stritch); "Bonjour Paris"; "God Bless the Child"; "Old Friend"; "Liza with a 'Z'"; "Sailor Boys"; "Some People"; "J'ai Deux Amours"; "Stepping Out"; "Losing My Mind"; "I Love a Piano"; "Cabaret"; "New York, New York"; Medley (with Aznavour): "Our Love Is Here to Stay"/"The Song Is You"/"Old Devil Moon"/"How High in the Sky"/"Let's Fall in Love"/"I've Got You Under My Skin"/"Dream"/"Unforgettable"/"I've Grown Accustomed to Her Face"/"These Foolish Things"/"Just a Dream Ago"/"How High in the Moon"/"Just in Time"/"Le Temps." Liza is only featured on the first two tracks of Disc One, but is on all of Disc Two. Total Playing Time: one hour and 17 minutes.

Among her commercially available recordings, this one is perhaps the most accurate audio representation of Liza in the 1990s. She is in both fine form and her voice is rich and powerful. A definite peak period vocally. The album also boasts superb sound, a great and vast orchestra, and an excellent program of songs, making this disc a must-have.

Liza Minnelli Live at Radio City Music Hall
(Album)

Recorded live on high-definition videotape at Radio City Music Hall, the first week of February, 1992. "Imagine" was pre-recorded spring 1991. Executive producers: Phil Ramone, Liza Minnelli. Produced by Phil Ramone. Released November 3, 1992, by Columbia Records (Sony) on CD and audio cassette. CD release: # CK 53169. Still available. Total playing time: one hour, 14 minutes.

Liza's sixteen songs: "Teach Me Tonight"; "Old

Friends"; "Live Alone and Like It"; "Sorry I Asked"; "So What"; "Sara Lee"; "Some People"; "Seeing Things"; "Stepping Out"; "I Wanna Get into the Act"; "Men's Medley"; "Imagine"; "Here I'll Stay"/"Our Love Is Here to Stay"; "There's No Business Like Show Business"; "Stepping Out" (reprise); "Theme from *New York, New York*."

Currently Liza Minnelli's best-selling CD—according to SoundScan reports, the album had sold 98,142 copies through January 25, 2004. The disc presents moments from Minnelli's act prepared for the venue's record-breaking spring 1991 engagement. A year later, when Sony recorded the return run, she was in spectacular form, if not at full vocal peak. (There were reports that Telarc—the same label that released the 1987 Carnegie Hall album—was going to be releasing the album.) While this album didn't chart, the video did—debuting on *Billboard*'s video chart at number 34 on December 12, 1992. It spent nine weeks on the charts, peaking at number 23 on January 9, 1993. The CD is highly recommended for the MMs and LLs out there, although the video may have a more powerful effect on the more casual fan.

Sondheim: A Celebration at Carnegie Hall

(Album; two-CD set; Liza sings on three tracks)

All-Digital Recording (DDD). Recorded June 10th, 1992, in concert at Carnegie Hall. Produced for Records by Jay David Saks. Released by RCA Victor/BMG Music, February 23, 1993, on audio cassette and CD : two CD-set #: 09026-61484-2. This recording has sold 5,732 copies from February 1993 through April 25, 2004, according to SoundScan. (Also issued by RCA on a single disc of highlights, as well as on home video: VHS and DVD.)

Liza's three songs: "Water Under the Bridge" (duet with Billy Stritch); "Back in Business" (with Stritch; ensemble); "Old Friends."

Liza closed the first act in this tribute to Sondheim, then returned at the evening's end, in the next-to-last number, "Old Friends." The home video omitted "Water Under the Bridge," but this was shown during the PBS telecast.

Frank Sinatra—Duets

(Album; Liza sings on one track)

Recorded and released in 1993 (released November 2, 1993) by Capitol Records, CD # CDP 0777 7 89611 2 3. Arrangement by Nelson Riddle. Liza's track recorded at Impressao Digital Studios in Rio de Janeiro. Produced by Phil Ramone. This recording has sold 2,980,595 copies from November 1993 through April 25, 2004, according to SoundScan.

Liza's song: "I've Got the World on a String" (duet with Frank Sinatra).

Sinatra's last major triumph was a set of two albums that paired him with some of music's biggest stars. Much was made of the fact that Frank had recorded these songs by himself first, and the guest artists taped their performances on separate occasions. Liza's recording took place while she was in Rio de Janeiro with Billy Stritch. There is a brightness to her voice here and a higher tone than had been on display recently. Another must-have for Minnelli maniacs and Liza loons: two icons together (if not at the same time and place).

"Liza Minnelli: The Day After That"

(Single)

Recorded in 1993 at Sony Music Studios, New York City; also at Manta Sound Studios in Toronto, Canada, on Sunday, June 13, 1993. Video shot in Toronto the week of November 23, 1993. Photography by Kevyn Aucoin. Recording produced by Phil Ramone, Billy Stritch, Don Sebesky, and Liza Minnelli. Released November 23, 1993, by Columbia Records/Sony Music on CD, # 44K 77189. This recording has sold 9,818 copies from November 1993 through April 25, 2004. There was also a short-form video available on VHS and laser disc from Sony, which featured a music video and a making of the recording. They are no longer available.

In perhaps the most important recording of her career, Liza Minnelli devoted herself to the AIDS cause. Singing one song in three versions—in English, Spanish, and French performances—Liza chose Kander and Ebb's moving song from their

Kiss of the Spider Woman Broadway musical. Donating "a substantial portion of net profits" from the CD to AmFAR, Minnelli made the recording and video in honor of the first World AIDS Day. Singing the song at the United Nations that December 1, 1993, and making the disc and video were ways the star found of reconnecting with the cause to fight the disease that had killed so many of her friends, including Peter Allen, the year before. Liza even directed the music video, and this recording is a testament to the heart and soul of this loving human being. A must-have for everyone, if it can be found.

Minnelli had mentioned she planned to record an album of songs from her father's movies, which Sony would release in 1994, but this did not happen, perhaps due to producer Phil Ramone being unavailable (although Liza had said she would work with another producer at Sony). There were also June 1994 reports that Liza would be performing a "duet" with her mother's voice for a studio recording. This did not happen. Nor did a noted "blues" album for Disney's Hollywood Records label—there were rumors of a million-dollar deal with the company.

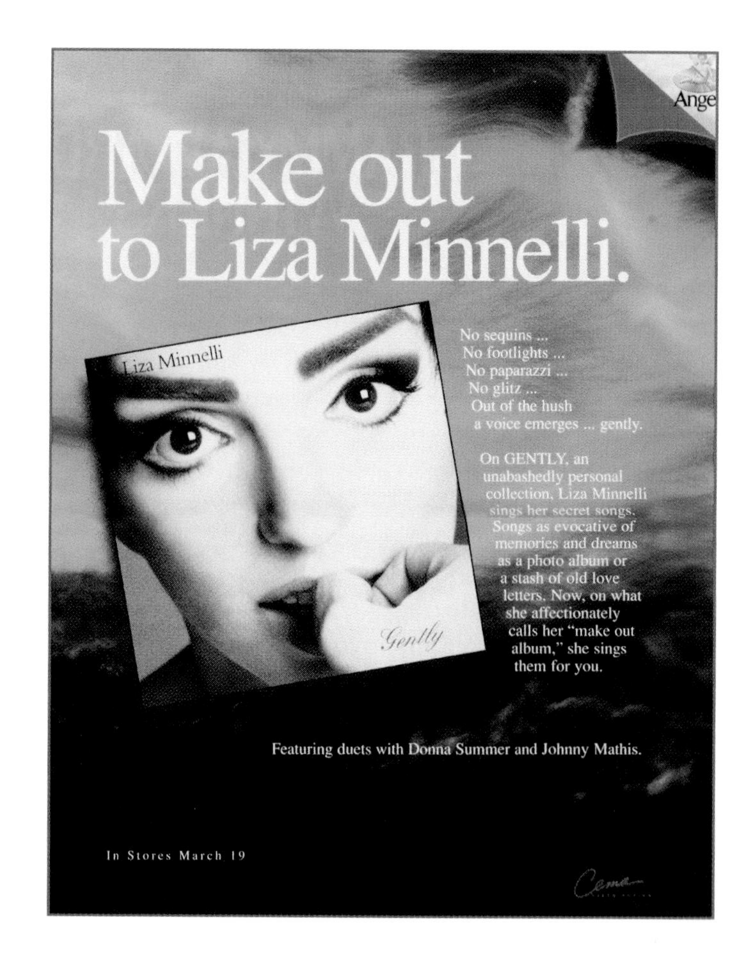

Gently
(Album)

All-Digital Recording (DDD). Recorded throughout 1995, in L.A., New York City, and Nashville. Executive producers: Jay Landers and Steve Murphy. Associate producer: Billy Stritch. Album produced by Brooks Arthur. Released by Angel Records on March 19, 1996, on cassette and CD: CD # 7243-8-35470-2-9. Total playing time: 42:25.

Liza's eleven songs: "Chances Are" (duet with Johnny Mathis); "You Stepped out of a Dream" (Melissa Manchester, Brenda Russell, Billy Stritch on background vocals) ; "Embraceable You"; "Close Your Eyes"; "Some Cats Know"; "Lost in You"; "I Got Lost in His Arms"; "It Had to Be You"; "Never Let Me Go"; "Does He Love You?"; "In the Wee Small Hours of the Morning."

One of Liza's most popular and profiled later albums—and another example of how diverse the singer's recording career has been. *Gently* is subtitled "The Makeout Album." Minnelli started talking about it in the fall of 1994 (during which time she also mentioned the desire to do a disc with four different trios, including the Andre Previn Trio and the Dr. John Trio, which didn't occur). Liza joked that one early title for *Gently* should be "*Extended Foreplay*!" There were other titles considered, including *Liza May Minnelli*, *Come Hither*, and *Lost in You*. Additionally, there were at least seven songs recorded that didn't make the album's final release: "I Remember You," "As Time Goes By," "Come Hither," and "I Hadn't Anyone Till You," "So in Love," "Some of These Days," and "You Fascinate Me So." A smoky, jazzy disc, *Gently* is richly orchestrated and lovingly done. Liza's singing shows some dryness, but at the same time has an abundance of depth to it, and is perhaps her most intimate work. As Liza herself said, "There is no glitter or pizzazz to my vocals. It's just raw me." The sales were fairly good—according to SoundScan reports, the album had sold 76,835 copies through January 25, 2004. *Gently* spent one week on *Billboard*'s Top 200 charts, where it appeared at number 156 during the week of July 6,

1996; (it has also been noted as reaching number 58 on the charts in the UK) and the singer was nominated for a Grammy for Best Traditional Pop Vocal. (During June 1997 interviews, Liza mentioned a follow-up being planned, with Billy Stritch producing, called *Desire*, but it was never released, nor recorded.) Although Liza would be in stronger voice mere months after completing this album, *Gently* is such a finely crafted album that it also is a must-have.

The Life: World Premiere Recording

(Album; Liza sings on three tracks)

Recorded March–October 1995. Liza's tracks reportedly recorded on February 9, 1995. Produced by Cy Coleman and Mike Berniker. Released by RCA Victor/BMG Classics May 21, 1996, CD # 09026-68001-2. No longer in print. (Disc had been announced back in July 1993 as an EMI release, but was never recorded till '95.)

Liza sings three songs on this album, presenting the score to Cy Coleman's new Broadway musical *The Life*. Recorded during the same period of *Gently*, Liza sounds exactly as she does on that disc: moving, if a bit dry vocally. Minnelli still wows on the uptunes "Use What You Got"; "People Magazine" (duet with Billy Stritch); and the lovely ballad "We Had a Dream."

Pavarotti and Friends for War Child, 1996

(Album; Liza sings one song)

Full-Digital Recording (DDD). Recorded June 20, 1996 live from the Parco Novi Sad, Modena—Released November 19th, 1996 by Decca Records/London Records on cassette and CD, and on also on a DTS 5.1 CD. This recording has sold 7,166 copies from November 1996 through April 25, 2004, according to SoundScan.

Liza sang "New York, New York" in a unique pairing with Pavarotti. She is in spectacular voice and form. The VHS/laser disc—and now DVD (as part of a Pavarotti box set)—also includes a lovely Liza solo: a medley of the beautiful ballad "I Have Dreamed," from *The King and I*, with "Long Ago and Far Away."

In the spring or summer of 1997, columnist Cindy Adams mentioned Liza would be doing a disc of duets with singer Sam Harris. It never happened. Army Archer announced on September 5, 1997, that Billy Stritch would be producing a new Liza album in October 1997—a Brazilian-flavored disc. That project never transpired either.

My Favorite Broadway: The Leading Ladies, Live at Carnegie Hall

(Album; Liza sings one song)

Recorded September 28, 1998; Liza's vocal re-recorded spring-summer 1999, before the fall 1999 airing on PBS and release on DVD and CD. CD released November 16th, 1999, by Hybrid Recordings/TVT Soundtrax, release # TVT 2010-2A. This recording has sold 25,598 copies from November 1999 through April 25, 2004, according to SoundScan.

Liza sings "Some People" on this live recording of the concert held at Carnegie Hall. That evening, she closed the first act; her segment consisted of being introduced by Rosie O'Donnell, with whom she dueted on "Liza with a 'Z.'" Minnelli's solos were "Sing Happy" and "Some People." Liza was still suffering from major vocal problems following failed vocal surgery early in 1997; after her voice healed to a remarkable degree in the spring of 1999, the star re-recorded her vocal for this track. Her singing is still not as strong as on some of her other renditions, but with a huge orchestra behind her, Minnelli socks it out of the ballpark, as they say, making this a favorite rendition of "Some People."

Minnelli on Minnelli: Live at the Palace

(Album)

Recorded live at the Palace Theater, New York City, December 27 and 28, 1999, and studio overdubs in

New York City, mid-January 2000. Produced by Phil Ramone and Billy Stritch. Released February 29, 2000, by Angel Records, CD # 7243 5 24905 2 3. Total playing time: one hour, 5 minutes. (According to SoundScan reports, the album had sold 20,628 copies through January 25, 2004.)

Liza's seventeen songs: "If I Had You"; "Taking a Chance on Love"; "Love"; "Limehouse Blues"; "Meet Me in St. Louis" Medley: "Meet Me in St. Louis"/"Under the Bamboo Tree"/"The Boy Next Door"/"Have Yourself a Merry Little Christmas"; "Guess I'll Have to Change My Plan"; "Triplets"; "Shine on Your Shoes"; "I Got Rhythm"; "Baubles, Bangles and Beads"; "The Night They Invented Champagne"; "I'm Glad I'm Not Young Anymore"; "What Did I Have That I Don't Have?"; "The Trolley Song" ("duet" with voice of Judy); "I Thank You"

A slightly abridged version of Liza's thoughtful and moving Broadway revue tribute to the music from her father's films, it's sad to say that this CD is probably the poorest study of Liza Minnelli's voice. While her instrument had come back to an astounding strength and clarity two years after vocal surgery, the star developed the flu during the end of her month-long engagement—when this disc was recorded. That cold comes through loud and clear in digital clarity: just listen when she says "my father's movies" before her second number; it sounds like "byed fadder's boovies." Minnelli's voice had actually been strong and bright the first two weeks in the run, before it was captured for this record. Hoping to improve matters, studio redubbing was done on many numbers—a common practice on almost every "live" recording ever made. Liza's flu had only gotten worse by that point, and much of *Minnelli on Minnelli: Live at the Palace* is actually painful to listen to, despite the brilliant thirty-four-piece orchestra and breathtaking arrangements. There are still *some* fine moments though, including "Love," a surprisingly strong "I Got Rhythm," and "Baubles, Bangles and Beads." There are two numbers on which Liza somehow manages to sound infinitely better: an astonishingly powerful and moving "What Did I Have?," and a lovely "I Thank You" finale, where she suddenly sounds like it's 1975. If this had been recorded the first week of the run instead of the last, the album might be another Minnelli masterpiece instead of a very inaccurate representation of what the lady was capable of in December 1999 at the Palace.

Grateful: The Songs of John Bucchino
(Album; Liza sings one song)

Recorded the first week of February 2000, at Sear Sound Studio C, New York City. Produced by John Bucchino. Released by BMG Classics in 2000. Still available. This recording has sold 8,302 copies through April 25, 2004, according to SoundScan.

Liza sings "That Smile" with Billy Stritch, a wonderfully fun, up-tempo love song. Unlike the *MOM* disc above, this recording is an accurate representation of Liza Minnelli's "new" 1999–2000 voice: she sparkles and soars here with her newly higher range, and this was recorded mere weeks after her *Minnelli on Minnelli* disc was completed. *Grateful* is another Minnelli must-have.

Broadway Cares—Home for the Holidays

(Album; Liza sings one song)

Recorded September 19, 2001, at Westrax Recording Studios, New York. Arranged, orchestrated and conducted by Michael Morris. Produced by Tony Moran & Nick De Biase. Released in October 2001 by Centaur Entertainment, CD # CEN 30047-2. This disc has sold 8,522 copies through April 25, 2004, according to SoundScan.

Liza sings "Baby It's Cold Outside" with Alan Cumming. Recorded within days of 9/11, she is in superb form and voice, and the recording is so much fun, too. A must-have. (Liza was also announced to be one of the singers at a Saturday, September 22, 2001, recording session at New York City's Hit Factory to record "We Are Family," which would aid terrorism victims.)

Liza's Back!

(Album)

Recorded live at the Beacon Theater, New York City, Friday, June 7 and Saturday, June 8, 2002—Liza's final two nights of her seven-night run at the Beacon. Album illustrations: Joe Eula. Photography: Greg Gorman. Executive producer: Clive Davis. Co-produced by David Gest. Produced by Phil Ramone. Released by J Records on October 29, 2002; CD #: 80813-20045-2. Total playing time : one hour, 13 minutes, 43 seconds.

Liza's eight songs: "Liza's Back"; "Something Wonderful"; "Cry" Medley: "Cry"/"Don't Cry Out Loud"/"Crying"; "City Lights"; "Don't Smoke in Bed"; "Some People" ; "Never Never Land"/"Over the Rainbow"; "What Did I Have That I Don't Have?"; "Rose's Turn"; "Mein Herr"; "Money, Money"; "Maybe This Time"; "Cabaret"; "But the World Goes 'Round"; "New York, New York"; "I'll

Be Seeing You." (There were reports of four bonus tracks that were to have been recorded at a Liza concert in Las Vegas, but Minnelli had not returned to Vegas to date.)

Liza is truly back, and her latest solo album proves it, reaching heights not heard on Minnelli records in years. A comparison of the *Minnelli on Minnelli* disc with *Liza's Back* certainly proves this. Clive Davis (who had signed Liza to Columbia in 1972) was so overwhelmed by Liza's opening night performance (May 31, 2002), he immediately offered Liza a recording contract. Although Liza was slightly stronger vocally on other nights of the Beacon run—and on closing night in London weeks before, as she would be again at Town Hall in December 2002—the *Liza's Back!* album is a miracle. There is an excellent mix of the expected hits and new material here. Another must-have for Liza lovers, and for anyone who wants a taste of the abundance Liza Minnelli still offers her audiences. The total copies sold of the *Liza's Back!* CD was 25,334, through January 25, 2004, according to SoundScan.

Sacha Distel: But Beautiful

(Album; Liza sings on one song)

Recorded on November 26, 2002, at Right Track Recording on West 48th Street in New York City. Session producer: Jay Messina. Liza Minnelli appears courtesy of David Gest Productions, Inc. Released by Prosadis / Mercury Records, a Universal Music Group (only released overseas, in June 2003; available on Amazon.com as an import through their European division).

Liza sings one duet with Sacha: "All the Way," high and brightly if not as astounding as she would be a week or so later at her Town Hall concerts in New York City on December 5 and 6, 2002. Still, she manages to put vast emotion into the lines of this duet, as she always does.

Liza Minnelli will certainly make more albums. There has been a disc of duets with contemporary artists mentioned recently as a possibility. This would be produced by Piere, possibly for Sony, and contain duets and different songs about Paris. It has also been rumored that she will record a duet with Charles Aznavour for his new duets CD. In the spring of 2004, reports again circulated that the star would indeed be recording an album of French songs—in French—during the summer of 2004. A noted title for this album may be "L'Air D'Paris." In December 2003, Liza told a reporter that she was planning two new albums: an album of songs by her godmother, Kay Thompson, and a first-ever Minnelli Christmas album (although she confessed she still had to "talk with Clive" about the projects, referring to Clive Davis, who was the executive producer on her most recent solo album, *Liza's Back!*). There were also reportedly two or four songs that were recorded as gifts to give during the presentation of an AIDS award Liza received in London, early in 2003. The songs included "Ever to Be Near You" and a new studio version of "New York, New York," with a possibility of "Crying" being another. In May 2004, Liza recorded four songs (in L.A. and Paris) for the duets disc: "Blues in the Night," "Rendez-vous," "Comme un Jeune Amant," and "Love Me Tender." The album was set to be mostly original pop songs, with several guest artists singing duets with Minnelli—including Aznavour, Johnny Halliday, Vanessa Paradis, and Bono—fourteen tracks in all, to be recorded July–August and completed end of October, for release in 2005. Regardless of when the next Liza album will surface, those of us who appreciate this artist should be grateful so much of her legacy has been documented on records.

CHAPTER THIRTEEN

Liza Live—In Concert, on Tour, and Personal Appearances

The relationship between Liza Minnelli and her audiences exceeds that of any other performer. Anyone who has attended a Minnelli concert can attest to the vast amount of affection that flows back and forth across the footlights. "This is the best game of tennis I know," Liza remarked at one recent New York City lovefest (*Liza's Christmas Spectacular*, Town Hall, December 6, 2002). There is no other performer today who longs to please and move her fans more than Minnelli. This living legend simply opens her heart and soul, and shares. Perhaps it is impossible to properly analyze any great magician's secrets, but this generosity could be at the core of why people respond to Liza live—obvious vast talent aside, for the moment. How could one not respond to someone who only wants to share, to give warmth and feeling to others?

The loyalty shown Liza is not limited to her audiences. In a business known for fleeting professional relationships, Minnelli has worked with the same creative personnel for her entire forty-year career. Marvin Hamlisch, the Oscar-winning composer, has been friends with Liza since the early 1960s, and helped select the

material for Minnelli's first live appearances (and still does, on occasion, such as the orchestrations he contributed for 1999's *Minnelli on Minnelli*). Bill ("Pappy") LaVorgna served as Liza's exclusive drummer and musical conductor from 1978 through 1999. Even though he retired from the road in early 2000, he still made time to work with Liza in 2002, during her appearances in *Liza's Back!* Jazz musician and arranger Billy Stritch has done the majority of Minnelli's vocal arrangements and orchestrations since 1991, and has been a producer on her albums. (Stritch is currently putting together a new concert for Liza in 2004.) The star has continually turned to dance coach Luigi to keep her in shape physically and to vocal coach Angela Bacari to make sure the legendary Liza voice is working at its best (Bacari brought Minnelli back to peak vocal ability in 2002.) Acclaimed artist Joe Eula first designed a Liza logo in 1970, and he has since done all of the illustrations to date for her concert programs, T-shirts, and album covers—including the famous *Liza with a "Z"* logo. Perhaps the most identified Minnelli collaboration is with Fred Ebb and John Kander, the songwriters who have supplied Liza with the majority of her songbook, including the scores to *Cabaret*, *New York, New York*, and a multitude of others. Ebb has contributed to, formatted, and/or directed every Liza Minnelli concert-live act since 1965. This chapter is about that first tour, and all the others that have followed.

To date, Liza Minnelli has performed approximately 3,303 concert/nightclub/"live" appearances, a staggering amount. While some years were spent mainly making movies or working in other media, there were others where Minnelli would perform a backbreaking two hundred concerts a year. You're about to see these figures confirmed in the following pages.

This chapter is a chronological log of Liza's live performances in concert halls, nightclubs, stadiums, and other venues around the world (other major personal appearances and benefit shows will be noted also), from 1961 to the present.

(*Note:* When audio and/or video preserving a particular performance is known to exist, there will be a notation made following the listing in brackets, representing: [A] for audio recording only, and [V] for video.)

1961

At age fifteen, Liza performed on her own for the first time, at a benefit for the Veteran's Hospital in Harlem, New York. Minnelli and a friend sang "Steam Heat."

1963

Herbert Berghof Studios, New York—February 3, 1963 (Opening). Presentation of dialogues and poems by the late Robert Frost. Liza performed "The Generations of Men" with Irven Rinard and Richard Morse, and performed two solo pieces as well: "People Keep Saying," and "The Last Word of a Bluebird." This was Minnelli's first known performance in Manhattan.

Central Park, New York—May 25, 1963. Not much information exists about Liza's first performance in the famed New York landmark, except this from

her summer 1965 fan club bio: "she sang to a capacity Central Park audience in the rain." Minnelli again sang in the Park thirty-one years later, for the Stonewall 25th Anniversary event on June 26, 1994.

October 26, 1963—Liza appeared at the "April in Paris" Ball, which was televised on NBC (on October 27). (See the photo on the previous page.)

1964

The London Palladium—November 8 and 15, 1964. The legendary live concert with her beloved mama at the London Palladium. This was Liza's first time working there, and likely her first concert (two-act, formal concert) ever. (Released on LP, and DVD/VHS; all in abridged versions; complete concert awaiting release on two-CD set. See additional information in the entries for *Judy Garland and Liza Minnelli: Live at the London Palladium*, pages 14 and 129.)

Liza at the 6-hour afternoon rehearsal for her London Palladium debut, November 8, 1964.

Actor's Studio, New York—December 31, 1964. Liza and family—Judy, Lorna, and Joe—all took part in a benefit performance.

1965

Carnegie Hall, New York—January 10, 1965. All-star benefit show. Liza sang "Meantime" and "Blue Moon," from her first solo album, *Liza! Liza!* (An audio tape did exist at one time, but is not known to have survived.)

World's Fair, New York—June 8, 1965. Liza made an appearance at the RCA Pavilion in conjunction with her first Broadway musical, *Flora, the Red Menace*. It was noted that Minnelli and her *Flora* costar Bob Dishy "made a public recording."

Brighton Beach and Coney Island, Brooklyn, New York—Summer 1965. Liza entertained on the John Lindsey-for-Mayor campaign, even singing during a downpour.

Following the July 1965 folding of *Flora, the Red Menace*, Liza performed her first solo nightclub act at the Blue Room, Shoreham Hotel–Nightclub, Washington, DC. The opening was September 14, 1965. Liza's songs: "One Life to Live"; "The Gypsy in My Soul"; "Too Marvelous for Words"/"When I Tell Him"/"Wait 'Til You See Him"/"A Wonderful Guy"/"You'll Never Believe Me"/"The Handsomest Boy"; "Liza with a 'Z'"; "There Is a Time"; "That's a Plenty For Me"; "All I Need Is the Boy" (with her two male dancers) "Where Did You Learn to Dance?" (with her two male dancers); (Dance by her two male dancers, while she changed her costume); "If I Were in Your Shoes"; "Songs I Taught My Mother": "I Got You Babe" and "Maybe This Time"; Encore: "Everybody Loves My Baby." Liza kept this act throughout 1965, into 1966, and would continue to sing much of the material throughout the 1960s and beyond. A review by

Don Hearn summed up the sensation in the next day's edition of the *Washington Daily News*:

"A star is born. Liza Minnelli. This vibrant, vivacious young lady made her nitery debut at the Shoreham Blue Room last night. It was, perhaps, one of the most exciting—certainly entertaining—evenings in the Room's history. . . . As it happens, this is Miss Minnelli's bow to the saloon set. . . .

"Blessed with a big, big voice, an electric personality, and an A-1 act, Miss Minnelli is a guaranteed box-office gusher. . . . This extremely talented and exuberant star uncorks a magnum of surprises with her dancing. . . . Rarely has this paragrapher seen a more vital, highly charged talent on the night club stage. . . . She's fantastic, nothing short of fabulous. Miss Minnelli is an emotional experience."

Latin Casino, Cherry Hill, New Jersey—October 1965 [A—10/23 performance]

International Club at the Shamrock Hilton, Houston, Texas—November 4–16, 1965. Twelve-day engagement, during which Liza broke all the club's previous records. A local critic wrote: "Her Saturday night house was one of the biggest in the club's history. She has that spark of magic that comes along seldom. She is alive and electric, and, at the same time, naive. She has a singing talent that just won't wait, and she dances like a dream on long and beautiful legs. The audience gave her a standing ovation before the show was over. This is the best show in ages."

Cocoanut Grove, Los Angeles—November 23–December 7, 1965. Opening (Judy, and kids, Mark Herron) [A—Opening night]

Sahara Hotel, Congo Room, Las Vegas—mid-December 1965. Liza appeared onstage for one

Variety, September 22, 1965:

Liza Minnelli—Songs, Dances—55 minutes—Shoreham Blue Room

Liza Minnelli, who still has six months to go as a teenager, debuted as a nitery performer in Washington's posh Shoreham Hotel Blue Room with an act which is a gasser. It is knockout showmanship. The Tony Award winner is the hottest new entry for clubs in a long time.

Her songs, dances and patter are magnificently written and staged to make the most out of her remarkable talent and personality. She even has the capacity to evoke the emotional response in the league with her mother and Barbra Streisand. She can sing as well as either of them, if not better, and can dance like Cyd Charrise. The membership rolls of the Liza Minnelli cult are due for a fast rise.

She can put the full house opening night audience on its feet, which is very unusual in the huge, sophisticated Blue Room. She is one of only 2 or 3 performers who have received a standing ovation in Bernie Bralove's swankery on opening night in the last 15 years. As a footnote, her reaction to the demonstration displayed superb stage presence in an unexpected, unrehearsed situation. "Oh, I can't believe it," she cried out, "You're too good to me." The sincerity drove the crowd into louder applause.

With her diversified talents, she is a vibrantly exciting powerhouse of talent by herself.

night of Judy's engagement at the Sahara, singing "Side by Side" with Judy Garland.

Sahara Hotel, Congo Room, Las Vegas—December 26, 1965–January 24, 1966, Opening (Liza's first time in Vegas as a live act).

1966

Persian Room, Plaza Hotel, New York (Liza's first time in "New York, New York," as live solo act)—February 9–March 7, 1966.

Deauville Hotel, Miami Beach—March 12–22, 1966 (date most likely wrong—Liza was in NYC).

Melodyland Theater, Anaheim, California—March 22–27, 1966. Liza appeared as guest star on the bill of "The Don Adams Show," opening for the star of the *Get Smart* TV series.

Talk of the Town nightclub, London—May 1966.

Monte Carlo Festival—June 14, 1966. Liza was invited by Princess Grace to represent the U.S. Charles Aznavour wrote a song for Minnelli to perform.

Olympia Theater, Paris—June 15–28, 1966. Liza's first engagement at this historic hall, as part of their International Festival of Variety Shows.

Elmwood Casino, Windsor, Ontario—July 14–23, 1966.

Sahara Hotel, Congo Room, Las Vegas—September 13–October 9, 1966. Return engagement.

Canadian appearance, 1966.

1967

Sahara Hotel, Lake Tahoe, Nevada—May 3 (or 16)–June 5, 1967.

Summer tour of Australia, Hawaii, Rome, and Monaco, with Peter Allen. Venues included the Chequers Club in Sydney, Australia and the "New 20's Club" in Melbourne.

In October 1967, Liza signed a five-year contract to appear at the Sahara hotel in Las Vegas, for anywhere between four and eight weeks a year, leaving it to Liza how often and how long her engagements would be. Salary was reported as $22,000 for every week she performed. Universal had Minnelli cancel her November 14 opening, as they wanted her free for *Charlie Bubbles* film work, "press prem & publicity," although a definite release date for the film hadn't been set as of that time.

New York—December 10, 1967: Actor's Temple Benefit. Liza sang "The Happy Time"; "Mammy"; and "Liza with a 'Z.'"

New York—December 11, 1967: Liza sang at the Hal Prince Ball, and also at Senator Javit's Tribute Show.

Eden Roc Hotel, Miami—December 26, 1967–January 1, 1968

There were reportedly plans for Liza to play Washington, D.C., early in 1968, with her new act (featuring the "boys" she worked with from her old/first act), as well as an offer from Madison Square Garden.

1968

Empire Room, at the Waldorf-Astoria Hotel, New York—January 8–February 3, 1968; new act. (Shows were nightly at 9:30 and 11:45 PM—no shows on Sunday—with a $6.00 per person entertainment charge during the week, and $7.00 on weekends.) Liza made a generous offer through her fan club to pay the cover charge for fans wanting to see her perform.

Sahara Hotel, Las Vegas, March 1968

Auditorium, Chicago—March 1968 (best reviews of her career so far, reportedly).

Westchester County Center, Westchester, New York—May 21, 1968

Sahara Hotel, Las Vegas, July 1968.

1969

Deauville Hotel/Nightclub, Miami—March 26, 1969

The Sahara Hotel, Las Vegas—May–September 1969 (exact date unknown)

Olympia in Paris, return engagement—December 1969 (A&M album recorded and a TV special. Video of the special exists in private collections.)

1970

Empire Room at the Waldorf-Astoria, New York—Early 1970

Cocoanut Grove, Los Angeles—Opened June 29, 1970 (Monday, June 15 has also been noted as opening night.) (Return engagement)

The Cave Theater–Restaurant. Vancouver, British Columbia—October 8–17, 1970

Empire Room at the Waldorf-Astoria, New York—December 2–19, 1970; Liza also did a benefit closing night between shows, for Ed Sullivan, which was also at the Waldorf. At her final show, Liza duetted with Lorna on "Cabaret," and sang "You Made Me Love You."

1971

Playboy Club, Miami—January 12–24, 1971

Greek Theater, Los Angeles—September 20–26, 1971

Riviera Hotel, Las Vegas—October 5–25, 1971. The hotel's resident band leader was Liza's uncle Jack Cathcart, who had played for Judy, and who had been married to Judy's sister Suzie. During this engagement, Liza sang "Smile" one night with Johnny Ray. She also visited illusionist/impersonator Jim Bailey, who was performing in Vegas as Judy. Liza wound up singing with him. She would later perform an entire show in Vegas with Bailey as Garland in 1973. This was the first engagement in which the orchestra introduced her with the song "Cabaret" instead of using the Gershwin song "Liza." Minnelli decided this herself, just hours before opening night.

Harrah's Club, Lake Tahoe, Nevada—October 28–November 10, 1971

O'Keefe Centre, Toronto—November 15–20, 1971. First time at the O'Keefe.

Olympia Theater, Paris—December 7–28, 1971. Return engagement. Opening night performance was a benefit for the United Jewish Appeal.

1972

El San Juan Hotel, San Juan, Puerto Rico—January 13—25, 1972

Playboy Club, Miami—January 26–February 5, 1972 (Lorna joined her onstage for several duets, and was offered her own appearance at the club the following December).

Cruise to the island of Martinique, end of March 1972, for one week; Liza sang twenty minutes nightly on this ship for a fee, the only known time she has performed professionally on a cruise line.

Garden State Arts Center, Holmdel, New Jersey—August 28–September 2, 1972. Liza's first time at this venue; she would appear there frequently over the years (1981–96). Her "extra" songs included "Mr. Bojangles" and "Everybody Loves My Baby." [A]

Riviera Hotel, Las Vegas—Opened mid-October 1972. A new act, which she continued to perform through 1974, featuring the songs "Yes"; "God Bless the Child"; "Exactly Like Me" (a new Kander-Ebb special material piece about how so many women think they look like her); "It Was a Good Time"; "Moonlight Bay"/"Side by Side"; "Natural Man"; "Six Lessons from Madam La Zonga"; "A Quiet Thing"; "I Can See Clearly Now"; "Shine On Harvest Moon"; "Maybe This Time"; and "Cabaret."

Riviera Hotel, Las Vegas—December 1–14, 1972. Engagement with Joel Grey. The pair opened with three numbers, Grey did a fifteen-minute set, then Liza had her segment. The show closed with their "Cabaret" hits and their encore "For All We Know."

1973

CONCERN Benefit (Cancer research), January 20, 1973

Diplomat Hotel, Hollywood, Florida—February 8–18, 1973

Century Plaza, NARM Convention, Los Angeles—February 28, 1973. Liza performed for an hour, then was given a plaque in honor of her mother's music ("As long as music is heard in our land, she will never be forgotten."). Minnelli didn't know about the award, it was a complete surprise to her. She encored with "The Very Thought of You."

Rice Davis Benefit, Los Angeles—March 11, 1973

Maple Leaf Gardens, Toronto—March 29, 1973 (Liza had just won the Oscar two days earlier): Benefit for CARIH (Asthmatic Children's Hospital).

HIC Auditorium, Honolulu—April 21, 1973

London Palladium—May 11, 1973. *Liza with a Z* show, with additional numbers, including a medley of "Up on the Roof"/"Peaceful." (Audio exists of selections from Liza's act at this venue; although the recording may be a *Royal Command Performance* TV show with a possible date of 1972.)

Royal Festival Hall, London—May 12, 1973

Rainbow Theater, London—May 13, 1973 (Concert promoters had wanted Liza to play Earl's Court, but she looked at it and "said 'no' right away. It was just too huge.")

Arie Crown Theater, Chicago—May 30 and June 1, 1973

Cook County Jail and House of Corrections, Chicago—May 31, 1973. Liza sang for 3,000 inmates.

Civic Theater, Baltimore—June 22, 1973. Start of three-city tour. Liza laughed when she saw the marquee on the theater and wanted a photo of it; under her name it read: "Wrestling Sunday; Roller Games Wednesday." (This was a 6,000-seat venue.) Liza wore the yellow Halston outfit she wore when she won her Oscar that spring. Her program was: "Yes"; "Don't Let Me Be Lonely Tonight"; "Oh, Babe, What Would You Say?"; "I Can See Clearly Now"; "Shine On Harvest Moon"; "Liza with a 'Z'"; "Natural Man" (with the girls); "Ragtime"; "A Quiet Thing"; "Someone to Watch Over Me"; "It Was a Good Time"; "Mammy"; "Cabaret"; and "Ring Them Bells."

Convention Center, Indianapolis—June 23, 1973

Public Gardens, Cleveland—June 24, 1973

Harrah's, Lake Tahoe, Nevada—July 19–August 2, 1973

Riviera Hotel, Las Vegas—August 8–21, 1973

Greek Theater, Los Angeles—August 27–September 1, 1973

Liza then started a twenty-seven-city tour through the rest of the year, with fifty people in her group (musicians and other personnel) traveling on a rented plane. The show consisted of her *Liza with a "Z"* act, along with songs from *The Singer* album, including "I Don't Want To Be Lonely Tonight"):

Dane County Coliseum, Madison, Wisconsin—September 20, 1973

Municipal Auditorium, Kansas City, Kansas—September 21, 1973

Civic Arena, Pittsburgh—September 22, 1973

Kiel Auditorium, St. Louis—September 23, 1973

Baton Rouge—September 28, 1973

Civic Auditorium, Atlanta—September 29, 1973 [A]

Bay Front Arena, St. Petersburg, Florida—September 30, 1973

New Orleans—October 1, 1973

Veteran's Memorial Coliseum, New Haven, Connecticut—October 5, 1973

Providence, Rhode Island—October 6, 1973

Music Hall, Boston—October 7 or 8, 1973 (both dates have been noted)

Coliseum and Expo Center, Phoenix, Arizona—October 11, 1973

Moody Coliseum, Dallas, Texas—October 12, 1973

Oral Roberts University, Tulsa, Oklahoma—October 13, 1973

Arena, Oklahoma City, Oklahoma—October 14, 1973

(There was talk at this time of a concert in New York, at either the Met or Radio City Music Hall; Liza would play New York in January 1974, but at a smaller, Broadway theater.)

Rainbow Theater, London, England—mid-late October, 1973: Filming of "Love from A to Z" NBC-TV special with Aznavour

Rochester, New York—November 1, 1973

Buffalo, New York—November 2, 1973

Binghamton, New York—November 3, 1973

Hershey, Pennsylvania—November 4, 1973

Memphis, Tennessee—November 8, 1973

Nashville, Tennessee—November 9, 1973. Liza's first concert in Nashville.

Columbus, Ohio—November 10, 1973

Dayton, Ohio—November 11, 1973

Richmond, Virginia—November 15, 1973

Hampton Roads, Virginia—November 16, 1973

Tuscaloosa, Alabama—November 17, 1973

Charlotte, North Carolina—November 18, 1973

Kennedy Center, Washington, D.C.—November 19, 1973. Benefit for the National Ballet.

Versailles fashion show, Paris, France, November 23–26, 1973. Liza sang "Au Revoir, Paris" and "Bon jour Paris," with special lyrics by Kay Thompson.

Riviera Hotel, Las Vegas—November 30–December 6, 1973

At some point during 1973, Liza appeared at the Flamingo Hotel, Las Vegas, with Jim Bailey as Judy, reprising part of the Judy-Liza Palladium concert. This was a one-time event only, on a Saturday night (rehearsals were all day Saturday).

1974

Winter Garden Theater, New York—January 6–26, 1974 (Liza gave a special midnight performance Friday night, January 25, for the Actor's Fund. This performance was videotaped on black-and-white tape, shot with two cameras. The tape can be viewed at the Theatre on Film and Tape Archive, a

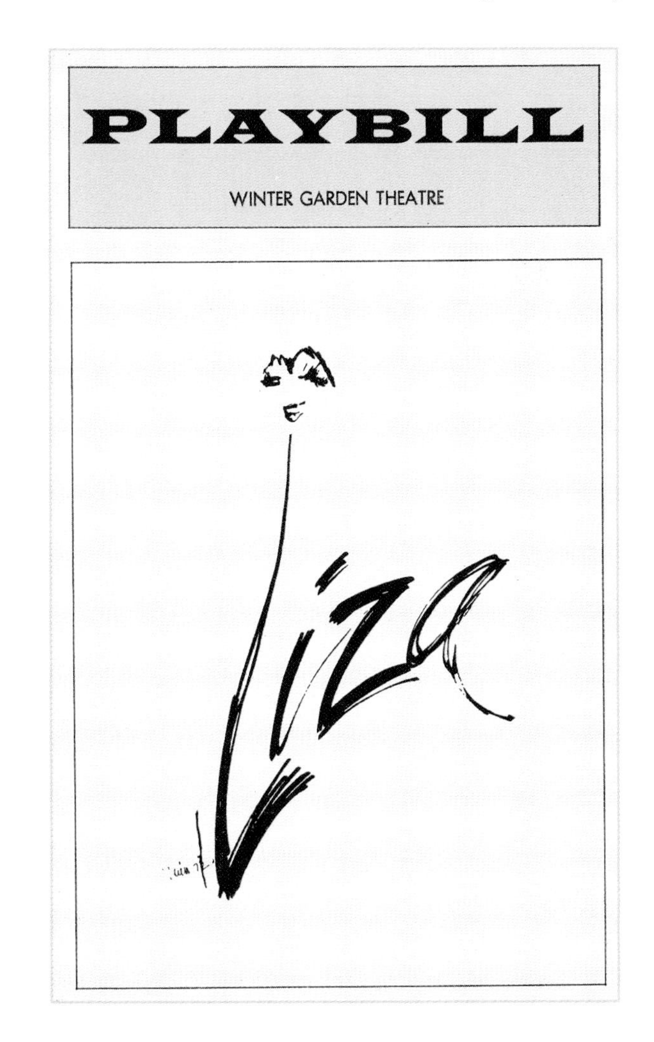

Liza onstage at the Winter Garden.

division of the New York Public Library for the Performing Arts in New York. The archive also has a fifty-minute talk with Liza and Kander and Ebb, videotaped on January 14, 1974. There were also two performances Saturday nights at 7:30 and 10:30, and two on Sundays, a matinee and an evening show.) Columbia Records recorded the show—known as *Liza*, then later *Liza at the Winter Garden*—for an LP. An audio tape made of a Saturday night performance exists. The January 25 performance was filmed and made part of the Stanley Prager Memorial Collection, part of Lincoln Center's Library. There were also silent color home movies made during this engagement that exist. Liza's songs for this engagement: "Yes"; "Meantime"; "Shine On Harvest Moon"; "Liza with a 'Z'"; "Exactly Like Me"; "If You Could Read My Mind"/"Come Back to Me"; "It Was a Good Time"; "I'm One of the Smart Ones"; "Natural Man"; "I Gotcha"; "Ring Them Bells" (Intermission); "Bye, Bye, Blackbird"; "A Quiet Thing"; "Anywhere You Are"/"I Believe You"; "There Is a Time"; "The Circle"; "I, in My Chair"; "Mammy"; "I Can See Clearly Now"; "Maybe This Time"; "Cabaret." ("You and I" had originally been the second song.) This engagement grossed a record $413,815, and Liza received a reported fee of $300,000. (The engagement completely sold out in 36 hours after the tickets went on sale—of course, the tickets had been printed as "Lisa," not Liza.)

"Liza makes it seem like it's summer again, and in every respect, Liza *is a winner. . . . Her vitality is unusual. . . . She has a voice that can purr, whisper, snarl, and roar. But why only three weeks, Miss Minnelli? Stay longer next time."* **—Clive Barnes, *New York Times*, review of *Liza at the Winter Garden***

Riviera Hotel, Las Vegas—January 30–February 12, 1974. Paul Williams opened her show. A song officially added to the act was "Meantime," from her first solo album, *Liza! Liza!* in 1964.

Nacional Hotel, Rio de Janiero engagement—February 16–23, 1974

Helio Isla Hotel, San Juan, Puerto Rico—February 28–March 6, 1974

Diplomat Hotel, Hollywood, Florida—March 8–18, 1974

Jim Stacy Benefit (with Sinatra, Sammy Davis Jr., and Connie Stevens) Los Angeles—March 24, 1974; Liza's songs: "Yes"; "I'm One of the Smart Ones"; "You're Nobody Till Somebody Loves You" (with Sammy); "Shine On Harvest Moon"; and "Don't Let Me Be Lonely Tonight."

Harrah's, Lake Tahoe, Nevada—April 5–18, 1974. (The night of the 15th was canceled when doctors refused to allow her on stage due to the flu.)

A.N.P.A. Benefit with Ed Sullivan, New York—April 23, 1974

Palace Theater, New York—May 9, 1974. Hemophilia and AMDA Benefit, honoring Jule Styne. Liza sang two of his songs: "Some People" and "I Guess I'll Hang My Tears Out to Dry."

White House Press Photograph Session—May 26, 1974

Riviera Hotel, Las Vegas—July 10–23, 1974

Great Allentown State Fair, Allentown, Pennsylvania—August 8–10, 1974. There were a total of six shows: Liza was the largest grossing single attraction in the Fair's history: $179,646 was the total gross for the six shows. (Color, silent home movies exist.)

August Beach Club, Marbella, Spain—August 15–17, 1974

Canadian National Exposition, Toronto—August 21, 1974

Minnesota State Fair, St. Paul, Minnesota—August 23, 1974

Iowa State Fair, Des Moines, Iowa—August 24, 1974

Indiana State Fair, Indianapolis—August 25, 1974

DuQuein State Fair, DuQuein, Illinois—August 26, 1974

Ohio State Fair, Columbus, Ohio—August 28, 1974

Spain—fall of 1974

Annual Thalian's Benefit Show, Los Angeles—October 1974

Riviera Hotel, Las Vegas—December 6–12, 1974 (fourteen shows)

1975

Overseas tour (Jack Haley Jr. had hoped to film the tour and present it as a TV documentary, but the filming has never been seen; Haley also shot footage on the set of Liza's *New York, New York* movie for a proposed documentary, which has also never been seen).

Congress Hall, Paris—January 4–5, 1975

100 Year Hall, Frankfurt—January 7, 1975

Stadhalle, Vienna—January 8, 1975 (sixty-six-minute show; Tickets $15 to $45)

Congress Center, Hamburg—January 9, 1975

Deutschlander, Berlin—January 10, 1975

Scandivanium, Goteborg, Sweden—January 11, 1975

Falkoner Hall, Copenhagen—January 13, 1975 (Tickets sold for $35.00 each and higher—the most expensive tickets for a performer Denmark had ever had up to that date; Lorna joined Liza onstage at this venue. This was where Judy Garland gave her last concert ever, on March 25, 1969. The venue was then known as Falkoner Centret. The top ticket price was $18 six years earlier. Jack Haley Jr. had captured this on film for his proposed TV special on this tour, but none of the footage is known to have surfaced, or even exists. Haley passed away in 2001.)

Madrid—January 15, 1975 ($50 top ticket price; Liza was paid $143,000 for the two shows she did that night.)

Barcelona—January 16, 1975

Nacional Hotel—January 31 and February 1, 1975

Rodeo Drive, Beverly Hills, California—May 25, 1975. CONCERN Cancer Charity Event. Liza and Lorna each performed at this event; Admission was from $100.00 up to $5,000 per person. $250,000 was raised.

CNE Grandstand Show headliner, Toronto—1975

1976

Lake Tahoe, Nevada—March 1976

Westchester Premiere Theater, Greenbrough, New York—April 15–24, 1976, with Marvin Hamlisch. Liza's songs included "Lucky Lady," and "Oscar" (with Marvin). Audio exists.

Shubert Theater, New York—May 2,1976. George Abbott eighty-eighth Birthday Tribute

The Forum, Los Angeles—October 2, 1976. Over 16,500 fans helped to raise money for this benefit concert for Permanent Charities; First noted public live performances of "But the World Goes 'Round," and "New York, New York." Other songs included "Lucky Lady," "There Goes the Ball Game," "My Man," and "I Am My Own Best Friend" from *Chicago*. Audio exists.

Riviera Hotel, Las Vegas—December 3–16, 1976. First solo "In Concert" show of Liza's career in Vegas, and first time the Rivera presented such a show without a star having dancers, etc. The final night, Liza also performed "My Ship" and "Some People" for Sammy Davis Jr's fifty-first birthday bash, then raced back to do her midnight show, and a 2:30 AM show for the gypsies (chorus people and dancers) on the strip. [A]

Diplomat Hotel, Miami Beach—December 31, 1976. Joint performance with Sammy Davis Jr. Tickets were from $100-$250 per person. [V]

1977

Harrah's, Lake Tahoe, Nevada—January 10–15, 1977

Latin Casino, Cherry Hill, New Jersey—January 17–27, 1977. Liza's orchestrations and costumes were lost in transit the first two nights of this week-long engagement. She went on wearing just jeans and a turtleneck, and with only the five musicians traveling with her (until the third night, when the charts and clothes were found; the additional musicians were then brought in). This was one of the first "live" engagements where Liza worked with drummer Bill LaVorgna, who had played on the *New York, New York* soundtrack. LaVorgna had worked with Judy Garland at Carnegie Hall, on her TV series, and other performances, possibly dating back to circa 1957, as Liza has said she knew Bill from the time she was eleven years old. The musician became like a true member of Liza's family—Minnelli even calls him "Pappy"—and Bill has remained with the star to this day. He served as her exclusive musical director and conductor from 1978 through the end of 1999 and retired early in 2000, but came back to work with the star as her drummer and musical conductor in 2002. Liza's songs of this tour (December 1976 through May 1977): Overture; "Lucky Lady"; "My Ship"/ "The Man I Love"; "Some People"; "Come In from the Rain"; "I'm One of the Smart Ones"; "My Own Best Friend"; "Hot"; "You're the Cream in My Coffee"; "And I in My Chair"; "Oscar" (with Fred Werner, her pianist); "But the World Goes 'Round"; "Cabaret"; "New York, New York." [A—1/17 or 1/18, and early show on 1/19]

Rio de Janeiro—February 11–24, 1977

Riviera Hotel, Las Vegas—March 3–9, 1977

Sunrise Musical Theater for the Performing Arts, Sunrise, Florida—March 14–20, 1977 (Prices were $12.75–$14.75)

Raleigh House Theater, Southfield, Detroit—March 23–25, 1977

Sabre Room, Hickory Hills, Chicago (1,400 seat nightclub)—March 26–28, 1977

Las Vegas—April 28–May 11, 1977. [A] [— Closing night, and also one night where Robert Goulet came onstage and duetted with Liza on "Birth of the Blues"; there is also an audio of closing night.]

1978

From September 1, 1978, through November 25, 1979, Liza performed the same two-act concert for this entire tour. (See the 1979 Carnegie Hall album for list of songs, page 144.) That album deleted only three of the show's songs: "Everybody Gets the Blues" (her second song); "Arthur in the Afternoon" (after "Come In from the Rain"); and "You Do Something to Me" (after "Arthur in the Afternoon").

Saratoga, New York—September 1, 1978

Blossom, Ohio—September 3, 1978

Merriweather Post, Maryland—September 6, 1978

Pine Knob, Michigan—September 11–14, 1978. During Pine Knob engagement, Liza sang "Suppertime" and "Don't Let Me Be Lonely Tonight" in her hotel lounge with a local band. [A]

O'Keefe Centre, Toronto—September 16 (or 18), 1978 [A]

Universal Amphitheater, Los Angeles—September 28–October 3, 1978. Liza encored with "My Mammy" on closing night. [A]

Lake Tahoe, Nevada—October 6–12, 1978

Pittsburgh—October 26–27, 1978 [A—closing night]

Syracuse, New York—November 3, 1978

Boston—November 4, 1978

Portland, Maine—November 5, 1978

Avery Fisher Hall, Lincoln Center, New York—November 12, 1978. Kander and Ebb Tribute: "Sing Happy." Liza sang: "Yes," "Liza with a 'Z'"; "Maybe This Time"; "Lucky Lady"; "A Quiet Thing"; "City Lights"; "Cabaret"; "Keeping It Hot" (with Chita Rivera and Gwen Verdon); "Pain" (with Chita and Gwen); "Finale." [A]

Copenhagen—November 15, 1978

Goteborg, Sweden—November 17, 1978

Stockholm—November 18, 1978

Hamburg—November 20, 1978

Dortmund, Germany—November 21, 1978

Zurich—November 23, 1978

Antwerp—November 25, 1978

Amsterdam—November 27, 1978

Munich—November 29, 1978

The London Palladium—December 4–9, 1978. Sammy Davis Jr. joined Liza for closing night, and they duetted on "Just in Time." Liza encored with "Maybe This Time." [A—closing]

Olympia Theatre, Paris—December 17–18, 1978. [A—closing]

1979

Rio de Janeiro—February 10–19, 1979

Lakeland Civic Center, Lakeland, Florida—March 15, 1979

Fox Theatre, Atlanta—March 17, 1979 [A—both the 7:30 P.M. and 11:00 PM shows]

Bay Front Civic Center, St. Petersburg, Florida—March 20, 1979

Theater of the Performing Arts, Miami Beach—March 22–April 1, 1979 (While in Miami Beach, Liza recorded "Song for You," I'm Glad There Is You," "My Buddy," "The Thought of You," "If I Love Again," "I Can't Give You Anything but Love," and "My Funny Valentine," in a local recording studio they'd rented, so that she could give the recordings as a birthday gift for Halston. They still exist.)

Ocean State Performing Arts Center, Providence, Rhode Island—April 20 and 21, 1979

Palace Theater, Cleveland, Ohio—April 24–29, 1979

Harrahs, Lake Tahoe, Nevada—May 2–10, 1979

Palace Theater, Cincinnati, Ohio—May 17–20, 1979 [A—last three nights]

Kiel Opera House, St. Louis, Missouri—May 22 and 23, 1979 [A—first show]

Music Hall, Dallas, Texas—June 5–10, 1979

Jones Hall, Houston, Texas—June 12–14, 1979

O'Keefe Center, Toronto—June 18–20, 1979

Place des Arts, Montreal, Quebec—June 22–24, 1979

Reiss-Davis Child Study Center Benefit, Beverly Hilton Hotel, Los Angeles—June 27, 1979

UNICEF Show, Berlin, Germany—August 23, 1979 (This was reportedly filmed for a UNICEF TV special, but is not known to have ever aired.)

Carnegie Hall, New York—September 4–14, 1979

2-LP set recorded, issued by Liza in 1981—see the listing for the Carnegie Hall album, page 144 for more info. Liza encored with "My Mammy" on closing night. [A—Opening; September 7; 8; and closing night] *Variety* stated:

"Minnelli is a vibrant, dynamic, potent entertainer, capable of bringing an audience to heights of appreciation it may not have really thought about. . . . She arrives at what, in her mid-30s, must be a high spot in her career. . . . She does most of the things one expects her to do, but she startles by doing them even better than can be recalled. . . . Minnelli brings it all home, punching, driving, singing, moving, carrying an audience with her to a bursting, rising tribute, which threatens to go on forever. . . . One knows that one has spent the evening in the presence of one of the best performers of our time." **(Meyr; 9/5/79)**

The *New York Times* said:

"Shifting from inner intensity to outward vocal power, but never losing the fine lines of her vocal control, never letting her belt shred into the shrill yell that is so apt to emerge in such situations. Miss Minnelli is very secure in her vocal movements and she can deliver, high or low, with gorgeous colors and fascinating textures along with her power. . . . It was a production in which every element

Liza's legendary first solo concert at Carnegie, featured her belting Broadway hit "City Lights."

was unusually strong, and each aspect came together in superb balance." **(John S. Wilson, 9/6/79)**

Arie Crown Theater, Chicago—October 4–7, 1979

Uihlein Hall, Milwaukee—October 9–11, 1979

Orpheum Theater, Minneapolis—October 13 and 14, 1979

Music Hall, Boston—October 18–20, 1979

Broome County Arena, Binghamton, New York—November 1, 1979 [A]

New Haven Coliseum, New Haven, Connecticut—November 3, 1979 [A]

Shubert Theater, Philadelphia—November 5–11, 1979 (Liza's first noted concert performance in Philadelphia.) [A—closing]

Kennedy Center, Washington, D.C.—November 13–18, 1979 [A—next-to-closing night]

Performing Arts Center, New Orleans—November 20–25, 1979 (Both shows on November 24 were videotaped by HBO, which aired the concert in 1980; ABC filmed closing night for their *20/20* series.)

1980

Wolf Trap, Virginia—June 3, 1980. Benefit. Liza's set included "Bobo's" from *The Act* and many other numbers, including "God Bless America" with the crowd at the end. [A]

September-October: Tour of "Liza Minnelli in Concert with Joel Grey." Set for October 1, 1980 through January 9, 1981. An April 3–May 1, 1981, tour of Australia set also. This tour was started, but then rescheduled for 1981 after the opening engagement in Massachusetts.

1981

March through September 4, 1981, with Joel Grey as Liza's opening act (rescheduled from the fall of 1980):

Shubert Theater, Philadelphia—March 16–22, 1981 (Start of tour). Liza's songs: "Yes"; "'But the World Goes 'Round"; "Some People"; "London Town"; "I'm One of the Smart Ones"; "(Theme from *Ice Castles*) Through the Eyes of Love"; "New York, New York"; "Cabin in the Sky" leading into "Showstopper" medley: "A Wonderful Guy"/"My Man"/"A Person Could Develop a Cold"/"Bewitched, Bothered, and Bewildered"/"Before the Parade Passes By"/"City Lights"/"The Man That Got Away" (Liza's first known performance of this song so identified with her mother)/"Showstopper Reprise"; "Money, Money" (with Joel Grey); "Cabaret"; "But We Will Always Think of You" (with Grey). [A—opening and the last two nights.]

Jack Lloyd wrote for the *Philadelphia Inquirer:*

"Miss Minnelli just kept stopping the show, cranking out the big songs with reckless abandon. She loved every minute of it, and so did the audience. There is a special bond between Liza Minnelli and her fans, you see. It is a passionate love affair."

Chateau de Ville, Framingham, Massachusetts—March 24–29, 1981

Bay Front Arena, St. Petersburg, Florida—April 1, 1981

Bob Carr Auditorium, Orlando, Florida—April 3 and 4, 1981

New Orleans Performing Arts, New Orleans—April 14–19, 1981

Fox Theater, Atlanta—April 21 and 22, 1981 [A—opening]

Palace Theater, Columbus, Ohio—April 24 and 25, 1981

Liza in Philly, March 1981.

The Garden, Louisville, Kentucky—April 27, 1981

Grand Ole Opry, Nashville—April 29, 1981 [A]

Executive Inn, Owensboro, Kentucky—May 15–16, 1981

Tulsa Ballet Theater, Tulsa, Oklahoma—May 18, 1981

Denver Auditorium, Denver—May 20–24, 1981

Greek Theater, Los Angeles—May 27–June 1, 1981

Riviera, Las Vegas—June 4–10, 1981

Warfield, San Francisco—June 13–17, 1981

Tarrant County Convention Center, Dallas/Forth Worth—June 20, 1981

University of Texas, Austin—June 21, 1981

Jones Hall, Houston—June 24–28, 1981

Garden State Arts Center, Holmdel, New Jersey—August 19 and 20, 1981. At this engagement, Liza added "Roses Turn," from *Gypsy*, to her act, for the first time. [A]

Saratoga Performing Arts, Saratoga, New York—August 23 and 24, 1981

Merriweather Post, Maryland—August 26 and 27, 1981

Poplar Creek, Illinois—August 29 and 30, 1981

Pine Knob, Michigan—September 1–4, 1981. Conclusion of tour with Joel Grey. All dates to follow in 1981 are solo concerts/performances, unless otherwise noted.

Festival Hall, Brisbane, Australia—September 11 and 12, 1981

Palais St. Kilda, Melbourne, Australia—September 14–20, 1981

Regent Theater, Sydney, Australia—September 22–30, 1981

Entertainment Center, Perth, Australia—October 2 and 3, 1981

Festival Theater, Adelaide, Australia—October 5–10, 1981

Sun Plaza, Tokyo—October 13–15, 1981

Sun Palace, Fukuoka, Japan—October 17, 1981

"Get a Feathered Hat for the Baby": Liza belts out her beloved "Some People" song, from *Gypsy*; Sydney, Australia, September 1981.

Kaikan, Kyoto, Japan—October 19, 1981

Shimin Kaikan, Nagoya, Japan—October 20, 1981

Festival Hall, Osaka, Japan—October 22 and 23, 1981

NHK, Tokyo—October 25, 1981

Kenmin Kaikan, Yokohama, Japan—October 26, 1981

Manila Hotel, Manila, Philippines—October 30–31, 1981

Blaisdell Center, Honolulu—November 4 and 5, 1981

Riviera Hotel, Las Vegas—December 3–12, 1981 ($30 minimum. Lorna sang "Happy Days/Get Happy" with Liza at one show). There was a midnight show and a special 3 AM show for Vegas gypsies, closing night. [A—12/12]

Flyer—signed by Peter Allen to me—to a December 27, 1981, Carnegie Hall benefit for the Tappan Zee Playhouse, that was canceled. It would have been a once-in-a-lifetime concert by this dynamic duo, who hadn't performed together since the late 1960s.

Diplomat Hotel, Hollywood, Florida—December 31, 1981 (Video of this show still exists in private collections)

1982

Carnegie Hall, New York, Tappan Zee Playhouse benefit—April 25, 1982. Liza's songs: "Arthur's Theme" accompanied by Dudley Moore on piano, sung as a duet; "Lucky Lady"; "Come Back to Me"; "Some People"; "Through the Eyes of Love"; "Rose's Turn"; "New York, New York." [A]

Ford Theater, Washington, D.C., Benefit—September 25, 1982. Liza's songs included "Yes." (Videotaped for TV; shown in 1983. See the entry for *The*

President's Command Performance on page 111 for more information.)

Sun City, South Africa—October 8–17, 1982. The *New York Post* stated on October 5 that Liza was "reportedly getting a cool million bucks for one week's work there." Minnelli's fall 1982 shows were very similar to her 1978–1979 shows, but added "Liza with a 'Z'"; "Through the Eyes of Love"; and "It Was a Good Time."

Via Reggio, Italy—October 23, 1982

Teatro Nuovo, Milan—October 24, 1982

San Remo, Italy—October 27 or 28, 1982

Bussaladomini, Via Reggio, Italy—October 29, 1982

Rome—October 30, 1982

Teatro Ariston, San Remo, Italy—October 31, 1982

Moulin Rouge, Paris—November 4, 1982. Liza was the first performer to appear solo at the legendary nightspot. A highlight of her two-and-a-half-hour show was "Shine On Harvest Moon," sung in French. (Clips from this performance were shown on ABC's *Good Morning America*; see page 111 for more information.)

Sunrise, Lauderhill, Florida—November 16–21, 1982

Centrum Stadium, Worcester, Massachusetts—November 26 and 27, 1982 (On the 27th Lorna sang "Get Happy"/"Happy Days Are Here Again"; Liza sang "New York, New York" *again*, after that.) [A]

Roy Thomson Hall, Toronto—December 4–7, 1982

Place des Arts, Montreal—December 16–19, 1982

Grand Hotel de L'Europe, Badgastein, Austria—December 31, 1982. Video of show shot with three cameras at dress rehearsal still exists. It was reported Liza was paid $300,000 for this one show. [V—show, and dress rehearsal]

1983

Chicago Theater, Chicago—February 16 and 17, 1983

Annenberg Theater, Palm Springs, California—February 19, 1983. Tribute to Vincente Minnelli; $1,000 a ticket.

Stehlin Foundation Benefit, Jones Hall, Houston—February 28, 1983

Chicago Theater, Chicago—March 4 and 5, 1983

Majestic Theater, Dallas—March 8–12, 1983 [A—3/9 show]

Symphony Hall, Phoenix—March 16–19, 1983

Universal Amphitheater, Los Angeles—April 7–10, 1983. New show, "By Myself" concert with two male dancers. This act included new material, such as: "The Sound of Your Name"; "Old Friends"; "Bilbao"/"September Song"; a revival of "All I Need Is the Boy" from Liza's very first act in 1965; "Through the Eyes of Love"; a revival of "God Bless the Child"; and a Vincente Minnelli tribute medley, during which Liza sang, for the first time, many of the songs she would sing in her 1999–2000 tribute concert to her father, *Minnelli on Minnelli*, such as "The Boy Next Door" and "The Trolley Song."

Paramount Theater, Seattle—April 16 and 17, 1983

Golden Gate Theater, San Francisco—April 23–May 1, 1983 [A]

Apollo Theater, London—May 16–June 8, 1983. "By Myself" show. [A]

New York, Tribute to Liz Smith—June 14, 1983. Liza with Liz and cast of *A Chorus Line* [V]

Garden State Arts Center, Holmdel, New Jersey—June 27–July 2, 1983. [A—opening]

At the end of July 1983, it was announced Liza would return to Carnegie Hall for another fourteen shows in September 1983 (she did fourteen concerts there in September 1979). The next day it was stated there wasn't enough time to make the arrangements for the engagement so quickly.

Wang Center, Boston—October 19–22, 1983

Palms State Theater, Detroit—October 31–November 3, 1983

Holiday Star Theater, Merrillville, Indiana—November 7–12, 1983

O'Keefe Center, Toronto—mid-late November, 1983

1984

No concerts in 1984; Liza was appearing in *The Rink* on Broadway

Shubert Theater, New York—April 29, 1984. Jule Styne Tribute. Styne introduced Liza, and she sang "Some People," "Rose's Turn" and "There's No Business Like Show Business." [A]

There were reports of a Liza-Sinatra concert in Central Park, which never happened.

1985

Carnegie Hall, New York—Monday, April 22, 1985, Annual New York Pops Concert. Liza's first official "live"/concert appearance since her stay at the Betty Ford Center the previous summer. Liz Smith introduced Minnelli, who sang "God Bless the Child," "Boys and Girls Like You and Me," and "New York, New York." [A]

Twenty-seven-city, six-month "Comeback" Tour (with "The Footlockers"). Program included such songs as "Pick Yourself Up"/"Blue Skies"/"I'm So Excited" as her opener; "Sad Songs"/"My Man"/"The Man I Love"; "I Don't Care Much"; "Girls Just Wanna Have Fun"/"Material Girl"; "London Town"; "Boys and Girls Like You and Me"; "I Love a Piano" (first time she sang this song in her act); "'But the World Goes 'Round." There was a dress rehearsal for the show on June 7, at the Edison Theater in New York, New York, for invited guests. Audio of that exists.

Paramount Theater, Seattle—June 18, 1985

Pavilion, Concord, California—June 25 and 26, 1985

Pacific Amphitheater, Costa Mesa, California—June 28 and 29, 1985

Denver—July 3, 1985

Starlight Theater, Kansas City, Missouri—July 5, 1985

V.P. Fair, St. Louis—July 6, 1985

Riverbend, Cincinnati—July 9 and 10, 1985

Hoffman Estates, Poplar Creek, Illinois—July 12 and 13, 1985

Pine Knob, Clarkston, Michigan—July 15 and 16, 1985

Kingswood, Toronto—July 18 and 19, 1985

Jones Beach State Theater, Wantagh, New York—July 26, 1985 [A]

Merriweather Post Pavilion, Columbia, Maryland—July 29–30, 1985

Performing Arts Center, Saratoga, New York—August 1 and 2, 1985

Finger Lakes, Rochester, New York—August 5 and 6, 1985

Garden States Arts Center, Holmdel, New Jersey—August 8–11, 1985 [A—August 10]

Worcester, Massachusetts—September 7, 1985

Kennedy Center, Washington, D.C.—September 10–15, 1985

Atlantic City, New Jersey—September 20 and 21, 1985. First known engagement there.

Fox Theater, Atlanta—September 26–October 2, 1985

St. Louis, Missouri—October 28–November 3, 1985

Jones Hall, Houston, Texas—November 5–7, 1985

Austin, Texas—November 9, 1985

Dallas, Texas—November 10, 1985

San Antonio, Texas—November 13, 1985

New Orleans—November 15–17, 1985

Pensacola, Florida—November 20, 1985

Tampa or Orlando, Florida—November 22, 1985

Sunrise, Florida—November 25–December 1, 1985

1986

London Palladium, March 7–23 (also noted as the 28th), 1986—Liza's 1985–1986 voice was possibly her best ever. Program of songs included "Opening Number Medley–With a Song in My Heart" (starting in the fall of 1986; before that it was "Pick Yourself Up"/"Blue Skies"/"I'm So Excited"); "Wherever He Ain't"; "I Don't Care Much"; "And I Couldn't Be Happier"; "My Own Best Friend"; "Here's to the Band"; "I Love a Piano"; and the expected hits, etc. (HBO videotaped during this engagement for broadcast that spring; See the entry on page 113 for more information.) [A—closing night]

The London Palladium / HBO concerts, March 1986. *Top:* Liza again sings her dynamic "Some People."

Other dates were Bournemouth, Brighton, Manchester, and Birmingham, March 25–30, 1986

Palais des Congrès, Paris—April 3, 1986

The Golden Nugget Opera House, Atlantic City, New Jersey—April 30–May 4, 1986. First known official performances with Frank Sinatra. $75.00 per person admission. [A]

Harrah's, Lake Tahoe, Nevada—May 9–12, 1986

Civic Center, Des Moines, Iowa—May 15–17, 1986

Wolf Trap, Virginia—May 28, 1986

Carlton Club, Minneapolis—May 30–June 2, 1986

River Hall, Milwaukee—June 5 and 6, 1986

Heinz Hall, Pittsburgh—June 11–14, 1986

Starlite, Indianapolis—June 18–22, 1986

July 4th / Liberty Weekend, Giants Stadium, 1986. Liza sang "New York, New York." (Broadcast on ABC-TV special)

Oakdale Music Theater, Wallingford, Connecticut—September 3–7, 1986 [A]

Golden Nugget, Opera House, Atlantic City, New Jersey—September 11–14, 1986

Westbury Music Fair, Westbury, New York—September 17–21, 1986. First concert engagement at this venue. Liza appeared there in 1966 in *Pajama Game*, and again in 1967 on Judy's opening night.

Valley Forge Music Fair, Devon, Pennsylvania—September 24–28, 1986. First concert engagement at this venue, although Liza also appeared there in 1966 in *Pajama Game*. [A—9/25 show]

1987

Academy of Music, Philadelphia—March 1, 1987. Benefit for the Institutes for the Achievement of Human Potential, Liza's main charity, located in Pennsylvania.

The White House, Washington, D.C.—March 8, 1987. Taping of PBS show, tribute to Rodgers and Hart. (Aired March 25, 1987, on PBS)

Owens Auditorium, Charlotte, North Carolina—March 17, 1987

Sunrise Musical Theater, Sunrise, Florida—March 19–23, 1987

Symphony Hall, Phoenix, Arizona—March 26–28, 1987

Friars Club Roast, Los Angeles—April 5, 1987

Ruth Eckerd Hall, Clearwater, Florida—April 13–16, 1987

Los Angeles—April–May 1987: "Happy Birthday, Hollywood" videotaping for ABC-TV special.

Pierre Hotel, New York—May 12, 1987

Carnegie Hall, New York—May 28–June 18, 1987. Shows from May 28–30; June 2–6; June 9–13; and June 16–18. (See the entry for *Liza Minnelli at Carnegie Hall*, page 146, for the entire program of songs.) On closing night, Liza encored with "He's Funny That Way" and "Shine On Harvest Moon." Liza toured many other venues with the same show. [A—at least two performances, including closing night]

Publicity photo for Liza's "3 Weeks at Carnegie Hall" 1987 concert (and tour).
Opposite: "Live" shot onstage at Carnegie Hall.

"If the electricity and power at Carnegie Hall for Liza Minnelli's homecoming could have been harnessed, there would be no worry for years about a power shortage. If the love flowing from the audience toward the stage and the heroine restored could be packaged, world peace would be assured. . . . Minnelli could do no wrong. . . . Never overdoing, always maintaining a classy sense of balance and, maybe most important, always in total control." **—*Variety*, June 3, 1987**

"The millions of dollars spent on renovating Carnegie Hall were almost nullified when Liza Minnelli appeared onstage before a forty-six-piece orchestra and practically demolished the rafters, the balconies, the ushers, the paying customers and anything/anyone else within earshot of her voice. Her stunning performance alone could have done it. . . . It was the quintessential concert performance; one female singer at the peak of her vocal powers singing some of the finest popular songs ever written." **—*Hollywood Reporter*, June 2, 1987**

"Liza is the greatest . . . [She has a] face you'd give your last penny to. . . . The audience that was eating out of her hand had a small banquet." **—Clive Barnes, *New York Post***

"Stunning! Liza underscored a sharpened sense of artistic and personal identity that was apparent from the moment she arrived on stage. Her songs were accompanied by a decisive, powerfully illustrative gesticulation . . . and her voice has never sounded stronger and surer." **—Stephen Holden, *New York Times***

"A night of such pure pleasure and excitement that I will never forget the privilege of it all. Liza not only sings but acts, in what has to be the most effective naturalistic manner of any performer alive." **—Liz Smith, syndicated columnist**

Performing Arts Center, Saratoga, New York—August 9, 1987

Great Woods, Mansfield, Massachusetts—August 11, 1987

Garden State Arts Center, Holmdel, New Jersey—August 13–16, 1987

Concord Pavilion, Concord, California—August 18–19, 1987

Pacific Amphitheater, Costa Mesa, California—August 22, 1987

Riverbend, Cincinnati, Ohio—August 24, 1987

Blossom Music Theater, Cleveland, Ohio—August 26, 1987

Pine Knob, Clarkston, Michigan—August 28, 1987

Poplar Creek, Hoffman Estates, Illinois—August 29, 1987

Merriweather Post, Columbia, Maryland—September 1, 1987

Golden Nugget Casino, Atlantic City, New Jersey—September 3–6, 1987

Ice Hockey Stadium, Stockholm—October 16, 1987

Scandinavium, Goteborg, Sweden—October 17, 1987

Borsen, Stockholm—October 19, 1987

Olympia Halle, Munich—October 23, 1987

Stadt Halle, Vienna—October 27, 1987

Schleyer Halle, Stuttgart, Germany—October 29, 1987

Westfalen, Dortmund, Germany—October 31, 1987

Kuppelsall, Hanover, Germany—November 1, 1987

Festhalle, Frankfurt, Germany—November 3, 1987

Operahaus, Berlin—November 5 and 6, 1987

C.C.H. Congress Center, Hamburg, Germany—November 8, 1987

Philips Halle, Duesseldorf, Germany—November 10, 1987

Royal Albert Hall, London—November 15–17, 1987

Meadowlands Arena, East Rutherford, New Jersey—December 4–5, 1987. With Frank Sinatra. Sinatra's musical arrangements were missing on the 4th, so that show was canceled. (Bootleg CD released of moments from the December 5 performance, from tapes made through the sound system.) [A—entire show]

Golden Nugget, Atlantic City, New Jersey—December 11–13, 1987. With Sinatra.

Harrah's, Lake Tahoe, Nevada—December 31, 1987

1988

Wang Center, Boston—April 29, 1988. Benefit for the National Kidney Foundation of Massachusetts. Liza headlined a bill that included Ben Vereen, and the Radio City Music Hall Rockettes making their Boston stage debut.

Trump Plaza, Atlantic City, New Jersey—May 5–8, 1988. Same weekend Lorna was playing in A.C. at Trump's Castle, another Donald Trump Hotel. They caught each other's acts.

Trump Plaza, Atlantic City, New Jersey—September 8–11, 1988

September 1988: "Ultimate Event" Tour—with Frank Sinatra, Sammy Davis Jr., and Liza—began. *Note*: You will see many Ultimate Event concerts from fall of 1988 through July 1990 listed as "UE." Other concerts listed are solo, unless otherwise noted:

The Summit, Houston, Texas—September 17, 1988 (UE)

Arizona St., Phoenix, Arizona—September 18, 1988 (UE)

The Omni, Atlanta—September 22, 1988 (UE)

Miami Arena, Miami—September 24, 1988 (UE)

Publicity portrait for the "Ultimate Event" concert tour with Frank and Sammy.

Sundome, Tampa, Florida—September 25, 1988 (UE)

Spectrum, Philadelphia—September 27 and 28, 1988 (UE) [V]

Bryne Arena, Secaucus, New Jersey—September 30 and October 1, 1988 (UE)

Nassau Coliseum, Uniondale, New York—October 3, 1988 (UE)

Centrum, Worcester, Massachusetts—October 6 and 7, 1988 (UE)

Summit, Houston, Texas—October 9, 1988 (UE)

Riviera Hotel, Las Vegas—November 17–20, 1988 (Solo) [A—11/18 show]

LA Forum, Los Angeles—November 26, 1988. With Frank and Sammy; Benefit for Barbara Sinatra Child Abuse Center

Fox Theater, Detroit—November 30–December 4, 1988. (UE) The shows were videotaped in Detroit for Showtime TV special/Kodak Home Video.

Trump Plaza, Atlantic City, New Jersey—December 8–11, 1988 (solo)

Milan, Italy—December 15, 1988

Waikiki Sheraton, Waikiki, Hawaii—December 29, 1988 (solo)

Hyatt Waikoloa, Honolulu—December 31, 1988 (solo)

1989

"Ultimate Event" Tour continued:

Reunion Arena, Dallas—January 17, 1989 (UE)

Miami Arena, Miami—January 20–21, 1989 (UE)

Betty Ford Center Benefit, Palm Springs, California—January 28, 1989 (solo)

Academy of Music, Philadelphia. Institutes for the Achievement of Human Potential, Benefit concert (Liza, with special guest Marvin Hamlisch)—Sunday, February 5th, 1989

Castle Hall, Osaka, Japan—February 23, 1989 (UE)

Tokyo Bay N.K Hall, Tokyo—February 25, 1989 (UE) (Bootleg CD released from this date, seemingly derived from a TV airing in Tokyo.)

National Tennis Center, Melbourne, Australia—February 28, and again on March 1, 1989 (UE)

Sydney Entertainment Center, Sydney, Australia—March 3 and 4, 1989 (UE) [A—opening night]

Blaisdell Arena, Honolulu—March 7 and 8, 1989 (UE)

Trump Plaza, Atlantic City, New Jersey—March 16–19, 1989 (solo)

Palace Trussardi, Milan, Italy—April 6, 1989 (UE)

Rotterdam, Holland—April 8, 1989 (UE) [A]

Ekasbas Hall, Oslo, Norway—April 13, 1989 (UE)

Scandinavium, Goteborg, Sweden—April 15, 1989 (UE) [A]

K.B. Hall, Copenhagen—April 16, 1989 (UE)

Royal Albert Hall, London—April 18–22,1989 (UE). Liza recorded *Results* album at night during this engagement. [A—closing night]

Paris Opera House, Paris—April 24 and 25, 1989 (UE)

Vienna—April 27, 1989 (UE)

Amsterdam—April 28, 1989 (UE) [A]

Munich—April 29, 1989 (UE) [A]

Dublin—May 3 and 4, 1989 (UE)

Radio City Music Hall, New York—May 1, 1989. Songwriters Hall of Fame 20th Anniversary. Videotaped for TV special; aired June 22, 1989.

Riviera Hotel, Las Vegas—May 18–21, 1989 (solo)

San Jose, California—Hospital Benefit, May 24, 1989

Monte Carlo, Red Cross Gala (with Sammy Davis, Jr.)—August 4, 1989

Perelada Castle and Casino, Bacelona, (with Sammy)—August 6, 1989

Riviera Hotel, Las Vegas—August 10–13th, 1989 (solo)

Reunion Arena, Dallas—August 24, 1989 (UE)

Garden State Arts Center, Holmdel, New Jersey—August 26, 1989 (UE) [A]

Trump Plaza, Atlantic City, New Jersey—September 7–10, 1989 (solo)

Reunion Arena, Dallas—September 20, 1989 (UE)

Bally's Hotel, Reno, Nevada—September 21–24th, 1989 (solo)

Reunion Arena, Dallas—September 27, 1989 (UE)

Skydome, Toronto, Ontario—October 2, 1989 (UE)

Capital Center, Landover, Maryland—October 5, 1989 (UE)

Charlotte, North Carolina—October 6, 1989 (UE)

Radio City Music Hall, New York—October 23, 1989 (Benefit)

Extensive Tour of Europe (to promote *Results* album)—November 1989

Riviera Hotel, Las Vegas—November 30–December 3, 1989 (solo)

Trump Plaza, Atlantic City, New Jersey—December 7–10, 1989 (solo)

1990

Drama League Benefit, New York—February 1, 1990. Tribute to Jule Styne. Liza sang "If Mama Were Married" with her sister Lorna Luft, then performed a solo of "Some People."

Europe; promotional tour for "Love Pains" single from *Results* album—February 1990

Sunrise Theater, Sunrise, Florida—March 14–18th, with Ben Vereen. Liza sang "Losing My Mind" and "Love Pains," both from the *Results* album; she encored on "Birth of the Blues," dedicating it to Sammy Davis. (Davis was battling cancer, and would die two months later, on May 16, 1990.) [A—3/14 and 3/16 shows]

Charlotte Coliseum, Charlotte, North Carolina—March 24, 1990 (UE; All following *Ultimate Event* concerts were with Liza and Sinatra only, as Sammy Davis Jr.'s illness kept him from the tour, which concluded a few months later, on July 1, 1990.)

Thompson Hall, Toronto—April 6, 1990 (Benefit)

Riviera Hotel, Las Vegas—April 19–22, 1990 (solo)

Benefit for the Betty Clooney Foundation for brain-injured people—April 24, 1990. Among Liza's songs was "Kiss of the Spider Woman."

Bally's Hotel and Casino, Reno, Nevada—April 26–29, 1990 (solo)

Harrah's, Lake Tahoe, Nevada—June 1–3, 1990 (solo)

Sands Hotel, Atlantic City, New Jersey—June 8–10, 1990 (solo). Liza's songs: "Yes"; "God Bless the Child"; "Old Friend"; "I Don't Want to Know"; "My Own Best Friend"; "Some People"; "Tall in the Saddle"; "Crying"; "Ring Them Bells"; "Losing My Mind"; "He's Funny That Way"; "Kander and Ebb Medley"; "Cabaret" intro/"Liza with a 'Z'"/"Mein Herr"/"Married"/"Money, Money"/"The World Goes 'Round"/"New York, New York." [A—6/9 show]

Hamburg or Berlin—June 21, 1990 (UE)

Brussels—June 23, 1990 (UE)

Zurich—June 24, 1990 (UE)

Tel Aviv—June 27, 1990 (UE)

Barcelona or Seville—June 30, 1990 (UE)

Madrid—July 1, 1990 (UE)

Riviera Hotel, Las Vegas—July 12–15, 1990 (solo) [A—7/13 show]

"Stepping Out for Starlight"—October 12, 1990. The final scenes of *Stepping Out* were filmed in front of an audience as a benefit for the Starlight Foundation (which grants wishes for terminally ill patients). Liza sang "Stepping Out," and also performed "Sara Lee," and "But the World Goes 'Round."

Riveria Hotel, Las Vegas—Weekend of November 30, 1990. [A—11/30, 11 PM show]

1991

Las Vegas—January 24–27, 1991

Drama League Benefit, New York—February 4, 1991. Tribute to Kander and Ebb. Liza sang "Lucky Lady" "But the World Goes 'Round," "Stepping Out" (first official concert/public performance of the title song from her new film), and "New York, New York" (reprise) with Fred Ebb (and John Kander at the piano).

Sands Hotel, Atlantic City, New Jersey—March 22–24, 1991

Radio City Music Hall, New York—April 23–May 12, 1991. "Liza Stepping Out at Radio City Music Hall." *Amusement Business* magazine announced at the end of 1991 that Liza's engagement at Radio City was the largest-grossing stand of the year—$3.8 million. *Newsday* called the show "a triumph!," and it *was* a complete triumph, artistically and commercially. Another monumental Minnelli moment in her career. (One of the songs not on the released video or CD—made a year later during Liza's return engagement—is "What Makes a Man a Man" by Aznavour, about a drag queen who lives with his mother.) [A—at least three shows, including opening, 5/9, and closing night]

The above Radio City show toured:

Cleveland, Ohio—June 6–9, 1991. In Cleveland, Liza sang a new arrangement of "Sing Happy," from *Flora*. [A—6/7, 6/8 and closing]

Blockbuster Pavilion Charlotte, North Carolina—July 16, 1991

Deer Creek Center, Indianapolis—July 18, 1991

Marcus Amphitheater, Milwaukee—July 20, 1991

Poplar Creek, Chicago—July 21, 1991

Chastain Park, Atlanta—July 23, 1991

Starwood Amphitheater, Nashville—July 25, 1991

The 1991 Radio City Music Hall show.

Starplex Amphitheater, Dallas—July 27, 1991

Woodlands Pavilion, Houston—July 28, 1991 [A]

Riverport Arts Center, St. Louis, Missouri—July 31, 1991

Merriweather Post, Baltimore—August 2, 1991. Liza added "Crying" to this show. [A]

Starlake Amphitheater, Pittsburgh—August 4, 1991

Capital Music Center, Columbus, Ohio—August 6, 1991

Riverbend Amphitheater, Cincinnati, Ohio—August 7, 1991

Lake Compounce, Bristol, Connecticut—August 9, 1991

Performing Arts Center, Saratoga, New York—August 11, 1991

Greek Theater, Los Angeles—August 30 and 31, 1991 [A—8/30 show]

Pacific Amphitheater, Costa Mesa, California—September 1, 1991

Riviera Hotel, Las Vegas—September 5–8, 1991 [A—9/7 show]

Sands Hotel, Atlantic City, New Jersey—September 27–29, 1991 [A—9/28 show]

Hollywood Walk of Fame—September 30, 1991. Liza received a star on the famed street, outside the Hollywood Roosevelt Hotel. The $4,800 fee to cover the costs of the star was raised mostly by Liza's fan club, with some final assist by Paramount Pictures. (Liza had flown in from Atlantic City the middle of Sunday night / Monday morning, after working there the previous weekend.) That day was proclaimed "Liza Minnelli Day" in the city of Los Angeles.

Stockholm—October 5, 1991

Turku, Finland—October 7, 1991

Copenhagen—October 9, 1991

Anvers, Belgium—October 11, 1991

Rotterdam, Holland—October 12, 1991

Frankfurt, Germany—October 16, 1991

Dusseldorf, Germany—October 18, 1991

Zurich, Switzerland—October 20, 1991

Berlin—October 22, 1991

Hamburg—October 24, 1991

Munich—October 26th, 1991

Royal Albert Hall, London—October 30 and 31, 1991 [A—10/30 show]

Dublin—November 2 and 3, 1991

Bari, Italy—November 8, 1991

Rome—November 9, 1991

Ravena, Italy—November 11, 1991

Florence—November 12, 1991

Genoa or Turin, Italy—November 14, 1991

Milan—November 16, 1991

Palais des Congrès, Paris, with Charles Aznavour: November 20, 22, 24, 26–30; December 1–15, 1991 (A CD and DVD were recorded during this engagement.)

Caesar's Palace, Las Vegas—December 28–31, 1991

1992

Radio City Music Hall, New York—January 24–February 2, 1992. Return engagement. A high-definition videotape was shot during this week; a CD and VHS/laser disc were released by Sony (Columbia Records) called *Liza Live at Radio City Music Hall.* [A—1/31 show]

Desert Inn, Las Vegas—March 11–15, 1992 [A—3/12 show]

Sands Hotel, Atlantic City, New Jersey—April 10–12, 1992 [A—closing]

Wembly Stadium, London—April 20, 1992. Freddie Mercury Tribute. Liza closed the show with "We Are the Champions" (Released on VHS/laser disc/DVD.)

Riviera Hotel, Las Vegas—May 14–17, 1992

Desert Inn, Las Vegas—June 3–7, 1992

Royal Albert Hall, London—June 23, 1992. Tribute to Sammy Davis Jr. Videotaped for British TV. Video survives.

UNICEF benefit, Miami,—Summer 1992.

Sands Hotel, Atlantic City, New Jersey—August 13–16, 1992

Garden State Arts Center, Holmdel, New Jersey—August 28–29, 1992 [A—closing]

Jones Beach, New York—August 30, 1992. Audio exists.

Desert Inn, Las Vegas—September 2–6, 1992

Symphony Hall, Boston—September 23–27, 1992 [A—opening]

Shea's Buffalo, Buffalo, New York—October 1–4, 1992

New York—October 5, 1992. "Save 890 Broadway" benefit with Liza, to save the rehearsal complex where Michael Bennett (*A Chorus Line*) worked.

City of Angels Hospice, Hollywood, California—Saturday, October 17, 1992

Circle Star Theater, San Carlos, California—October 21–25, 1992

Desert Inn, Las Vegas—October 28–November 1, 1992 [A—Closing, 9 PM show]

Fox Theater, Detroit—November 11–15, 1992. Liza sang "Yes I Can" (opener); "All the Lives of Me" by Peter Allen—who had recently passed away—leading into "But the World Goes 'Round," which she would repeat during 1993 dates, and on her 1996 tour. [A—all shows]

Universal Amphitheater, Los Angeles—November 18, 1992. AIDS Project Los Angeles 6th annual Commitment to Life. Liza sang; as did Streisand. [A]

Performing Arts Center, Providence, Rhode Island—November 19–22, 1992

Desert Inn, Las Vegas—December 30–31, 1992; January 1–3. 1993

1993

Stamford Performing Arts Center, Stamford, Connecticut—January 9, 1993

Pasadena Civic Center, Pasadena, California—January 29, 1993 [A]

Desert Inn, Las Vegas—February 3–7, 1993

Maxwell King Center, Melbourne, Florida—February 13, 1993

Harborside Convention Center, Ft. Meyers, Florida—February 14 and 15, 1993

Peabody Auditorium, Daytona Beach, Florida—February 17 and 18, 1993

Ruth Eckerd Hall, Clearwater, Florida—February 20 and 21, 1993

Van Wezel Performing Arts Center, Sarasota, Florida—February 22 and 23, 1993

Broward Performing Arts Center, Ft. Lauderdale, Florida—February 25–28, 1993. Liza was still doing mostly the material from her Radio City show/tour, along with "Cryin'," and the "All the Lives of Me"/"But the World Goes 'Round" medley. [V] [A—opening, closing]

Kravitz Center, West Palm Beach, Florida—March 2–4, 1993

Sands Hotel, Atlantic City, New Jersey—March 19–21, 1993

Desert Inn, Las Vegas—April 7–11, 1993

Chicago Opera House, Chicago—April 13–18, 1993 [A—4/16–4/18 shows]

Orange County Performing Arts Center, Costa Mesa, California—May 19–27, 1993

Around this time (May 1993) there had been talk of Liza appearing in concert at The Met in 1995. This did not happen. Minnelli has not concertized at that great landmark to date, although she appeared with the Martha Graham Dance Company in *The Owl and the Pussycat* at the Met in 1978 and 1980.

Carnegie Hall, New York—June 1–5, 1993. Joint concert with Charles Aznavour. Liza did three additional dates with Aznavour. [A—closing]

O'Keefe Center, Toronto—June 9–13, 1993. With Aznavour. [A—closing]

Warner Theater, Washington, D.C.—June 16–20, 1993. With Aznavour.

Place des Arts, Montreal—June 23–28, 1993. With Aznavour.

Sands Hotel, Atlantic City, New Jersey—July 8–11, 1993 [A—7/10 show]

Desert Inn, Las Vegas—August 3–8, 1993. During this engagement, Liza did a sexy song and dance routine to "I've Got Your Number," with Billy Stritch accompanying her on piano.

Luna Park, Buenos Aires—August 18–22, 1993. Songs included "Cryin'," "Lover Man/The Man I Love," "Ring Them Bells," "Sailor Boys," the complete Kander and Ebb medley, and "The Day After That." Video exists.

Olympia Theater, Saõ Palo—August 24 and 25, 1993

Municipal Theater, Rio de Janeiro—August 27 and 28, 1993

Liza signed with Krost/Chapin Management, Inc. with Barry Krost as her manager in September 1993, with a focus on films.

Children with AIDS Charity Softball Game, Passaic, New Jersey—Saturday, October 3, 1993

Desert Inn, Las Vegas—October 5–10, 1993 [A—10/9 show]

Abravanel Hall, Salt Lake City—October 13 and 14, 1993 [A—closing]

Fair Grounds, Minot, North Dakota—October 16, 1993

Ak-Sar-Ben Coliseum Arena, Omaha, Nebraska—October 18 and 19, 1993 (Liza's first appearance in Nebraska.) The governor of Nebraska awarded Liza the title of admiral in the Nebraska navy. [A—opening]

Washington, D.C.—October 23, 1993. Ceremonies in honor of the bicentennial of the Capitol Building and the return of the Statue of Freedom to the top of its dome. Liza sang "America, the Beautiful."

Royal Albert Hall, London—November 4–5, 1993

A European concert tour—Germany—with Ray Charles and Shirley Bassey, November 1993. Shirley opened the show, then Ray performed, and then Liza. There were no duets:

Utrecht, Holland—November 6, 1993

Grugahalle, Essen, Germany—November 8, 1993 [A]

Festhalle, Frankfurt—November 9, 1993

Deutschlandhalle, Berlin—November 10, 1993

Olympiahalle, Munich—November 12, 1993

Baltimore—November 21, 1993. AIDS Benefit. [A]

United Nations, New York—December 1, 1993. Liza sang "The Day After That," in honor of the first annual World AIDS Day.

Sidewalk of Stars, Radio City Music Hall, New York—December 14, 1993. Liza was the first to be awarded a star.

The Meadowlands, East Rutherford, New Jersey—December 31, 1993. Joint concert with Frank Sinatra.

1994

Roundabout Theater, New York—January 17, 1994. Benefit for the Singer's Forum.

AIDS Project Los Angeles—January 27, 1994. Liza sang "The Day After That."

MGM Grand, Las Vegas—February 17–20, 1994 [A—opening]

Bob Hope Theater, Palm Desert, California—February 23–27, 1994

Bally's Grand, Atlantic City, New Jersey—March 4–6th, 1994. Liza's first engagement at Bally's, as part of a long-standing contract; the first year was reported as "at least $75,000 per show, for a total of $675,000 for 1994." [A—all three nights]

McCallum Theater, Palm Springs, California—Early March, 1994

Arena Theater, Houston—March 19, 1994. AmFAR AIDS Benefit.

Auditorio Nacional, Mexico City—March 24–27, 1994

Rainbow Room, New York—May 10, 1994. Liza sang at the Martha Graham Centennial Benefit.

MGM Grand Hotel, Las Vegas—May 19–21, 1994

New York—May 22, 1994. Theater Development Fund/Hal Prince Tribute.

Plaza Hotel, New York—May 24, 1994. Benefit for the Foundation of Neurosurgical Research.

Paramount Arts Center, Aurora, Illinois—May 26–28, 1994 [A—all three shows]

Grugahalle, Essen, Germany—June 3, 1994

Rossia Hall, Moscow—June 6 and 7, 1994

Essen, Germany—June 8, 1994. Private event, for which Liza was reported to have been paid $500,000. She did the show despite dislocating her hip in a fall, two hours before the show.

Turkey—June 10, 1994

World Cup, Chicago—June 17, 1994

The Mark, Moline, Illinois—June 19, 1994 [A]

Meadowlands Arena, New Jersey, World Cup—June 24, 1994

Gay Pride, New York—Sunday, June 26, 1994. Liza sang "The Day After That" to over half a million people gathered in Central Park. This performance is available on VHS from Stonewall 25. (See this book's Appendix for listings of videos and DVDs available for sale.) It had been thirty-one years since Minnelli sang in Central Park—see the entry for May 25, 1963, page 160–61 for more info.

Harbor Lights Pavilion, Boston—June 30–July 1, 1994. Liza sang "Lucky Lady," and "The Man That Got Away" at this concert. They were not an official part of her program at this time, although she did sing "Lady" in her 1977 shows, and "Man" during her 1981 tour. [A—both shows]

Tanglewood Festival, Tanglewood, Massachusetts—July 2, 1994

Oakdale Theater, Wallingford, Connecticut—July 5, 1994

Warwick Music Theater, Warwick, Connecticut—July 6, 1994

Starlite Music Theater, Latham, New York—July 8, 1994 [A]

Lake George, New York—July 9, 1994. Convention for Pepsi-Cola employees, closed event. (It's been rumored Liza receives in the area of $250,000 for every private/cooperate event/convention appearance.)

Bally's Grand, Atlantic City, New Jersey—July 15–17, 1994 [A—opening]

Chastain Park, Atlanta—August 14, 1994 [A]

Merriweather Post, Baltimore—August 16, 1994 [A]

Riverbend, Cincinnati, Ohio—August 18, 1994 [A]

Polaris Amphitheater, Columbus, Ohio—August 19, 1994 [A]

Poplar Creek, Chicago—August 21, 1994

Festival Theater, Stratford, Ontario—September 12, 1994. Benefit for the Stratford Festival.

Center for Performing Arts, Anchorage, Alaska—September 15–17, 1994

Opera House, Seattle—September 20–21, 1994. Liza sang "Just in Time" as a tribute to Jule Styne, who had recently passed away. [A—both shows]

Queen Elizabeth Theater, Vancouver, B.C., Canada—September 23–25, 1994.

Bally's Grand, Atlantic City, New Jersey—September 30–October 2, 1994. Liza's new songs: "Yes I Can"; "Blues in the Night," and in the lounge after one show, she sang "Love for Sale," and "The Man I Love." [A—opening and closing]

La Jolla Playhouse, La Jolla, California—October 6, 1994

Century Plaza Hotel, Los Angeles—Saturday, October 8, 1994. The Thalian's 39th Annual Ball honored Liza for her AIDS work. Goldie Hawn presented the award to Liza, praising her as "a beacon of light" for being "the first public person to speak out about AIDS." Liza sang, including a "Happy Days Are Here Again"/"Get Happy" duet with Lorna.

Tavern on the Green, New York—October 13, 1994. Liza was honored by the Arlene Walters Foundation , which offers help to parents and families of drug and alcohol-dependent children.

Marriot World Center, Orlando, Florida—October 18, 1994

Majestic Theater, New York—October 23, 1994. Fight for Sight benefit.

Beverly Hilton Hotel, Los Angeles—October 28, 1994. Carousel Ball benefit.

Westbury Music Fair, Westbury, New York—November 2–6, 1994. Liza opened with "Here's to Us." Other new material included "Tall Hope." [A—11/3 and another show]

Wexner Center for the Arts, Columbus, Ohio—November 12, 1994. Benefit. [A]

Marriot Marquis, New York—November 15, 1994. Liza performed at *Billboard* magazine's benefit for the National Music Foundation's art center to be built in Lenox, Mass.

Valley Forge Music Fair, Devon, Pennsylvania—November 16–20, 1994 [A—at least four shows, including 11/18, two on 11/20, and at least one other, date not known]

Kennedy Center, Washington, D.C.—Saturday, December 10, 1994. "Concert of the Americas." Liza opened the show with "Old Friends," closed it with "New York, New York," then encored with the all-star cast in singing "Freedom." (Videotaped for TV; See the entry for *Concert of the Americas*, page 117, for more information.)

1995

Beverly Wilshire Hotel, Los Angeles—February 8, 1995. BAFTA's bash honoring Anthony Hopkins. Liza's first date post-surgery for her hip (the surgery was December 17, 1994). Liza sang three Aznavour songs, including "What Makes a Man a Man."

Dallas—May 7, 1995. Benefit.

New York—May 22, 1995. Benefit.

State Fair, Pueblo, Colorado—June 3, 1995 [A]

Center of Performing Arts, Cerritos, California—June 7–11, 1995.

Stanhope, New Jersey—June 21, 1995. Benefit.

Bally's Grand, Atlantic City, New Jersey—June 22–25, 1995 [A—both shows on 6/23, and shows on 6/24 and closing] [There is also an audio of Liza singing "I Hadn't Anyone 'Til You" at Gatsbys Bar in Atlantic City, after a show]

New York—July 4, 1995. Benefit.

Garden State Arts Center, Holmdel, New Jersey—July 10, 1995 [A]

Sporting Club, Monte Carlo—July 14–16, 1995

Israel—July 22–25, 1995

Civic Arts Plaza, Thousand Oaks, California—August 9–12, 1995

Bally's Grand, Atlantic City, New Jersey—August 15–17, 1995

NHK Symphony Hall, Tokyo—August 22–24, 1995. Videotaped and shown on TV in Japan, and was announced as probable airing on the Disney Channel. It never aired in U.S.; however, video exists. Liza opened with "Yes I Can." Other numbers included "Blues in the Night," "Sailor Boys," "Crying," "I Love a Piano," "Shine on Harvest Moon," "At Sammy's House" medley (with Billy Stritch), Kander and Ebb medley.

Hershey Auditorium, Hershey, Pennsylvania—September 14, 1995

Bally's Grand, Atlantic City, New Jersey—September 15–17, 1995 [A—9/16 and closing night]

Dortmund, Germany—November 18 and 19, 1995

Paris—December 6, 1995. Benefit.

Bally's Grand, Atlantic City, New Jersey—December 8–10, 1995. Liza sang Judy's "Paris Is a Lonely Town" for the first and only known time. [A—all three nights]

Caesars Tahoe, Lake Tahoe, Nevada—December 29–31, 1995 [A—12/30]

1996

New York—January 22, 1996. Benefit for New York Hospital.

Bally's, Las Vegas—January 24–27, 1996 [A—all nights except for 1/25]

Jackie Gleason Theater, Miami—February 13, 14, 16 and 18, 1996 [V, A—all shows]

Bally's Grand Casino, Atlantic City, New Jersey—March 1–4, 1996 [A—all but closing night]

River Hotel, Palm Beach, Florida—March 29, 1996

Foxwoods Casino, Ledyard, Connecticut—May 10–12, 1996 [A—opening and closing nights]

Atlanta—May 19, 1996. Jewish National Fund Benefit. Liza opened with "I Feel a Song Coming On."

Bally's Grand Casino, Las Vegas—May 22–26, 1996. Liza received Liberace Award on her opening night. [V, A—opening; A—all but 5/24]

Sheraton Hotel, New York—June 12, 1996. Songwriter's Hall of Fame.

Parco Novi Sad, Modena, Italy—June 20, 1996. Pavarotti and Friends War Child benefit. Liza sang "New York, New York" with Pavarotti, and a solo of "I Have Dreamed." CD and video/laser/DVD released.

Arthur 15th Anniversary Tour with Dudley Moore:

Garden State Arts Center, Holmdel, New Jersey—July 3, 1996. [A]

Saratoga Performing Arts Center, Albany, New York—July 7, 1996. [A]

Rochester, New York—July 9, 1996. [A]

Oakdale Theater, Wallingford, Connecticut—July 11 and 12, 1996. [A—7/11 show]

Great Woods, Great Woods, Massachusetts—July 14, 1996.

Harbour Lights, Boston—July 15, 1996. Rescheduled from July 13. [A]

Michigan State University, East Lansing, Michigan—September 18–21, 1996 [A—all shows, including two on closing night]

Bally's Grand, Atlantic City, New Jersey—October 11–13, 1996

Beacon Theater, New York—October 21, 1996. Benefit.

Westbury Music Fair, Westbury, New York—October 23–27th, 1996. Closing night was an absolutely perfect show in every way—form, voice, program of songs, clothes, audience—all sheer perfection. Liza encored with an a capella version of Judy's "You Made Me Love You." [A—closing]

Valley Forge Music Fair, Valley Forge/Devon, Pennsylvania—October 31–November 3, 1996 [A—11/2 and closing night]

Palo Alto, California—November 6, 1996. Benefit.

Davis Symphony Hall, San Francisco—November 7, 1996

Bally's, Las Vegas—November 14–17, 1996

Mystic Lake Casino, Mystic Lake, Minnesota—November 20 and 21, 1996

Palm Springs, California—December 7, 1996. Barbara Sinatra Children's Hospital Benefit.

Foxwoods Casino, Ledyard, Connecticut—December 13–15, 1996

Bally's, Las Vegas—December 29–31, 1996 [A—closing]

1997

New York—May 12, 1997. Singer's Forum Benefit.

Tallahassee, Florida—May 13, 1997. Benefit.

Hilton, Atlantic City, New Jersey—May 16–18, 1997. First stop of tour/first dates after Liza's March 1997 vocal surgery to remove polyps on her vocal cords. [A—5/17]

Davis Hall, San Francisco—May 29–May 31, 1997

New York—June 2, 1997. At the conclusion of the Broadway show *The Life*, Liza sang "Use What You Got to Get What You Want," from the show, and then sang "You Made Me Love You."

Boston—June 6, 1997. Benefit show.

Le Cabaret Casino, Montreal—June 18–20, 1997

Guild Theater, New York—June 23, 1997. AIDS Research Gala, with Miramax's premiere of *Shall We Dance?* Also on same date—Lena Horne Tribute at Avery Fisher Hall—Lena's eightieth birthday.

Mexico City—June 27–29th, 1997

Monterey, Mexico—July 1, 1997

Bally's, Las Vegas—July 24–27, 1997 [A—all but opening]

Pantages Theater, Los Angeles—July 31–August 2, 1997. 2,700 seats; Tickets were $77.50 top price. [A—closing]

Music Circus, Cohassett, Massachusetts—August 6, 1997

Warwick Theater, Warwick, Rhode Island—August 8, 1997 [A]

Cape Cod Melody Tent, Cape Cod, Massachusetts—August 9, 1997. This was the highest-grossing engagement in venue's history.

Beverly Hilton, Los Angeles—August 16, 1997. Humane from Hollywood Gala.

Sporting Club, Monte Carlo—August 22–24, 1997

Sicily—August 27th–30th, 1997

Verona, Italy—September 3, 1997

New York—November 17th, 1997. Liza appeared at the 25th Anniversary screening of *Cabaret*, to benefit Broadway Cares/Equity Fights AIDS.

Kremlin Palace, Moscow—December 13–14, 1997

Bally's, Las Vegas—December 29–31, 1997 [A—all nights]

1998

Foxwoods Casino, Ledyard, Connecticut—Early 1998

Memorial Arena, Lowell, Massachusetts—February 21, 1998 [A]

University of North Carolina, Wilmington—April 4, 1998 [A]

New Amsterdam Theater, New York—Tuesday, April 14, 1998. Eighth Annual Easter Bonnet Benefit for AIDS research. Liza hosted, with Nathan Lane.

Palace, Myrtle Beach, South Carolina—April 23, 1998 [A]

Atlantic City, New Jersey—May 1–May 3, 1998. [A—5/1 and 5/2]

Reno, Nevada—weekend of May 16, 1998 [A]

Bally's, Las Vegas (also noted as Reno)—Weekend of May 24–27, 1998. The rest of Liza's tour was canceled to allow more time for her voice to heal from its surgery.

Carnegie Hall, New York—September 28, 1998: "Broadway's Leading Ladies" taping. Liza's songs: "Liza with a 'Z'" (sung with Rosie O'Donnell, who introduced her); "Sing Happy"; "Some People." [A]

Kennedy Center, Washington, DC—December 5, 1998. "Kennedy Center Honors," CBS special taped. Liza sang "New York, New York" as part of the tribute to honorees Kander and Ebb.

Houston, Texas—December 9, 1998. Benefit. Liza sang for one hour, accompanied by Billy Stritch.

1999

Town Hall, New York—April 5,1999. MAC Awards. Liza received the Board of Directors Award and sang "Stormy Weather." [V, A]

Washington, D.C.—May 3, 1999. Helen Hayes Awards. Liza sang "Maybe This Time."

Beverly Hills Hilton Hotel, Los Angeles—June 7, 1999. RADD (Recording Artists, Actors, and Athletes Against Drunk Driving) "Entertaining Liza" tribute.

Radio City Music Hall, New York—October 4,1999. Gala Reopening. Videotaped by NBC and aired December 18, 1999.

Palace Theater, New York—December 1, 1999–January 2, 2000; 24 performances. *Minnelli on Minnelli* show. Official opening December 8, 1999. On December 7 it was announced that a fifteen-city tour would follow a possible extension/move to New York, New York's Gershwin Theater in March; Liza later admitted she'd be willing to tour all over the world for two to three years with this show. (See the *Minnelli on Minnelli: Live at the Palace* entry on pages 155–56 for a list of her songs in this show, on the CD. That disc ommitted "Happiness Is a Thing Called Joe," and made some of the other songs and dialogue shorter.) [V—at least two shows, Friday, December 10, and Saturday, the 11; A—many shows, including December 1–4, December 7–11, December 21, 27, 28, January 2, and others]

From *Variety*: *Minnelli on Minnelli* (Concert—Palace Theater; 1,743 seats; $125 top ticket price) Reviewed December 7, 1999. Running time: 2 hours, 20 minutes. Review by Charles Isherwood: "A creditable, courageous achievement. Minnelli gracefully received salvos of affection from the audience throughout the evening: 'We love you, Liza!' 'Welcome back, Liza!' And she gave a warm, energetic performance. . . . She still has a unique instrument that couldn't be mistaken for anyone else's, as well as decisive, dramatic phrasing and distinctive elocution. . . . When Minnelli catches and holds a climactic note, the thrill is still there. . . . *Minnelli on Minnelli* is ultimately as much support group as it is a concert. It may seem odd to ask audiences to pay for the privilege of providing an entertainer with emotional succor, but Liza's fans seem eager to give back a small measure of the pleasure they've been given by the performer over the years. Minnelli is one of the last practitioners of a particular strain of showbiz that draws on this mutual, personal give and take: We sustain our favorites with our love and loyalty as they have sustained us with their artistry. Call it a healthier kind of co-dependence."

From the *Hollywood Reporter*, review by Robert Osborne, December 9, 2003:

> "Liza Minnelli should maybe consider doing a remake of Frank Capra's *The Miracle Woman.* That title certainly applies. After all sorts of hip replacements, knee surgeries and other aggravating kerfuffles in her life . . . Liza is, bottom line, terrific . . . especially topnotch when she uses her sense of humor and inclination for comedy—she is a born comedienne. . . . Liza, in person, singing part of 'The Trolley Song' with seven images of Judy Garland on film. It's prime stuff. . . . An eventual transfer to television also seems a likely bet."

Minnelli on Minnelli set a house record for first-day phone sales at the Palace, taking in $436,845 on October 25, 1999. (The first day of phone sales for Disney's *Beauty and the Beast*, on September 26, 1993, resulted in a tally of $100,488, the previous record.) With tickets ranging from a $125 top price, down to $35, the show earned $435,280 in its first four previews. Its advance on opening day was $1.2 million. On December 21, 1999, *Variety* reported that only five shows in New York had improved their grosses from the previous week: *The Lion King*, *Minnelli on Minnelli*, *Rent*, *Swing!* and *Jackie Mason.* Liza's show jumped $53,951, to close at $558,664 with a gross potential of $782,623. Her average ticket price was the street's highest, $91.84. Liza's engagement sold out her final week, and also broke its gross potential ($626,098), climbing $209,827, for a close of $630,503.

2000

Pierre Hotel, New York—January 31, 2000. Liza was honored by the Drama League.

San Francisco—March 9–12, 2000. The first stop of the *Minnelli on Minnelli* tour.

Town Hall, New York—April 9, 2000. Liza was a presenter at the annual MAC Awards.

Kennedy Center, Washington. D.C.—April 12–16, 2000. Second (and final) stop of *MOM* tour. The *CBS Sunday Morning* TV show videotaped portions of the show for their segment on Liza. On Friday, April 28, Chicago was canceled. It was to be the next engagement, at the Shubert Theater, for two weeks, May 3–17, 2000; $120 top price. It was selling out, too, even at that theater's highest legit engagement price ever. Minneapolis was also canceled on April 28. All other engagements for the rest of the entire tour were canceled, due to Liza requiring back and knee surgeries.

2001

Drama League Benefit, New York—February 5, 2001. Tribute to Chita Rivera.

AIDS Charity, Center One / Community Healthcare Benefit, Bal Harbour, Florida—April 21, 2001. Liza was honored with a Life Tribute Award, and sang "Maybe This Time," with Peter Matz on piano. This was Liza's first official public performance since her near-fatal attack of viral encephalitis in October 2000.

Feinstein's at the Regency, New York—May 20, 2001. Liza attended Keely Smith's performance.

Tribeca Grand Hotel's Screening Room, New York—June 4, 2001. Fine Line Cinema's premiere of Alan Cumming's *The Anniversary Party.*

Madison Square Garden, New York—September 7 and 10, 2001. "Michael Jackson 30th Anniversary" concert. Aired on CBS on November 13, 2001. Liza sang a medley of "You Are Not Alone" / "Over the Rainbow," backed by a choir. CBS omitted "Rainbow," but later airings on VH-1 included Minnelli's final bars of the song.

Shea Stadium baseball game, Flushing, New York—September 21, 2001. Liza sang "New York, New York" (broadcast live during the game's telecast).

Century Plaza Hotel, Los Angeles—October 31, 2001. Thalians' 46th annual tribute; Liza sang "Dear

Mr. Haley," in honor of Jack Haley Jr., who had recently passed.

Madison Square Garden, New York—December 18, 2001. Annual "Miracle on 34th Street" concert. Liza sang "God Bless the Child" with Chaka Khan, and soloed on "New York, New York" [A]

2002

Royal Albert Hall, London—April 2–7, 2002. "Liza's Back!" concert. (Five shows) [A—closing night]

A tour had been announced at a January 24, 2002 press conference at London's Dorchester Hotel, including stops in Denmark, Paris, Germany, Austria, and Switzerland, but she only played London and then New York.

From *Variety*: *Liza's Back!* (Royal Albert Hall; 3,800 seats; £140 ($200) top) Running time: 2 hours, 35 minutes; Review by Matt Wolf:

> "On the evidence of *Liza's Back*, the Royal Albert Hall concert show signaling her first U.K. appearance since 1995, the fifty-six-year-old is indeed back, and in fighting form. . . . Minnelli is looking good and sounding ready for a creative rebirth. . . . What's astonishing, in entertainment terms, is how childlike and guileless Minnelli remains, even when the specifics of her life might have turned most people sour. . . . Her rapport with the crowd, meanwhile, redefined a kind of rapture whereby a performer and her fans seemed to be urging each other on, rather as if Minnelli's road to recovery somehow tallied with her public's own. . . . In a stroke, you could feel the Albert Hall understanding Minnelli, as a one-of-a-kind creature made for and by the stage whom we thought we had lost—and had, instead, all over again and thrillingly, found."

Beacon Theater, New York—May 31, June 1, 3, 4, 6, 7, 8, 2002. Seven shows. 3,332-seat venue. $1,000/$2,500 top ticket prices. Engagement grossed over $1.4 million for the week. The last two nights were recorded by J Records; the resulting disc was culled mostly from closing night, and omitted the songs "Yes," "Liza with a 'Z,'" "Family Affair," and "I Believe You," all from the first act. [A—every show] [V]

From the *Hollywood Reporter*—June 4, 2002. Review by Frank Scheck:

> "Looking and sounding better than she has in eons, Minnelli delivered a historic comeback evening that will long be remembered."

From *Variety*, posted on June 10, 2002; reviewed June 6, by Robert L. Daniels:

> "With seasoned razzle-dazzle and a generous dose of showbiz savvy, Liza Minnelli has returned to Gotham to reclaim her place on the roster of Broadway divas. Relaxed and assured, the well-weathered entertainer, fully recovered from a devastating illness and substance abuse, pulled out all the stops. She planted herself cen-

terstage and seduced her audience with a vigorous display of old-fashioned chutzpah. She is an instinctive interpreter of song, and she knows how to balance the humor and heart of a tune. She has developed a warm rapport with her fans. Her hip dance steps and theatrically planted physical stances drove her devoted followers—and they are legion—to plateaus of repeated ecstasy. Indeed, they lavished her with a standing ovation on nearly every number. It all has to do with showmanship, and Minnelli is a veteran of the art. . . . Minnelli's voice is as big and as richly flavorful as ever, despite a husky edge that adds to the coloring of a well-traveled singer. The repertoire is balanced with old and new material, from 'I Believe You' (assisted by a gospel choir) to the old teary-eyed Johnny Ray chart-topper 'Cry.' With the assistance of novice teen rapper Little Leroy, Minnelli had great fun putting a new spin on her trademark tongue twister 'Liza with a "Z".' . . . For a while, it seemed the showstoppers would never stop."

Town Hall, New York—December 5 and 6, 2002. "Liza's Christmas Spectacular." There were two performances on the 6th, at 7 PM and at 10 PM. Liza's songs included: Overture; "What a Lovely Night"/"When You Wish Upon a Star"; "Winter Wonderland"; "Christmas Is an Island"; "Something Wonderful"; "Maybe This Time"; "Jingle Bells"; "And I in My Chair"; "Ever to Be Near You" (a song credited to Liza's then-husband, David Gest); "Some People" (first act closer); "Where the Boys Are"/"Hold Me, Thrill Me"/"You Don't Know Me"; "You Don't Own Me" (with new additional lyrics for Liza by the song's writer, Leslie Gore); "What Did I Have?"; "Christmas Memories"; "Wilkommen"/"Cabaret"; "New York, New York"; "Have Yourself a Merry Little Christmas"; and "You'll Never Know" (sung a capella). (Petula Clark joined Liza onstage to sing her hit "Downtown" at the last show.) [A—all three shows]

Madison Square Garden, New York—December 18, 2002. "Miracle on 34th Street" concert. Liza's songs included "Georgia," with Ray Charles.

2003

February 2003 concert tour:

World Arena, Colorado Springs—February 10, 2003

Schottenstein Center, Columbus, Ohio—February 12, 2003 [A—2nd Act only]

Westbury Music Fair, Westbury, New York—February 14–16, 2003. Joel Grey was Liza's guest star at this one stop on her tour. It was reported in the March 15, 2003 issue of *Billboard* that this 3-show stint grossed $407,175 total; 6,827 people saw the shows, out of a total of 8,226. This, in spite of a massive snowstorm in the Northeast area, including New York and New Jersey. [A—all three shows; V—about 40 minutes of closing night]

American Airlines Arena, Miami—February 20, 2003 [V]

Palace of Auburn Hills, Auburn Hills, Michigan—February 21, 2003

Bryce Jordan Center, University Park, Pennsylvania—February 23, 2003

Turning Stone Casino, Verona, New York—February 24, 2003

Sovereign Bank Arena, Trenton, New Jersey—February 27, 2003. Liza's songs: "Liza's Back"; "Something Wonderful"; "Cry"; "Don't Cry Out Loud"; "Crying"; "Sara Lee"; "Don't Smoke in Bed"; "Some People"; "Never, Never Land"/"Over the Rainbow" (Act Two): "Where The Boys Are"/"Hold Me, Thrill Me"/"You Don't Know Me"; "You Don't Own Me"; "What Did I Have?"; "Rose's Turn"; "Wilkommen"/"Money, Money, Money"/"Maybe This Time"/"Cabaret"; "But the World Goes 'Round"; "New York, New York"; "I'll Be Seeing You." [A]

Italy—May 27, 2003. Pavarotti benefit concert. Liza sang an a capella version of "Cabaret," via a remote TV feed from her hospital room. She had broken her kneecap during a fall in her hotel two days earlier while in Italy to appear at the concert, and was having surgery the day after the concert, but she insisted on honoring her commitment to this event.

King Kong Room at the Supper Club, New York—Monday, August 4, 2003. Liza sang "My Shining Hour" a capella, at her friend Jim Caruso's weekly Cast Party event.

New York—September 18, 2003. Launch party for Liza's MAC Cosmetics line.

San Francisco—Last week of September 2003. Liza appeared at two AIDS events.

Luckman Fine Arts Complex, Los Angeles—October 25, 2003. S.T.A.G.E. Too benefit for the Actor's Fund, Sing Happy, saluting Kander and Ebb. Liza closed the concert with "Cabaret," "But the World Goes 'Round," "Liza with a 'Z'," and "New York, New York." This was recorded by LML Music, who plan to release the concert as a two-CD set.

New York—October 30, 2003. Liza appeared at a MAC Cosmetics event, honoring the company for their AIDS charity work.

Carnegie Hall, New York—November 3, 2003. Tribute to John Kander and Fred Ebb, at The Lauri Strauss Leukemia Foundation Benefit Concert "Reach for Tomorrow." Liza performed with the ninety-piece New York Pops Orchestra, and sang "Liza with a 'Z'," "Cabaret," and "New York, New York."

The Plaza Hotel, New York—November 5, 2003. The Landmark Conservancy Gala. Liza sang "Liza with a 'Z'", "Cabaret","But the World Goes 'Round," and "New York, New York." Kander and Ebb were made Living Landmarks, along with Elaine Stritch. Liz Smith (another Living Landmark) hosted.

2004

Robinson Center Music Hall, Little Rock, Arkansas—Friday, January 30, 2004. (Tickets were $60–$100; Tony Bennett had been the original artist slated for this performance, but he had to bow out when the original date was set for November 1, 2003 and he proved to have a prior booking; Minnelli took his place, but she had to reset the date anyway.) Liza appeared in concert with the Arkansas Symphony Orchestra, who performed the first half (including a suite from *The Wizard of Oz*). Minnelli performed an 80–90 minute extended second act. Her brilliant musical mainstay Billy Stritch (whom Liza referred to as "my friend, my family, my soul mate") conducted the thirteen-piece jazz band used in her act (three woodwinds, four brass, drum set, bass, synthesizer, percussion, piano, and guitar). Eric E. Harrison wrote in the next day's edition of the *Arkansas Democrat-Gazette* that "it was Liza with a 'wow.' . . . Minnelli . . . got plenty of love. . . . [The audience] gave her a bunch of standing ovations (starting with her entrance). . . . The lady has an incredible set of pipes and an incredible amount of energy, and she gave the crowd everything it expected, and more." Liza's songs: "What a Lovely Night (On the Atchison, Topeka, and the Santa Fe)"/"How Long Has This Been Going On"/"The Miracle Is You" (Liza used this medley first on her 1978–79 tour, again in 1981–82, and occasionally thereafter, but hadn't really sung the complete arrangement in years); "Here I'll Stay With You/Our Love Is Here To Stay," "Old Friends," "Live Alone and Like It," "Don't Smoke in Bed," "So What?" "What Did I Have I Don't Have Now?" (Billy Stritch then played and sang "Teach Me Tonight" while Liza changed from a white two-piece top with dark slacks into a black sequined top with short skirt and dark hose), "He's Funny That Way" (with just Billy on piano), "Liza with a 'Z'," "Mein Herr," "Money, Money," "Maybe This Time," "Cabaret," "New York, New York," "But the World Goes 'Round, and "I'll Be Seeing You."

Ars Nova Theater, New York—Monday night, March 1, 2004. Jim Caruso's cast party. With the show's musical director Mark Hartman at the piano, Liza sang "Teach Me Tonight," "Oscar," and "God Bless the Child."

Gershwin Theatre, New York, New York—Saturday, March 20, 2004. Liza attended the evening performance of the Broadway musical *Wicked*, based on *The Wizard of Oz* characters. Minnelli appeared onstage at the end of the show to help with the Broadway Cares/Equity Fights AIDS auction of photographs taken by one of Wicked's stars, Joel Grey. Liza sang a few bars of the song "Wilkommen" with Grey from their joint classic, *Cabaret*.

New York City Recovery Centre, New York—Monday, March 22, 2004. Liza appeared at the opening of the Caron Foundation's Manhattan treatment center for adolescents suffering from the disease of chemical dependency.

Walt Disney Concert Hall, Los Angeles—Tuesday, April 13, 2004. Liza attended a tribute to the music of Henry Mancini.

Grand Hyatt, New York—Tuesday, April 20, 2004. National Italian American Foundation (NIAF) East Coast Gala. Liza presented a student with the NIAF/Vincente Minnelli Scholarship in music, in honor of her father.

Kennedy Center, Washington, D.C.—Sunday, April 25, 2004. *Ellington, Etc.* Liza sang at this Tribute to the music of Duke Ellington. Liza closed the all-star concert, substituting for an ailing Aretha Franklin, and sang "But the World Goes 'Round," "I Got It Bad and That Ain't Good," and "What Did I Have?" Tickets started at $500.

Mandarin Oriental, New York—Monday, April 26, 2004. Liza appeared at the Roundabout Theatre Company's spring gala celebration. Kander and Ebb received the company's Jason Robards Award for excellence in theatre. Tickets started at $1,000.

Caesars Palace, Las Vegas—Saturday, May 1, 2004. *Michael Douglas and Friends* sports-showbiz gala, benefiting the Motion Picture and Television Fund. Scheduled to be videotaped and broadcast on ABC Sports, Sunday, July 18, 2004. Liza sang thirty minutes of material during her "Liza Minnelli and Friends" benefit cabaret.

Concerts set as we went to press were: Harrah's, Atlantic City, July 2–3, 2004 (tickets were $125); Chastain Park in Atlanta, on Friday, July 23, 2004; Montalvo Garden Theatre, Saratoga, California, on Sunday, August 15, 2004 (with guest Sam Harris; tickets $90–$150); Humphrey's Concerts by the Bay, San Diego, Tuesday, August 17, 2004 (tickets $95); Pier 62/63, Seattle, Friday, August 20, 2004 (tickets $55).

Of Liza's latest concert, Liz Smith had this to report in her syndicated column of July 8, 2004: "Liza Minnelli was a sellout for her two-night stint at Harrah's in Atlantic City over the Fourth of July weekend. The lady looked trim—maintaining her recent 20-pound weight loss. (Although she joked, 'This blouse was looser last week—too much barbecue!') She was in fine, strong voice, too. And as usual, she was on top of everything pertaining to her show and her presentation. Liza said, 'I could use more bass on this microphone. I sound like a bad trumpet. Can you help me out? Turn me into a flute or a horn?' "

As appearing in concert remains Minnelli's favorite vehicle in which to express her art, there is no doubt she will continue to lavish her gifts on her adoring public for years to come.

CHAPTER FOURTEEN

Minnelli Musings

"Up there onstage, I'm not haunted by people's opinions of me. I am what I do."

Since *The Liza Minnelli Scrapbook* has focused on the star's career, I felt it might be interesting to take a glimpse into Liza's thoughts *about* her work, about what she does for a living. Over the years, she has expressed her feelings about her life as a performer during various interviews on TV and in print, and I've culled some of those comments here—intertwined with Liza's reflections on fame, about how her mother should be remembered, and on life.

"Other people have been icons. I just get up there and sing and dance."

"My first love is music and dance."

"You put what you go through in your life up there on that stage. That's part of my job. If there is any truth to your life as your art, you might as well throw it up there."

"Most of the time it is fun being Liza, but what aggravates me is when you read something about yourself that you haven't done or haven't said. And you think, 'Wow, how do people get away with doing that?' Then there's the assumption that you don't have all the ordinary feelings that everybody else does. That you are not like everybody else, that you are special. When, in fact, you are not special, you just have a talent in a certain area, and you're lucky to have that talent. As far as everything else goes, you're exactly like everybody else."

"There are times in one's life when one is gripped with a curious bravery; when all your instincts tell you to move in a new and unknown direction, even though it may scare you. When you act on those instincts and move forward despite the fear—that's stepping out."

"Don't be too rough on yourself, it's too hard. If you're not gentle with yourself, nobody else is gonna be."

"Being famous is like being royalty. Royalty that the public has made. They are willing to invest in you what they invested in your parents—if you prove yourself. The other side of the coin, which I took a long time to realize, is that you can't invest your self-esteem in their thoughts. I mean, I don't know how ballplayers do it. One minute, it's 'Yea, yea, we love you!,' and then they strike out and it's 'You bum!' . . . I was always in the position—I was born *into it—where if I was good, people said, 'Of course.' If I wasn't good, people said, 'Of course.' If I'm healthy and working, they say, 'Well, of course.' If I die tomorrow, they'd say, 'Well, of course.' And it's true. And it's something you have to deal with—you make it lucky or you make it a hassle."*

"Show business is so . . . it can fool the shit out of you. It can just fool you to death. Because you think you work so hard and you get here and that's where you stay. No. No interesting career has ever stayed level all the time. It does kind of go up and down. And I think there is a point where you don't think that will happen to you. And that's exactly when it happens. Then you go, 'Wait a minute. What's happening?'"

"My father said to me right before he died, 'You haven't scratched the surface yet.' And I agree with him."

"I don't understand—I don't know how to say this, because they are my friends—but certain people's attitudes about not wanting publicity or having their picture taken. It is literally part of the deal and it's not a lot of trouble to let somebody snap your picture without slugging them. I think people who are doing that are copping an attitude of either Garbo or Brando that they thought was glamorous."

"My thoughts and the songs that I sing are about people who can get along, who will make it, who have *to make it!"*

"I think there's a lot of people around who would be doing what they wanted to be doing, instead of what they are doing, if they'd just had one other person at the right moment saying, 'Give it a try, go ahead!' Encouragement."

"The perspective on Mama is that people should just look at any of her films. Look at A Star Is Born, *look at* The Wizard of Oz, *look at* Meet Me in St. Louis. *Listen to* Judy at Carnegie Hall. *Remember what that tiny woman could give, and what she did give. The immense enjoyment that she gave to the* world, *I think. And that's it! That's what she left. She left her love here. And she touched* everybody! *Everybody in the world she touched! Who hasn't seen* The Wizard of Oz?*"*

"Keep your own council. And usually if you are in a stressful situation, if something is really bothering you, if you just sit down and take it easy and listen to some good music and look at the colors that are around you, you'll suddenly realize that you're not the most important thing in the world. That there are other things happening, a lot of other things going on. And it takes those pressures away, and you can put in in perspective. Whatever it is! And then get up and work it out. It's like taking a break—like if you're writing something at the piano, and you get stuck for a moment? If you get up and walk around and forget about it and go back to it, you usually can overcome it."

"Be a nice person. Just make nice to other people. I don't care what you do or what area of the world you want to work in, but for God's sake, be nice to other people. Life is too short to get picked at and—nailed! Even at school as a kid. Remember at school there was always that one kid who was always such a nasty kid? First thing I'd tell my kid is, 'Don't pay any attention. This child is a moron: you are a smart person. Don't talk to this child. If she hurts you, go away. Don't talk to her.' It's that kind of thing. And, 'Look around—keep your eyes open.'"

"Life goes foward, not backward."

"Work makes me very happy, and the audience makes it all worth it. I get off from audience energy. I'm totally conscious of what's out there. Wherever I play, I insist they keep the lights up so I can see everybody, and I swear I can. You see, I always think from the audience point of view. What would strike me as funny? What would touch me?"

"I just love what I'm doing. I feel so at home on the stage, it seems silly, I guess. But more than that, there's an incredible sense of joy, 'cause no matter what you give, you do get it back. It comes right back at you; you can almost feel the energy level. It feels like heat when it hits you in the face. I guess what we all strive for is to be happy, and that makes me happy."

"I'm married to everybody who has sent me a letter saying, 'You made me so happy.'"

"I'm best when I've had enough rest, I'm with people I love, and I'm working."

"The greatest gift I ever received was my God-given humor, talent, and strength."

"I've always chosen people that I always thought were better than I was, to take from, to learn from, to observe from."

"I like my fans. I think I would hate it without them. The only thing I do object to is that sometimes you go someplace and you can't do what you'd like to do when you get there, like the other night in Fort Lauderdale, Florida. After the show, we went to a discotheque, and for no reason at all there were so many security guards around me that it was impossible to get up and dance. And you know, I love to dance. I didn't ask to be guarded. The people around you sometimes get carried away. They become overprotective and they can overprotect you right out of a good time. Also, the people who meet me under those circumstances never get to meet me. *That's the part of it I don't like."*

"You don't worry about your price, for God's sake. Sure, a lot of actors say they want to return to the stage, but look how many do. I don't want to make any enemies, but there aren't too many ladies who go back. What happens is, you get spoiled by a marvelous cinematographer. But you have to go back to those little dressing rooms that you're forced to share. Or you absolutely lose your perspective."

"I never really cared why people came in to see me perform, I just cared what they thought when they went out."

"What have you been reading about me? That I'm difficult? I don't believe in that. It takes up too much time. Journalists build you up, then knock you down. It gives them something to do because they're bored with their own lives."

"I'm the ultimate survivor and believer. I just love life and am basically a happy person, which some find hard to believe. At times fame has been difficult, but only when I've been around the wrong people. You get into trouble when you avoid your problems, or

when you're told you don't have to deal with them now. It can't have had that bad an effect, though, otherwise I wouldn't be sitting here."

"We all think we're going to live forever. We have to, although the 'reality' of death isn't a real reality. If it were, you'd never do anything except lie in bed all day and worry. You have to take the exact opposite attitude, which is 'Thank God I'm alive today,' and get on with it. I don't worry about getting old—no more than anyone else."

"The public has known me their whole life and I'm like family in a funny kind of way, and I consider them to be that as well."

"The audience is my family. Whatever is printed about you is unimportant. What's important is to stand out there with your legs planted apart and sing, damn it."

"I have the most passionate heart. It needs to attach to something else. I don't feel entirely fulfilled unless I'm in love, but I think I'm wiser now. Love needs to be tempered by good sense or it quickly becomes obsessive."

"I'm a singer, not much else. Other people have been icons. I just get up there and sing and dance. I tread the boards for a living and sing my guts out. Sometimes my heart, too."

"Regret is a huge exercise in futility. There's no point in dwelling on the past, and the only thing is to take today and do it different, which is what I think most people try to do. I've made mistakes and I've done some dumb things, but I don't think there's any point in regretting anything. I'm far too old for that."

"I find it difficult to get parts now, but then everybody does. You look at the best actresses in America and they're all playing someone's wife. But in music, women are taking over the world. Look at Joan Osborne and Alanis Morissette, Sheryl Crow and Tori Amos; these dames talk like people do on the street, they're making the folk music of today."

"The main thing I like doing is performing live. I'm a road rat, and I just love getting out there. Singing is what I do, it's what I'm made of."

"There's this guy who walks along the street one day and falls straight into a hole. And the next day he walks down the same street and tries to jump over it, but falls in again. Then on the third day he approaches the hole really slowly, and tries to walk around the edge but still falls in. The day after that, he takes a different street. You know what I mean? Sometimes it takes a while to learn how to deal with the world."

"What's important, what counts is getting a piano player and going to the hospitals and hospices, and singing and talking and being there. That's important. The hands-on stuff—OK? That's the trenches. I'm not about being a victim. I'm singing about survival. About surviving life. What I'm saying is, we'll get through it, damn it. It might break our hearts and do in our heads, but at the end we'll be standing."

"Life is adversity. Just getting up is adversity. But the decision to be happy is a conscious choice. I like that, that it's up to you."

"In this art form, performance, what you are looking for is to get rid of anything that's not the truth. Suddenly you find yourself relying on gestures, a certain type of song. Kick it away, it's something you're leaning on. What you want is to be able to stand, without any tricks, in the light. To be pure, to be truthful."

"My survival mechanism is to always try and find the humor in every situation. It's always a lifesaver."

"The truth is, I'm a very adaptable creature. I don't have many hang-ups. I have my bad days—so what else is new? At heart, I'm really an Italian broad. I really am a nice person, and I think nice people are ultimately rewarded."

"Yes, I get down. But I don't let it eat away at me. I've worked out an antidote. I go where there's laughter and I can be with sympathetic people. If there's anything I know it's when you're negative, drown yourself with the company of positive people!"

"I think I'm comfortable with stardom. I think so. I'm just comfortable working. There are people who are stars, and people who are workers. I like to think of myself as a worker."

"I always find it baffling that people think I resent where I came from—I'm thrilled with where I came from. I was a witness to all this incredible talent and taste, and there's something nice about tradition. From my mother, I got the 'knock-'em-dead' style of performing that comes out of vaudeville, and from my father I took a European, more intricate approach. So I don't mind the idea of carrying on traditions, as long as I've made them my own."

"I am the kind of person who would feel rude if I was flippant to anyone. Being flippant is a cover."

"Things come up and life is full of surprises, and that's what I love. I love taking new roads and exploring new ways to have fun and to work and to develop spiritually and emotionally and in my work."

"You realize that there are a lot of people that really care about you, and realize that everyone is born with the same feelings and same stresses and the same everything. You just do your job and you just get through it and keep going. We do our job and I like my job. You do what you do."

"I think the thing I like to do most in my life is to work, and to work hard. And I think the thing I like second best is when someone says 'You did a good job.'"

Exit Music

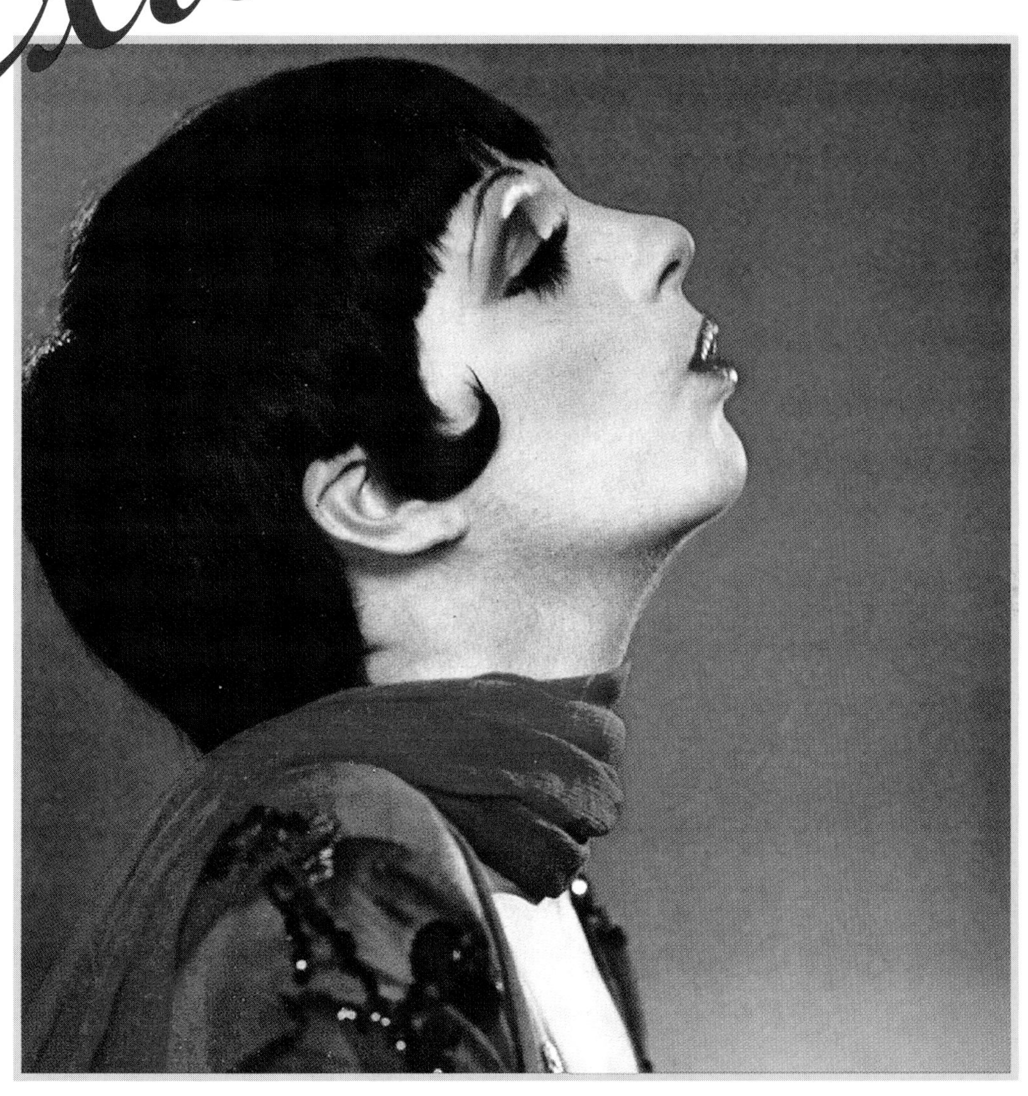

The very first issue (Winter 1965, *left*) of Liza's official fan club journal, *Limelight on Liza* (which ran from 1965 to 1997), and the final issue, the "30th Anniversary Edition 1965–1995"

Appendix

Liza Online; CDs, DVDs, and Videos; Suggestions for Collecting Liza's work

The wonderful world of the Internet has made following the career of Liza Minnelli—and collecting her work—much easier and more fun than ever before. In the days before the web, there was only Liza's official fan club: Limelight on Liza was founded in December 1964 by Nancy Barr (now Nancy Barr-Brandon), at Liza's request. In 1976, Suzan Meyer became the club's president, issuing the journals and updates, until the club ended in early 1997, as the Internet was rising. The Internet has since been able to bring even more Liza lovers together. Please keep in mind, though, that one should always exercise some caution in dealing with people you don't know online. There are two major e-mail lists or groups that are wonderful sources for getting the latest info on Liza:

love_liza—The oldest and largest e-mail chat group around (started in May 1998 and run by BJ and Annie; owned by Dixie). Liza has endorsed the group, and even gave a "live" online chat for it in the summer of 2000. Homepage: www.groups.yahoo.com/group/love_liza

TheLizaMinnelliFanClub—Founded February 2003; run by Alan Rice. Liza has supported this group also: www.groups.yahoo.com/group/LizaMinnelliFanClub

See their website: www.hometown.aol.co.uk/bidgy002/myhomepage/favstar.html

Both of the above groups are excellent ways to keep updated on Minnelli's career.

There are also several websites with Liza material, but two that seem to have fairly extensive content or are the most up-to-date are www.lizaonline.co.uk and www.angelfire.com/musicals/lizaminnelli

Two newer web sites have also come along just as we were going to press: Community.webtv.net/markspics/lizamay and www.lizamayminnelli.com

Liza herself does not have her own website running at this time. She does have a page through J Records' site (lizaonline.com), but it has not been updated for over a year as of this writing. Liza did have her own authorized site from circa 1998 or 1999 through 2001 (lizamay.com).

Since I have always felt the most important thing to focus on in Liza's life is her work, I'd like to offer these reminders as testaments to her craft. Here is a list of the currently available Liza Minnelli CDs, listed chronologically (See Chapter Twelve: "For the Record," for previously listed information such as label, release number, etc.).

Liza with some of her loving and devoted fans.

Liza's Currently Available CDs

1. *Best Foot Forward*
2. *The Judy Garland Show: The Show That Got Away*
3. *The Judy Garland Christmas Album*
4. *Liza Minnelli: The Capitol Years*—Released by EMI as a British import in 2001 (CD # 7243-5-32576-2-0). Available at Footlight Records, New York City, www.footlight.com Phone (212) 533-1572 (This shop remains the best place to find Liza albums, CDs, and DVDs/Videos.) This CD contains Liza's entire first solo album—1964's *Liza! Liza!* for Capitol Records—and tracks from her second and third albums for the label (1965 and 1966).
5. *Judy Garland and Liza Minnelli: Together.* Released on Curb Records in 1993. A twenty-eight-minute disc of "highlights" from the 1964 Judy-Liza London Palladium Concerts.

6. *Flora, the Red Menace*
7. *Liza Minnelli: When It Comes Down to It . . .* 1968–1977. Released March 9, 2004, by Raven Records in Australia (www.ravenrecords.com.au; available at Footlight Records, etc.). A superb collection covering Liza's A&M and Columbia studio recordings, focusing on the more unique singer-songwriter tracks (Randy Newman, Gordon Lightfoot, Lennon & McCartney, James Taylor, John Denver, Aretha Franklin, Mac Davis, Stevie Wonder, and Peter Allen, etc.). Ten of the twenty-six songs are new-to-CD tracks, and the sound is spectacular. Excellent liner notes and some fine artwork too. A new must-have.
8. *Cabaret*
9. *Liza with a "Z"*
10. *Alice Cooper—Muscle of Love* (import CD)
11. *New York, New York*
12. *Tropical Nights*
13. *The Act*
14. *The Rink*
15. *Remember: Michael Feinstein Sings Irving Berlin*
16. *Liza Minnelli at Carnegie Hall* (a.k.a. *Three Weeks at Carnegie Hall*) (1987) (two-CD set, and single "highlights" disc)
17. *Results*
18. *Billy Stritch*
19. *Aznavour - Minnelli: Paris—Palais Des Congres* (two-CD Set)
20. *Liza Minnelli Live at Radio City Music Hall*
21. *Sondheim: A Celebration at Carnegie Hall* (two-CD set, and single disc of "highlights")
22. *Frank Sinatra—Duets*
23. *Gently*
24. *Pavarotti and Friends for War Child*
25. *My Favorite Broadway: The Leading Ladies, Live at Carnegie Hall*
26. *Minnelli on Minnelli: Live at the Palace*
27. *Grateful: The Songs of John Bucchino*

Liza fans love wearing her concert T-shirts. Our own official Liza *Scrapbook* model, Scott Brogan, displays Liza "T's" from over the years.

28. *Broadway Cares—Home for the Holidays*
29. *Liza's Back!*
30. *Sacha Distel: But Beautiful*

Currently Available DVDs and Videos

DVDs

1. *In The Good Old Summertime*. Released in April 2004, from Warner Home Video. Liza made her film debut at the end of this 1949 release. (Also on VHS, most recently issued on April 1, 1992, from MGM/UA/Warner Home Video.)
2. *The Judy Garland Show—Volume One*. Released June 15, 1999, from Pioneer Entertainment/Classic World Productions, Inc. Liza's 1963 solo guesting on Judy's TV series. (Excerpts appear on the *Judy Garland and Friends* VHS tape, but in poor quality.)
3. *The Judy Garland Show—Volume Three*. Released November 23, 1999, from Pioneer Entertainment/Classic World Productions, Inc. Liza appears in this 1963 Christmas episode from Judy's TV series. (Also on VHS, from Classic World Productions, Inc.)
4. *Judy Garland Live at the London Palladium with Liza Minnelli*. Released November 19, 2002, from Kultur Home Video. Fifty-five minutes of excerpts from the second of two concerts, November 15, 1964. (Only fair quality) (Also on VHS)
5. *Judy Garland: The Concert Years*. Released November 19, 2002, from Kultur Home Video. A 1985 PBS-TV documentary on Garland's concert career, features a few seconds of silent, color home movie footage of Judy and Liza onstage together at the Palace Theater in 1967. (Also on VHS)
6. *Cabaret*. Released August 19, 2003, from Warner Home Video. (Second release on DVD, but same as the first one from 1997, only the packaging changed.) Contains extras, such as a 1997 interview, etc. (Also on VHS—the VHS "25th Anniversary Edition," which spent one week on *Billboard*'s Top Video Chart at number 38, for the week of November 22, 1997.)
7. *Andy Warhol, Superstar*. Released May 27, 2003, from Sony Music. A documentary on Warhol, includes brief shots of Liza.
8. *That's Entertainment!* Released October 19, 2004, from Warner Home Video. Box includes 1974 ABC television special on the movie.
9. *The Muppet Show*. Available from Time-Life Home Video. Liza's 1979 guest appearance on this TV series.
10. *Arthur*. Released August 22, 1997, from Warner Home Video. Liza's 1981 movie hit. Includes the trailer. (Also on VHS)
11. *The Muppets Take Manhattan*. Released June 5, 2001, from Columbia/Tri-Star Studios. Liza's 1984 release. (Also on VHS)
12. *Rent-A-Cop*. Released May 23, 2000, from Vidmark/Trimark. Liza's 1988 release. (Also on VHS)
13. *Dame Edna: Complete Series*. Released October 5, 2004, from Warner Home Video. Includes Liza's 1989 TV appearance.
14. *Palais des Congrès de Paris*—Charles Aznavour and Liza Minnelli. Released January 9, 2003, from Musicrama, Inc. Liza's November-December 1991 concert with Aznavour. Make sure you get the one with the white cover and drawing with the two stars, and not the one from Brazil with photos—that one is a bootleg and is poor quality.
15. *The Freddie Mercury Tribute Concert*. Released November 26, 2002, from EMI. Liza's appearance at the April 20, 1992, tribute to Mercury.
16. *Sondheim—A Celebration at Carnegie Hall*. Released November 30, 2001, from BMG Special Products. Liza's appearance at the June 10, 1992, tribute to Sondheim. (Also on VHS)
17. *Jerry Herman's Broadway at the Hollywood Bowl*. Released July 29, 1997, from Varese Sarabande/UNI. Liza introduces this June 1993 concert, via videotape. (Also on VHS)
18. *West Side Waltz*. Released September 2, 2003, from FreemantleMedia Home Entertainment, through UAV Entertainment. Available at Amazon, Wal-mart, etc. Liza's 1995 TV movie.

19. *My Favorite Broadway—The Leading Ladies.* Released February 16, 2001, from Image Entertainment. Liza's 1998 appearance at this all-star show, from Carnegie Hall. (Also on VHS)
20. *Jackie's Back.* Released March 19, 2002, from Xenon Home Video. Liza is "interviewed" in this "mockumentary" (a "mock" documentary about fictitious singer "Jackie," which aired in 1999).
21. *Meet Me in St. Louis*—60th Anniversary Edition. Released April 6, 2004 from Warner Home Video. A two-disc set featuring spectacular restoration, the DVD also features a new on-camera introduction with Liza, which was videotaped by Stephen Bogart's company in the fall of 2003.
22. *Arrested Development* DVD box set. Released October 19, 2004. Liza's 2003–2004 season.
23. *A&E Biography.* Website DVD-R (and VHS) release of the June 2004 bio on Liza.

VHS (the following are not yet available on DVD)

1. *Journey Back to Oz.* Released by various low-budget labels. Liza's 1962 work in this animated feature. (Can be hard to find, but is a great treat for kids and adults.)
2. *The Dangerous Christmas of Red Riding Hood.* Released circa 1985–1986; various low-budget labels. This 1965 color special has appeared on a few bootleg videos over the years, all in B/W film prints, and not from the color videotape. (A wonderful treat for kids and for adults.)
3. *The Sterile Cuckoo.* Released March 20, 1985, from Paramount Home Video. Liza's 1969 movie release.
4. *Silent Movie.* Released July 1, 1997, from Fox Home Video. Liza's 1976 movie release.
5. *That's Dancing!* Released October 12, 1994, from Warner Home Video. Liza's 1985 movie release.
6. *Minnelli on Minnelli: Liza Remembers Vincente.* Released November 10, 1993, from MGM/UA Home Video. Liza's 1987 PBS-TV documentary tribute to her father's films.
7. *Arthur 2: On the Rocks.* Released January 6, 1998, from Warner Home Video. Liza's 1988 movie release.
8. *Stepping Out.* Released January 27, 1993, from Paramount Home Video. Liza's 1991 movie release.
9. *Liza Minnelli: Live from Radio City Music Hall.* Released November 10, 1992, from Columbia/Sony Home Video. Liza's 1992 concert return to Radio City. This VHS debuted on *Billboard*'s Top Video Chart on December 12, 1992, and spent nine weeks there, where it peaked at number 23 during the week of January 9, 1993.
10. *Parallel Lives.* Released March 7, 1995, from Paramount Home Video. TV-movie featuring Liza, aired in 1994.
11. *Stonewall 25.* Released Spring 1995. Liza's complete performance of "The Day After That," from the *Stonewall 25* celebration of June 26, 1994. Write Stonewall 25, PO Box 2038, New York, NY 10113.

For Collecting Liza's Work on CD and DVD/VIDEO

For new fans, or for those fans who want to share their love of Liza with friends, here are some guidelines.

Suggested CDs

1. *Liza Minnelli: Ultimate Collection, 2001* (Hip-O Records/UNI Music). While perhaps not perfect (missing tracks from Tropical Nights, and the single "All That Jazz"), this is the only commercially available collection that covers nearly the whole of Liza's recording career. Here are reasons for suggesting this disc (and not because this writer was involved with the project): This set spans twenty-five years, from her first solo album in 1964 to one of her more recent and best albums, *Results*, in 1989. The hits are all here, as are the unexpected, and even a rare never-before-on-CD track ("Simon"). Liza has also "endorsed" it, as it is mentioned in her current concert souvenir program.

2. *Liza Minnelli Live at Carnegie Hall (Three Weeks at Carnegie Hall)*, 1987, two-CD set (Telarc Records). Liza is foremost a live performer, and this two-disc set captures the star in peak form and voice, backed by a superb and vast forty-four-piece orchestra.
3. *Liza with a "Z"* (TV Soundtrack), 1972 (Columbia Records). Liza in her peak seventies period with a superb selection of current hits and standards, all delivered in fantastic voice.
4. *Liza Minnelli: The Capitol Years, 2001* (EMI Records). Liza's first solo album from 1964, and five tracks each from her second and third albums, all for Capitol Records. A superb taste of the young Minnelli.
5. *Liza Minnelli: Liza's Back, 2002* (J Records). A fine example of the current-day Liza. A good mix of hits with new material. She's in superb form and in strong voice.
6. *Results* (Epic Records 1989). Liza at her most unusual, and "un-Liza-like." A collection of dance tracks and ballads, all richly orchestrated. She is in peak form and voice.
7. *Tropical Nights* (Columbia/DRG Records 1977). Here Liza sings seventies California-type pop-rock, with some jazz and a closing ballad "A Beautiful Thing" thrown into the mix. Great arrangements, and another vocal peak for the star.
8. *Liza Minnelli: When It Comes Down to It . . . 1968–1977.* Presenting a forgotten side of the singer, this "songwriter collection" is a testament to Minnelli minus the sequins.

Suggested DVDs/VIDEOS

1. *Palais des Congrès de Paris—Charles Aznavour and Liza Minnelli.* Released January 9, 2003, from Musicrama, Inc. Liza's November-December 1991 concert with Aznavour. The best commercially available representation of what the lady can do onstage. She is in superb form and voice during her hour-plus set, and in her duets with Aznavour. (Make sure you get the one with the white cover and drawing with the two stars. Available from Footlight Records in New York City, phone 212-533-1572, or online at Amazon.com and other sites).
2. *Cabaret* (1972) Warner Home Video DVD. Liza's most acclaimed movie and film performance. (The VHS actually features a superior print.)
3. *Stepping Out* (1991) Paramount Home Video VHS. Liza's most recent theatrical release, features a fine performance and some spectacular dancing too.
4. *Liza Live at Radio City Music Hall* (1992) Columbia/Sony VHS. While not in as strong form vocally as she is two months earlier on the Aznavour DVD, Liza still thrills in a superb show.
5. *The Judy Garland Show—Volume One* (1963) Pioneer Entertainment/Classic World Productions, Inc. DVD. A great treat to see Liza as a seventeen-year-old dazzler, working with her mom.

I hope you've enjoyed this journey through one of the great careers in entertainment. Liza Minnelli continues to dazzle in her fifth decade as a performer, and has many new exciting projects ahead of her. What will likely always remain on her schedule are concerts—Liza's lifeblood is contact with the audiences that love her as much as she loves them. Although the legend will soon be turning sixty, it's doubtful she would ever retire completely, even if large-scale tours are eliminated. One can't imagine Liza Minnelli ever tiring of wanting to share her gifts with the world, for which those of us who still care about the art of sharing are grateful.

ALTMAN